TRAVERSING THE MIDDLE

TRAVERSING THE MIDDLE

ETHICS, POLITICS, RELIGION

Gavin Hyman

CASCADE *Books* • Eugene, Oregon

TRAVERSING THE MIDDLE
Ethics, Politics, Religion

Copyright © 2013 Gavin Hyman. All rights reserved. Except for brief quotations in critical publications or reviews, no part of this book may be reproduced in any manner without prior written permission from the publisher. Write: Permissions, Wipf and Stock Publishers, 199 W. 8th Ave., Suite 3, Eugene, OR 97401.

Cascade Books
An Imprint of Wipf and Stock Publishers
199 W. 8th Ave., Suite 3
Eugene, OR 97401

www.wipfandstock.com

ISBN 13: 978-1-61097-447-9

Cataloging-in-Publication data:

Hyman, Gavin, 1974–

    Traversing the middle : ethics, politics, religion / Gavin Hyman.

    xx + 210 p.; 23 cm—Includes bibliographical references and index.

    ISBN 13: 978-1-61097-447-9

    1. Ethics. 2. Philosophy. 3. Christianity and politics. 4. Postmodern theology. I. Title.

BR115.P7 H96 2013

Manufactured in the USA.

Scripture quotation is from the New Revised Standard Version Bible, copyright 1989, Division of Christian Education of the National Council of the Churches of Christ in the United States of America. Used by permission. All rights reserved.

CONTENTS

Acknowledgments · vii
Introduction · ix

PART I *The Ethical*
   1 Anxiety · 3
   2 Complacency · 49

PART II *Between the Ethical and the Political*
   3 Between · 81

PART III *The Political*
   4 Passivity · 103
   5 Violence · 137

PART IV *The Religious*
   6 Faith · 163

Bibliography · 199

Index · 205

ACKNOWLEDGMENTS

If there are readers of my first book, *The Predicament of Postmodern Theology* (2001), who are now being so generous as to embark upon this one, I must first express my thanks to them for their constancy over such a long period. They will notice, I hope, that the author of this book is identifiably the same as the author of the first, because there is, I believe, an underlying continuity of thought between them. I still endorse most of the conclusions reached in that first book, and this one should be seen as an extension rather than a repudiation of it. Nonetheless, such readers will also, I hope, notice a development, in that I now see and express certain things rather differently from the way I did a decade ago. Insofar as this is the case, this is largely due to my more recent immersion in the writings of the late Gillian Rose, Charles Taylor, Rowan Williams, and Slavoj Žižek in particular. Furthermore, I have continued to be stimulated and provoked by the work of John Milbank and Don Cupitt. I must therefore acknowledge my deep indebtedness to them without in any way suggesting that they would agree with all of what follows (or, indeed, with each other). I am aware that they would explicitly disagree with me at central points, and there are places where I develop criticisms of at least some of them. Nonetheless, my thought, such as it is, has been indelibly shaped by theirs, and for that I am grateful.

This book was written at the University of Lancaster, initially in the Department of Religious Studies, and later in the Department of Politics, Philosophy, and Religion. Both have served as excellent contexts for the writing of this particular book, and I am grateful to all my colleagues in both departments for their support and friendship. I should particularly express my thanks to Brian Black, the late Paul Fletcher, Paul Heelas, Shuruq Naguib, Chakravarthi Ram-Prasad, Graham Smith, and Alison Stone, for stimulating conversations that have left their marks on these pages. Beyond Lancaster, I am very grateful for extended conversations—over more than a decade now—with my American friends and colleagues, Eric Boynton,

Acknowledgments

Clayton Crockett, Jeffrey Robbins, Noelle Vahanian, and, more recently, Vincent Lloyd. There are enough differences between us—but sufficient common ground—to make such conversations always stimulating and thought-provoking.

Some parts of this book or ideas within it were first aired in papers delivered at various conferences or university seminars over the last few years: the Modern Theology seminar at the University of Oxford, in December 2009; the "Future of Continental Philosophy of Religion" conference at Syracuse University, New York, in April 2011; the "New Visibility of Atheism in Europe" colloquium at the Donner Institue, Abo Akademi University, Finland, in January 2012; and the Modern Theology seminar at the University of Durham, in March 2012. I am grateful to all those who responded on those occasions with comments, questions, and criticisms, especially George Pattison, Joel Rasmussen, Johannes Zachhuber, Ruth Illman, Teemu Taira, Mattias Martinson, Gerard Loughlin, Christopher Insole, and Marcus Pound.

Some sections of this book have been previously published elsewhere, and I am grateful to the following publishers and editors for permission to use that material here: Ashgate Publishing for parts of chapters 1 and 2 excerpted by permission from "Disinterestedness: The Idol of Modernity," in *New Directions in Philosophical Theology: Essays in Honour of Don Cupitt*, edited by Gavin Hyman (Farnham: Ashgate, 2004), 35–52. Copyright © 2004; Ruth Illman and Teemu Taira for parts of chapter 6 excerpted from "Dialectics or Politics? Atheism and the Return to Religion," published in *Approaching Religion* 2 (2012) 66–74.

INTRODUCTION

After several decades of dominance in the Western academy and beyond, "postmodern" thought now finds itself in decline. In particular, it is being eclipsed by new discourses that call for the "return of the metanarrative" or a recovery of the domain of the "universal." The particular universal metanarratives being invoked vary enormously, from Marxism in various guises (Terry Eagleton, Fredric Jameson, Michael Hardt, and Antonio Negri) to a postsecular Augustinian theology (John Milbank and the theologians of "radical orthodoxy") to complexity theory as applied to network culture (Mark C. Taylor) to a Lacanian-Marxist revolutionary Christianity (Slavoj Žižek and Alain Badiou). For all their differences, these respective responses are in each case motivated, above all else, by ethical and political concerns. The perceived "relativism" and consequent impotence of postmodernism in ethical and political terms have, it is believed, brought us to an impasse at a time when the logic of global capitalism is preeminent.

Indeed, such criticism often appears in a stronger form than this. For it is claimed that postmodernism is not merely relativistic, impotent, and ineffectual, but is actually complicit with and, further, reinforces that from which emancipation is sought. That is to say, there appears to be a close familial relationship between global capitalism on the one hand and postmodern philosophy on the other, such that the two are expressions of each other in different spheres of discourse and activity and, consequently, reinforce and mutually sustain each other. One of the first to make such an argument was Fredric Jameson in his seminal book *Postmodernism, or, the Cultural Logic of Late Capitalism* (1991). As the title of his book makes clear, Jameson argued that postmodernism was an *expression* of late capitalism, a symptom of a deeper economic malaise. In classically Marxist terms, postmodernism is the superstructure that is determined by, is a reflection of, and serves to reinforce the economic base, namely, late capitalism. In the ensuing decades, Jameson's contention has gained widespread assent from

Introduction

Marxists and non-Marxists alike. Disillusionment with the postmodern intellectual trajectory has become widespread. For Alain Badiou, it is not only postmodernism that is complicit with global capitalism in this way, but the entire edifice of Western liberal democracy itself, and for similar reasons. It has lost any sense of a "universal," of "truth," and of "justice," and is instead fuelled by "preferences," "opinions," "information," and "spin." As such, it has become the ideal accomplice of global capitalism. It embodies a political order that services and does not challenge the economic one. This is why Badiou refers to the regime of "capitalo-parliamentarianism." As was the case with postmodern philosophy, therefore, there is little point in looking to contemporary democratic politics to resist or confront the sovereignty of global capitalism; on the contrary, in its current configuration, it merely reflects and reinforces it.

While the various thinkers mentioned at the outset would disagree with Badiou in many respects, almost all of them would agree with this general contention. In such circumstances, it is little wonder that they have been advocating a shift from talk of "difference" and "particularism" to the reassertion of "truth" and "universalism"; little wonder that talk of the "end of the metanarrative" has been giving way to calls for the "return of the metanarrative." But to what extent should this emerging consensus itself be contested? As the prioritizing of particularity has been increasingly shown to be wanting, should our response be to allow the pendulum to swing back so as to assert the sovereignty of the universal? To what extent would this be to remain caught up in many of the problems here at stake? In relation to this recently emerging consensus, this book will acknowledge its diagnosis while seeking to question its cure. That is to say, it will be acknowledged that while the postmodern philosophical trajectory has made invaluable interventions in Western thought in recent decades, it is in itself insufficient as an ethical and political resource. The need to move in some sense *beyond* postmodernism is frankly acknowledged. At the same time, however, the various recent attempts to do this by seeking unequivocally to *prioritize* the universal will here be contested. This will be done by asking two central questions. First, is the move from postmodern "particularism" to postsecular "universalism" still to remain caught within a wider structure that is itself problematic? If postmodernism was felt to be too passive and ineffectual, is it not the case that the return to unequivocal universals inaugurates a violent absoluteness that, in turn, destroys the ethical and political? In other words, does this move not reinscribe the same problem, albeit in an inverted form? It will be the burden of the following chapters to argue that this is indeed so. But insofar as this is the case, this will lead inevitably to a second central question, namely, that if the new universalisms are as ethically and politically problematic as were the postmodern particularities, then to which theoretical disposition are we now to turn?

These questions will be addressed by examining the nature of the ethical and political themselves. It will be suggested that the ethical and political are constituted by an enigma or *aporia* that is manifested in the central Judeo-Christian commandment to love your neighbor as yourself. This commandment, as has often been recognized, is strictly and logically unrealizable. But its very impossibility has served only to intensify its allure; the ethical, it seems, is constituted by precisely this impossible call. Recasting Kant's distinction between "legality" and "morality," we might say that if the ethical were simply realizable, it would in fact belong to the domain of legality and not to that of the ethical at all. This is why the notion of an ethical "system" is fundamentally misguided; it rests on the assumption that the ethical can be "determined" and "realized" by means of a properly implemented universal system. But for the ethical and political as such to be preserved, this enigmatic *aporia*, this irreducible impossibility, must itself be perpetuated. Critically, this impossibility does not induce paralysis but serves to fuel the movement or labor of the ethical and political themselves. For ethics and politics are fundamentally processes or activities rather than systems or templates—processes that seek to bear witness to the aporetic brokenness of thought without concealing or mending it. In contrast, both modern and postmodern philosophy, in their different ways, recognized the reality of this enigma but conceived it as a problem to be "resolved" or "mended," thereby ultimately destroying both the ethical and the political.

What would it mean to enact the ethical-political enigma in practical terms? Inspired by the work of Gillian Rose and other contemporary post-Hegelian thinkers, it will be suggested that such an enactment must pay due obeisance to the essentially *triune* structure of the ethical/political, such that each ethical/political decision or action is constituted by a process of labor or negotiation between the domains of the universal, the particular, and the singular. What the nature of the ethical/political reveals is the necessity of each of these three domains, and in such a way that no one is prioritized over the other two. Any final rest or stability is precluded, and the enigma is revealed in the very labor of the dialectical interplay between them. This interminable interplay may be understood as a manifestation of what Rose has called the "equivocation" of the ethical. Where one domain is prioritized (which is essentially what ethical and political systems attempt to do), the *aporia* is mended, and the result is both ethically and politically destructive.

In this respect, it will be argued that *both* postmodern approaches to ethics and politics *and* some of the most prominent recent corrections of them are found wanting. For although both do acknowledge the

Introduction

equivocation of the ethical and political, both nevertheless seek ultimately to overcome it through the unequivocal prioritizing of one domain over the other two. Postmodern approaches (by which I mean primarily the Derridean-Levinasian philosophical trajectory) prioritize the domain of particularity or singularity while recent correctives (such as those of Badiou, Milbank, and Žižek) prioritize the domain of universality. The effect of these respective prioritizations is to mend the brokenness of the ethical and political, to smooth away equivocation, albeit in different ways. On the one hand, postmodern approaches elevate particularity or singularity to such an extent that the universal content is robbed of its force. The result is a passivity and impotence that is ethically and politically fatal. On the other hand, recent correctives prioritize universality to such an extent that its content is unleashed with a force that threatens the violent destruction of that very content itself. For the force of the universal, unconstrained by the particular, threatens a violence that is both unethical and anti-political. It stands in marked contrast to the *content* of the universal, by virtue of which it is indeed judged to be universal. The challenge, therefore, is to negotiate a path between passivity and violence, a path that is difficult because it cannot unequivocally be stated in a system or a procedure that would guarantee any such mediation. There can be no question of a settled and mediating "balance" between the three domains of the universal, the particular, and the singular, precisely because they are irreducibly in tension. But this tension is itself productive and is indeed constitutive of the ethical and political as such. Judgments must indeed be made about which domain must be prioritized but they are never a priori in character and must be made repeatedly and anew in each singular instance.

Just as the singular and particular stand in need of the universal, so too, it will be argued, the ethical and political stand in need of the religious, as both Žižek and Milbank have, in their different ways, insisted. But much is at stake in the *manner* in which religion returns, and it is at this point that an important difference with both Žižek and Milbank is registered. It is therefore the case that the reader will observe a marked ambivalence on the role of the religious in relation to the ethical and political. On the one hand, the invocation of theology can serve to "mend" what I take to be the necessary "brokenness" of the ethical and political. It can too easily serve to "resolve" some of the tensions that must necessarily remain unresolved if the ethical and political processes are to remain fruitfully in movement. On the other hand, it will be shown how the ethical and political *require* the religious precisely in the interests of perpetuating this brokenness. So the challenge will be to articulate a theological disposition that fulfils the ethical and political requirement without at the same time closing down the open dialectical interplay that the ethical and political equally require.

In this respect, it is important to clarify the structural methodology of the analysis that follows. At first sight, it would appear that the study begins with a "neutral" account of the ethical and political as such (unencumbered by any theological presuppositions), which then *leads to* the conclusion that the religious or theological is necessary. But this is a misleading way of understanding the nature of the analysis. For the discussion of the ethical and political is itself informed by certain theological presuppositions, even if this is not immediately self-evident. There is a necessary and unavoidable circularity here. Perhaps the best way of clarifying the nature of this methodology is by way of analogy with the "natural theology" expounded by St. Thomas Aquinas. As numerous recent scholars have repeatedly insisted, Aquinas's "Five Ways" unfolded in the *Summa Theologiae* are in no way neutral philosophical investigations that lead him to the rational conclusion that there is a God. On the contrary, Aquinas makes only too clear the way in which faith in God is presupposed at the outset of the discussion. But with a view to persuading those who are not already within the circle of faith, Aquinas seeks to show how accounts of motion and causality, among other things, are incomplete without a theological supplement; theology "perfects" these kinds of naturalistic explanations. This is somewhat akin to the methodology being employed in this study, the aim of which is to make a case for a particular understanding of the nature of the ethical and political and, furthermore, to show how such an understanding is perfected through the invocation of a theological supplement. This is so even if the understanding of the ethical and political is itself informed by certain theological presuppositions.

Many readers will be aware, of course, that to argue for the return of theology on ethical and political grounds is hardly novel in the context of recent contemporary thought. The central purpose of this study, however, is not simply to add another voice to an already voluble chorus, but also to register a note of caution with regard to the way in which theology is actually returning in much recent thought. For it will be argued that theology can serve to close down rather than open up the ethical and political. In this respect, the study will develop arguments against some of those who have recently invoked theology on ethical and political grounds. A central purpose of this book will therefore be to negotiate this necessary tension between the simultaneous necessity and impossibility of theology.

The book is divided into three sections—the ethical, the political, and the religious. But it will be evident from what has thus far been said that this is in many ways an artificial division. Both the ethical and political analyses

Introduction

are informed by the religious; there is a pervasive anticipation of that which is more explicitly discussed in the final section. Furthermore, it is intrinsic to the understanding being developed here that the ethical and political are not two distinct and logically incompatible modes of discourse. The contrary has been argued, of course, by thinkers as diverse as Levinas on the one hand and Žižek on the other. Rather, it will be suggested that the two are essentially the same thing viewed from different vantage points. This, indeed, will be the burden of the argument in the linking chapter between the ethical and political sections. So the structural division of the book should be regarded as merely heuristic and in no way should be taken to suggest that the ethical, political, and religious are at all easily separable.

The book begins with an exercise in historical contextualization, with the first chapter taking as its starting point the assumption that our ethical inheritance in the West is encapsulated in the Judeo-Christian commandment that one should love one's neighbor as oneself. In line with much recent scholarship as well as a much older tradition of Judeo-Christian commentary, it is also assumed that this commandment embodies a fundamental enigma or *aporia* that resists "resolution." Rather than being problematic, this situation is taken as being revelatory of the nature of the ethical as such. The chapter will then proceed to consider the contrasting (and converging) ways in which modernity (particularly as exemplified by Kant) and postmodernity (particularly as exemplified by Levinas) responded to this *aporia*. Both acknowledged its reality, but both understood it as something to be overcome; herein lies their convergence. But whereas Kant resolves it through an unequivocal elevation of the domain of universality, Levinas does so through an ultimate elevation of the domain of singularity. In Kant's case, I shall examine the practical outcome of his prioritizing of the universal through a detailed analysis of his conception of disinterestedness as being a constitutive aspect of the moral. I show how the resulting system drains love away, is ultimately suicidal for the self, and instrumentalizes the neighbor. It is therefore fatal for the ethical enigma that is expressed in the command to love your neighbor as yourself.

In Levinas's case, his elevation of the domain of singularity might appear to be a revolutionary departure from Kant's thought. But in fact, I shall suggest that it ultimately only inverts Kant's approach, while leaving its structure and thus its problematic outcome intact. Although Levinas acknowledges the equivocation of the ethical much more explicitly than does Kant, he ultimately shares the impulse to "overcome" it by means of the a priori subordination of the universal to the singular. This inversion is given expression in the move away from Kant's subjective foundationalism (where the subject is rendered in a nominative mode); Levinas conceives of the subject as being itself constituted by a radical passivity in its primordial experience of being called to an infinite responsibility for the other (where the subject is rendered in an accusative mode). But he perpetuates the Kantian division between "self" and "other," where each is hypostasized and where the affirmation of one appears to be at the expense of the other. Once again, we see that the infinite responsibility to which the self is subjected ultimately gives rise to a suicidal logic of self-negation that easily tips over into its opposite, whereby such self-negation is inverted into an excessive self-promotion. The paradox exposed here in both modern and postmodern thought is that attempts to "resolve" equivocation actually result in anxious fragmentation. In both Kant and Levinas, we see the subject anxiously engaged in the simultaneous pursuit of self-negation and self-promotion, two antithetical and impossible quests.

In the second chapter, I examine two attempts to rescue the subject from the anxious fracture identified in Kant and Levinas. This rescue is effected by the invocation of a third term that mediates between the apparently irresolvable ethical antinomy between self and other—in one case, this is the excessive plenitude of God and in the other, it is the empty nothingness of the nihil. As far as the theological response is concerned, I discuss in particular Julia Kristeva's reading of Thomas Aquinas, where she argues that Aquinas's invocation of God is able to overcome the psychological torture inflicted on the subject by the pathological oscillation between love of self and love of other that otherwise obtains. Love of self is not at the *expense* of love of the other, on this reading, because both are constituted by the love of God, which serves as the mediating third. As for the nihilist response, I shall discuss Slavoj Žižek's reading of Spinoza, whose ontology of absolute immanence means that there is no Hobbesian "self" abstracted from and separated out from the world. When understood thus, self-affirmation is not at the *expense* of the wider world, as Levinas seems to suggest, but is itself simultaneously an affirmation of it. The opposition between egotism and altruism is thereby overcome through the positing of absolute immanence.

I shall argue, however, that these two "resolutions" are complicit in the cultivation of a certain complacency through the invocation of their respective mediating thirds. That is to say, they succeed in overcoming the anxious fracture brought about by Kant and Levinas, but at the price of smoothing away the necessary tension that should lie at the heart of ethical equivocation. In other words, the invocation of God or the nihil can serve to provide ethical "solutions" to questions that should be addressed through complex processes of deliberation and judgment that constitute the labor of the ethical. The chapter will go on to consider the nature of this labor, developing an account of the ethical as triune. Avoiding both anxious paralysis and

Introduction

easy complacency, this account of the ethical involves a difficult and always ongoing process of discernment and labor, recognizing the ethical reality of the phenomena of enigma, diremption, and inversion, which together preclude the possibility of any final ethical "closure." The chapter will also point to the necessity of the universal and, specifically, a theological universal. But, it will be suggested, this theological universal will itself need to be rendered in such a way as to avert the kind of ethical complacency that will have been identified in the first part of the chapter. This will be to point forward to arguments that will be developed more fully in chapter 6.

At this point, the book begins to make its passage from the ethical to the political, and chapter 3 will raise the critical question of the relationship between them. It will do so by juxtaposing two influential contemporary accounts of this relationship, namely, those of Levinas and Žižek. Both agree that there is a structural incompatibility between the ethical and political, although they disagree as to the way in which this should be resolved. Levinas gives an unequivocal phenomenological priority to the ethical, with the political emerging as a secondary (and logically contrary) supplement. Žižek, on the other hand, gives an unequivocal priority to the political, arguing that justice must be *liberated* from its being embedded in a particular situation, and must be restored to its proper dimension of universality, with ethics, the particularity of love, emerging as a secondary supplement. In this chapter, I argue that this dispute has been miscast. While the ethical *may* be defined by its valorization of the singular (as Levinas does) and the political *may* be defined by its valorization of the universal (as Žižek does), there is no necessity for them to be so, and, indeed, the outcome of their being so is decidedly problematic. For to define each in this way is to isolate and elevate one element of what should be an essentially triune structure in *both* the ethical *and* political. For this reason, the accounts will always be partial and phenomenologically inadequate, as well as being undesirable in their ethical-political outcomes. So the ethical and political are by no means incommensurable as both Levinas and Žižek would insist. Rather, both the ethical and the political are constituted by a triune interplay of universal, singular, and particular, one in the domain of the relational (the ethical) and the other in the domain of the public (the political). The relationship between ethics and politics should thus be understood as being one of "dependent co-origination."

In chapter 4, I proceed to an explicit discussion of the political as such. It follows from what will have been argued in the preceding chapter that this will be an account that is continuous rather than incommensurate with the account of the ethical developed in the first two chapters. As with the ethical, it will be argued that the perpetuation of the political depends upon the

Introduction

unresolved and ongoing interplay between the universal, the particular, and the singular. But in the domain of the political, this takes on a distinctive inflection in that the political depends upon the maintenance of a tension or juxtaposition between what I call (following Gillian Rose and Vincent Lloyd) "norms" and "practices." As such, this account will be seen to be distinct from both classical Marxism (with its envisaged *telos* of a dissolution of "norms" in favor of spontaneous "practices") and actually existing Soviet Marxism (with its subordination—through rigid, indeed, totalitarian discipline—of "practices" to "norms"). Both of these entail the "end of politics," the former through the subordination of the universal to the particular and the latter through the subordination of the particular to the universal. But if the political depends on the maintenance of this tension, it depends also on another tension between *current* norms and practices on the one hand and *future* norms and practices on the other. In this sense, it sets itself also against liberal democracy, with its confidence in *current* norms and practices and its a priori ruling out of a revolutionary giving way to future ones. Once again, I suggest, this is to subordinate the universal to the particular—in this case, the particular being constituted by the current, the prevailing, what is. Where this tension is eradicated by this kind of subordination, we again see the "end of politics," admittedly of a very different kind from that envisaged or enacted by the two Marxist ones, but the reality of which we may say we are experiencing today. That is to say, in currently prevailing norms and practices, the domain of the universal has been resolutely subordinated to the domain of the particular, and herein, I suggest, lies the problem—and indeed impasse—of our current political predicament.

In much current political thought, the same structural subordination of the domain of the universal may be found, albeit without explicit acknowledgment, and with equally problematic results. I seek to demonstrate this in the following part of chapter 4, in which I examine the work of Simon Critchley, Michael Hardt, and Antonio Negri. Although these thinkers would by no means agree with each other in every respect, I nonetheless suggest that they have in common this structural elevating of the particular or the singular over the universal. In this sense, although they would not (all) care to admit it, they are in this specific sense following in a broadly Levinasian trajectory. Through analyses of their respective projects, I show how their thought is ultimately detrimental to the political, and moves toward the "end of politics" through their respective subordinations of the universal. Indeed, it is precisely this subordination, I suggest, that gives rise to a corresponding—and fatal—subordination of future norms and practices to current ones. Insofar as this is so, they are in danger of repeating rather than contesting the central feature of the current political predicament.

Introduction

Hardt and Negri may well be right to say that a "postmodern" appeal to the fragmentary and the marginal are useless in the current political context, as these are the very features that sustain the universal sway of global capital. But equally, we might say that an unequivocal prioritizing of particularities—or singularities—is just as culpable and for the same reason. If there is to be a genuine contesting of current norms and practices opening out onto the possibilities inherent in future ones, some kind of universal horizon, it will be argued, must be invoked.

In this respect, the recent return to universals in the work of Alain Badiou and Slavoj Žižek, among others, has come as a welcome corrective, and it is their work in particular that I discuss in chapter 5. Their invocation of universals is to be welcomed because it has undoubtedly led to the revivification of a genuinely radical leftist political thought, of a kind that has been conspicuous by its absence in much late twentieth-century philosophy. They have insisted that forms of thought that seek only to "deconstruct" or "overcome" universals will always be condemned to a political passivity. They have insisted on a trenchant return of universals so as to enable a genuine political revolution. But while this insistence may be necessary, not least in the specific philosophical and political context in which Badiou and Žižek began articulating their own projects, such an approach carries its own dangers, not least of which is an *unequivocal* prioritizing of the universal over the particular, and this indeed is what we see in the work of both Badiou and Žižek. Such an unwavering commitment to the universal, which makes itself impervious to the call of particularity, would again enact the "end of the political," albeit in the opposite sense to that enacted by the thinkers considered in chapter 4. I shall show how it would be an inhuman legalistic imposition of justice without mercy, and the totalitarian abolition of that which questions or escapes the sovereignty of the universal. It would entail the steeling of oneself *against* the call of the neighbor, a refusal of the neighbor in his or her stubborn particularity, a refusal that ultimately renders the universal call to justice meaningless. For the universal call to justice is not one that is made in the abstract; rather, what is sought is justice for *particular* neighbors. When particular neighbors are sacrificed on the altar of universalism, the latter becomes ultimately self-subverting and the end of politics ensues. This is because engagement with the particularities of current norms and practices are renounced in favor of *future* norms and practices. This is enacted not through violent revolution, but through a passive withdrawal, a refusal to participate in norms and practices as they are, in favor of a stubborn witnessing to the universal truths in future norms and practices, what Žižek has called a "Bartleby politics." This is a peculiar form of violence, very different from the kind of violence usually associated with totalitarianism. But it may be said that they share a common structural logic, a common steeling of the political subject against the call issued by the particular neighbor and, indeed, against the lure of particularity as such. But, I shall argue, this is to renounce the tension between current norms and practices and future ones, the necessary tension wherein all political thought and activity is truly located. Whereas the thinkers considered in chapter 4 elevate mercy over justice, those considered in chapter 5 elevate justice over mercy. In contrast to both, the political is to be found in the constant negotiation of the difficult but necessary tension—never a priori resolved—*between* mercy and justice.

This brings us finally, in chapter 6, to an explicit discussion of that which has been implicit—but by no means absent—in the preceding chapters, namely, the religious. Having argued, on specifically ethical and political grounds, for the necessity of a universal, I shall show that the specific universal invoked should be so not on the basis of its *form* (that is to say, tautologically, *because* it is a universal) but because of the specific character of its *content* (by virtue of which it is judged to be universal). By virtue of its content, and in light of the foregoing analysis, the Christian universal will be seen to be both ethically and politically *necessary*. As already noted, in the context of recent ethical and political thought, such a conclusion is by no means controversial or original; almost all of the ostensibly secular philosophers and theorists considered in this study have advocated a return to religion in some form or another. But this very commonality masks a considerable plurality, for they by no means all advocate a return to religion in the same way. Indeed, in light of the cumulative analysis developed in this book as a whole, it will become evident that much is at stake in the *manner* in which the Christian universal returns. For we will have seen, particularly in chapter 2, how Christian theology can serve potentially both to *disable* the ethical and political through a "mending" of brokenness, as well as to *enable* them through the opening up of a dialectical interplay.

I shall suggest that a disabling process occurs when there is an ontological resolution of a predicament that should remain unresolved. Furthermore, these ontological resolutions may be enacted in two antithetical ways, as can be seen in the work of John Milbank and Slavoj Žižek in particular. Milbank returns to theology as a means of reinstating an unequivocally theistic ontology; Žižek, meanwhile, does so against the backdrop of a resolutely atheistic ontology. But both resolutions serve to skew the ethical and political interplay between universal, particular, and singular through their respective "mendings" of ontological brokenness. In Milbank's case, his resolutely theistic ontology means that many of the universal aspects of the ethical and political tasks can be arrogated to God, leaving finite creatures to attend to particularities—to our immediate neighbors, to our nearest and dearest, and so forth. In Žižek's case, his unequivocally atheistic ontology, in which contingent particularity is all there really is, means that the domain of the particular can look after itself, and human beings must take on the task of instantiating universal justice for themselves. But both approaches entail an a priori privileging of the universal or of the particular, which, I shall have argued, is ethically and politically problematic. In order to avoid any such privileging, such ontological questions must necessarily be left unresolved, for it is only such ontological openness or incompleteness that allows for the ethical and political dialectics to play themselves out in a creative way. In the interests of the ethical and political, therefore, we should return to religion in a way that is neither unequivocally theistic nor unequivocally atheistic; we should rather traverse the terrain of the middle.

This, indeed, is the message of the book as a whole, and the way in which it seeks to intervene in current debates. The last decade or so has witnessed an increasing disillusionment with the postmodern thought that had held sway for so long. Its ethical and political impotence became increasingly evident and impossible to ignore. But in seeking to put into question its a priori privileging of the domain of particularity, recent thinkers have too quickly sought refuge in an antithetical reassertion of the domain of universality. In contrast to both, I hope to show, in the chapters that follow, why we should instead traverse the middle—ethically, politically, and religiously.

Part I
THE ETHICAL

1

ANXIETY

Can there ever be an ethical system? Can ethics ever be systematic? Western philosophy, through much of its history, has answered in the affirmative. Indeed, its history is littered with doomed and discarded attempts to discover its holy grail—an ultimate and universal ethical system. All such quests have repeatedly failed because they are found to come up against irresolvable aporias and, ultimately, subversions of intention.

The explanation for the repeated failure of Western philosophy in this respect may well lie in its most distinctive feature. What may be said to underlie Western philosophy, in all its multifarious manifestations, is its quest for a "singular" system of truth, a legacy, it might be thought, of a Judeo-Christian (but especially Christian) commitment to monotheism. What distinguished Christian monotheism from the Judaism out of which it had grown was its much more emphatic universalism, and this universalism only served to reinforce its commitment to a "singular" truth. This quest persisted even after the commitment to monotheism declined. The modern relocation of authority from God to the human subject was in many ways a change of location that left much else intact. It constituted, in effect, the same universal and singular principle immanentized. In other words, the universal God was displaced by universal man—the modern abstract subject. Furthermore, it inevitably gave rise to the notion of a universal, abstract ethical system that must be followed by all people in all times, places, and circumstances.

Viewed in global terms, this notion of universal humanity, with its ideal abstract subject and its corresponding ethical system, was peculiarly unique. This was noted by the poet and writer Christopher Isherwood when he said that "the mistake of the West is the mass-application of all its standards. 'If a thing is good for me, it is good for everybody.' Indian thought

Part I: The Ethical

does not agree. It discriminates between different types of people and the different approaches which are helpful for each."[1] In this brief comment, Isherwood recognizes that outside the West, subjects are viewed as being multiple and heterogeneous; on this view, it is a peculiar and arbitrary fantasy to suppose that they could be homogenized into a universal abstract subject and that there could be a corresponding universal abstract ethical system prescribing in advance the right course of action in ignorance of the particularities of time, individual, and circumstance. Such a concept would likewise be viewed with incredulity by much Chinese thought, as well as by Indian thought. As Chakravarthi Ram-Prasad points out,

> in different ways, both the major Eastern traditions conceive of the individual in very *particular* terms. The responsibilities, entitlements and authority of individuals depend on their specific natures: people are not interchangeable in their rights and duties. If asked whether an individual either can or should do something, the classical Chinese or Indian would answer that it depended on that particular person's nature.... This particularity of the individual contrasts with that great modern Western idea, "generic" individualism.... In both classical Chinese and Indian thought, there is a contrasting "microindividualism": each individual in a sociopolitical collective has specific burdens and freedoms.[2]

What the East considers to be a necessary precondition for ethical reflection, namely, knowledge of the *particularities* of contingent circumstances, the West has regarded as a contaminating hindrance to be shunned at all costs.

Only recently has the West become aware of the peculiar arbitrariness of this notion of a universal subject and, with it, the notion of a universal ethical system. As Alain Badiou has commented, "If there is no ethics 'in general,' that is because there is no abstract Subject, who would adopt it as his shield. There is only a particular kind of animal, convoked by certain circumstances to *become* a subject—or rather, to enter into the composing of a subject."[3] In the wake of this, the challenge has been to develop a distinctively Western approach to ethical reflection that is free from the deformities by which Western thought has for so long been unconsciously disfigured.

1. Isherwood, *Diaries*, 128.
2. Ram-Prasad, "Great Divide," 23. For further elaboration, see his *Eastern Philosophy*.
3. Badiou, *Ethics*, 41.

The Equivocation of the Ethical

In what follows, I want to suggest that the ethical is a site of tension between contrary principles. These contrary principles are multiple and may be seen to proliferate. They include tensions between the universal and particular, autonomy and heteronomy, love of self and love of neighbor, interestedness and disinterestedness, and so forth. The ethical actually depends upon these tensions, and the labor of the ethical consists in the tarrying with these tensions, and judging and acting in the midst of them. Perhaps foremost among these tensions is that between the universal and the particular. As Terry Eagleton has observed, "There is a tension at the heart of ethical thought between the universal and the particular. Moral behaviour is a material affair, bound up with the needs and desires of mortal animals, part of their expressive or symbolic communication and so ineluctably local; but it is also supposed to stretch beyond this specificity into some more universal domain. . . . Like language, ethics is both grandly general and irreducibly specific."[4] But if ethics is indeed grandly general and irreducibly specific, the critical question at the heart of the ethical is one of how this tension should be negotiated. We shall see that a recurring temptation, to which much Western thought has succumbed, has been to "resolve" the tension by elevating one of the two principles over the other. This, in many ways, solves a difficulty, but it is at the price of the dissolution of the ethical itself. This has been the path pursued by many of the ethical theorists of Western modernity. But as we shall see below, it is a temptation to which contemporary thinkers, outside of the constraints of the tradition of Enlightenment modernity, continue to succumb. This is ethically problematic, and in what follows, we shall be looking at some of the various ways in which this is so.

But there is another fatal temptation. Rather than "resolving" the tension, there is a danger of succumbing to an anxious paralysis, of allowing the tension to induce sclerosis. This would be to remain caught in a constant flux and reflux between the two contrary principles, such that no negotiation would be possible. In other words, the ethical challenge is to negotiate the tension without thereby dissolving it. It is for this reason that Gillian Rose has insisted that the two contrary principles in tension must be supplemented by a third.[5] For her, therefore, the ethical consists in a constant struggle to configure what is fundamentally a "triune" structure. So the universal and the particular must be configured and reconfigured alongside the singular. That is to say, every ethical moment is an attempt

---

4. Eagleton, *Trouble with Strangers*, 111.
5. I am grateful to Vincent Lloyd for discussions around this point.

to configure—through negotiating—the universal, the particular, and the singular.[6] Central to this process of negotiation is the recognition that the universal has to be instantiated in the particular; the way in which this instantiation takes place cannot be prejudged; it is always the outcome of an irreducible tension.[7] It can only be negotiated repeatedly and anew in each singular instance. This is why there is also an indispensable singular aspect to each ethical moment, in the sense that each such moment is unique and nonrepeatable. The absolute singularity of each ethical moment, which is as integral to it as its universal and particular aspects, means that the ethical as such can never be unequivocally stated. In this sense, the heart of the ethical is equivocal.

Neither is it possible to state unequivocally what will constitute the universal, the particular, and the singular in any specific instance. While the negotiation of the tension often takes the form of the instantiation of the universal in the particular, we shall see in what follows that often the negotiation takes the form of how the singular is to be instantiated in the universal. In other words, the site of the negotiation of the tension between the two contrary principles can itself shift, and which are the two primary principles being negotiated in tension can also shift. So although we shall discuss many instances of the interplay between the universal, the particular, and the singular in what follows, we shall see that interplay being manifested in diverse ways. This too is an aspect of the equivocation of the ethical.

Given the multiple ways in which the ethical tension between the universal and the particular manifests itself, it may be helpful to look at some specific instantiations. I want to begin here by looking at the way in which the ethical enigma may be observed to be at work in the tension between autonomy and heteronomy, exploring this particularly through some suggestive comments of Rowan Williams. The temptation here, as before, is to ask whether the tension between autonomy and heteronomy can be "resolved."

---

6. See, for instance, Rose, *Broken Middle*, xii and passim, and *Judaism and Modernity*, especially chapter 6. Furthermore, it is not only the ethical that is constituted by this "triune" structure, but also "recognition," "concept," and spirit. See Rose, *Hegel contra Sociology*, 71.

7. The warning against "prejudging" is issued by Rose repeatedly throughout her works. She says that once it is shown that the criteria for the finite/infinite distinction is created by consciousness itself, this *implies* a notion that does not *divide* consciousness and reality in this way. "But it is not pre-judged as to what this notion, beyond the distinction between finite and infinite, might be. It is not pre-judged in two senses: no autonomous justification is given of a new object, and no statement is made before it is achieved." *Hegel contra Sociology*, 46.

On the contrary, the sustaining of the ethical depends precisely upon the perpetuation of the tension in a way that is dynamic rather than disabling.

To begin with, it ought to be clear that the ethical is not solely about autonomy. There is something clearly problematic about an ethical understanding that sees the self as "freely" and "autonomously" *choosing* to adopt moral principles or courses of action. Quite apart from the difficulties with the understanding of selfhood that such language clearly entails, we have also to ask whether such language is, in fact, ethically intelligible. What would it mean to say that we freely choose to adopt moral principles? This question has been well expressed by Williams: "The point is that 'I *choose* to concern myself with apartheid etc.' is a rather peculiar moral remark. A puzzled interlocutor might say, 'Of course you do, I can see that. But have you any reason for choosing[?]: because if not, the relative importance of moral issues will depend wholly on an individual's whims.'"[8] In other words, without "reasons" for our moral choices—which immediately qualify the extent to which they are "freely" chosen—we risk reducing them to being simply matters of arbitrary preference or self-assertion.

It should not be thought, of course, that the invocation of "reasons" here is in some way a rehabilitation of foundational rationality. There is certainly no suggestion here that rationality or rational procedures can somehow "ground" or "determine" the ethical life. But it is to claim that our ethical commitments can only really be intelligible if we say that we are adopting an ethical disposition or pursuing an ethical action *because* we see the world in this way, *because* we have a conception of what constitutes the "good," *because* we believe that the world should be ordered in accordance with that conception, *because* of what we have experienced of ourselves and of others. As Williams suggests, this "'because' relates the option to a vision"; it contextualizes the ethical commitment in terms of a tradition, a way of seeing the world. We judge thus not simply through an arbitrary preference or "free" assertion of the will, but because we see the world in this way, which in turn impels us to judge or act in certain ways.[9] There is, of course, the potential for regression here, to suppose that the way we view the world, our tradition of "seeing," is itself an unconditioned free choice. But it ought to be clear that our worldview, our vision of reality, is at least partly conditioned by factors quite beyond our rational control and willful assertion, through all sorts of contingent factors that collectively make up a process of life formation.

8. Williams, "Religious Realism," 6–7.
9. Ibid., 7.

Part I: The Ethical

In this respect, we can agree with Levinas (however much this agreement might be qualified in what follows) when he says that the "antecedence of responsibility to freedom would signify the Goodness of the Good: the necessity that the Good choose me first before I can be in a position to choose, that is, welcome its choice. That is my pre-originary *susceptiveness*. It is a passivity prior to all receptivity, it is transcendent. It is an antecedence prior to all representable antecedence: immemorial. The Good is before being."[10] There is thus a sense in which our ethical worldview or, indeed, our worldview generally, far from being something that we actively choose, is on the contrary something by which we are passively seized, something to which we are "susceptible." We know too that our worldview is conditioned by our own accumulated experiences and perceptions. What we *undergo*—what we experience and perceive—is as important to worldview formation as what we *will*. This is why Williams says that

> if we are trying to elucidate a moral attitude we now hold, we may well do so partly by adverting to a kind of experience which has led us to this point. "Why are you, as a Christian, indulgent towards divorce (or homosexuality, or whatever)?" may well be answered with, "If you had seen what I have seen and felt something of the demonic complexities and tensions of sexuality, you might judge likewise." There is nothing necessarily irresponsible in the admission that I judge thus because my experience prompts me to; because this is how I see [that] the world goes; because I see human well-being thus and not otherwise.[11]

This is why there *is* an element of heteronomy in moral life; it is to be answerable to a vision, a calling, that is beyond my willing and beyond my rational control. But to understand the ethical exclusively in terms of heteronomy would involve us in the inversion of the difficulties that are involved in an exclusively autonomous conception of ethics. If, for example, our participation in the ethical life were perceived as a process of our being imposed upon heteronomously, as though from the outside, irrespective of our will and without any active assent and commitment on our part, we would once again find it difficult to make much sense of the notion of moral responsibility. This, perhaps, is an instance of what Kant teaches us, namely, that a so-called moral life that is marked by servility and eudaemonism is not really a moral life at all. If ethical life is marked by pure submission and passive acceptance, to what extent can we really "own" our ethical commitments and endeavors? And if we cannot so do, what could it possibly mean

---

10. Levinas, *Otherwise than Being*, 122.
11. Williams, "Religious Realism," 7.

to talk about ethical "responsibility" in such a context? So if we are to reject a notion of ethical commitment as being the result of an unconditioned "free choice," so we are equally constrained to reject a notion of ethical commitment as being the outcome of an unconditioned "heteronomous command." As such terminology brings to mind, there are times when Levinas almost seems to suggest the latter conception of the ethical, where the ethical subject is reduced to absolute passivity in the wake of the unconditional and absolute call of the other. But at the same time, Levinas *does* teach us the necessary lesson that the ethical involves a degree of submission or answerability to a call that is beyond my own will, desires, and control. There is a sense in which we are passively caught up in the ethical in a way that precedes our rational reflection.

So if, as I shall argue in this and the following chapter, Kant and Levinas are cautionary examples of what can occur if the enigma of ethical commitment is "resolved" by the elevation of autonomy on the one hand and heteronomy on the other, they also at the same time teach us the necessity of both. In ethical commitment, there must be an element of both autonomy and heteronomy, and the heart of the ethical may be viewed as consisting in the enigmatic interplay between the two. So it seems that central to participation in the ethical is a dynamic interplay between a "tradition" of seeing the world, a "vision" of the Good, a *telos* to which we are passively susceptible, on the one hand, and, on the other, our active commitment to a realization of that *telos* in the midst of our lived experience. The experiences and perceptions that constitute life in its particularity can serve to criticize and question the tradition that we espouse. But conversely, the experiences and perceptions that constitute life may themselves stand under the judgment of the worldview we take to be authoritative. As Williams again puts this, "responsibility is being answerable for one's choices *in terms of* being prepared to own and explore one's perceptions. These are qualities which make sense only if we see the moral life as the process in which 'given' perceptions are tested and modified in the painful crucible of our own experience—and vice versa: moral vision enlarges its interpretative scope as tradition and personal discovery or response criticize each other."[12]

So tradition and experience criticize each other; the ethical movement is not only in one direction. We may see this as one manifestation of the tension between the universal and the particular and the mutually critical relationship that pertains between them: "The issue can be put another way, in terms of the unresolvable tension between attention to the particular and commitment to the universal. Since the abstract universal is present

12. Ibid.

in our history only as a disempowering and would-be timeless sameness, and since the purely arbitrary assertion of the particular can never found a social practice, with its necessary temporal involvement, truthful action is inescapably shadowed, but destined to achieve only by confronting its shadow."[13] There is therefore no foundationalism here; neither the universal nor the particular is given unequivocal priority. Insofar as there is such a priority, it lies in the very process of the dialectical movement itself. The tense negotiation between the universal and the particular is interminable.

But if interminable, it must not induce paralysis. If, as we insist, there is no unequivocal resolution or rationally calculable balance between the universal and the particular, between the particular and the singular, the danger is that this will induce a hopeless despair and that ethical action (and political interaction) will become paralyzed. But difficulty, labor, equivocation, and provisionality do not in themselves entail impossibility. Rather, singular decisions must be made and actions taken in the midst of equivocation, in the middle of a tension between contrary principles. But the way in which the tension is to be negotiated, the decision made, the action taken, cannot be prejudged in advance, cannot be *a priori* resolved. This means that every act, every decision, entails a risk, the risk of inversion of intention, the risk of a certain unavoidable implication in violence, the risk of acting in a way that might ultimately be judged unethical. Furthermore, these risks may themselves be manifestations of a larger risk: the risk of "suspending" the imperatives that our moral worldview would seem to demand. In making a specific ethical judgment, we may feel called to "suspend" the ethical norms under which we operate; in order to instantiate the universal good in the particular, we may make a singular judgment that entails acting contrary to the way in which the universal good is usually generalized. To "suspend" ethical norms is to take a risk even if such a risk is judged necessary. Such risks are intrinsic to the ethical, and to act ethically is to act with an awareness of these unavoidable risks. This is deemed to be justified and, further, necessary, on account of two considerations in particular. First, such risk must be ventured if one is to avoid falling into the ethical impotence and paralysis already mentioned. One can only avoid the risk entailed in the attempt to negotiate the ethical tension by not acting at all, which is to enact the dissolution of the ethical. As Williams puts this (in the context of a discussion of Gillian Rose's work), "there is no way of being actively and historically within the ethical without such risk, since the ethical without risk is powerless—that is, it is incapable of truthfully

---

13. Williams, "Between Politics and Metaphysics," 13.

negotiating the otherness, the differences, that it always contains (in both senses of the word)."[14]

But secondly, such risk is also justified by the recognition that the universal is "suspended" but not "abolished." Gillian Rose discusses this point in relation to Kierkegaard's pseudonymous author's discourses on the *akedah*. In this context, she says, "to posit that the ethical is 'suspended' is to acknowledge that it is always already presupposed. It grants a momentary licence to hold the ethical fixed and unchanging. But once this is granted, the moment will be imperceptible, for the movement of faith does not always take place in time, or, it takes place in every moment of time; whereas, if the ethical is abolished, then a time outside time, or a social reality outside social reality, must, illogically, be posited."[15] Jacques Derrida has also spoken of this in the context of a discussion of the *akedah*: "In both general and abstract terms, the absoluteness of duty, of responsibility, and of obligation certainly demands that one transgress ethical duty, although in betraying it one belongs to it and at the same time recognizes it. The contradiction and the paradox must be endured *in the instant itself.* The two duties must contradict one another, one must subordinate (incorporate, repress) the other."[16] So the universal law is not abolished, which would entail the arbitrary self-assertion of the individual will, the triumph of sheer particularity; rather, the universal is suspended in the knowledge that that very suspension and the violence that it inevitably brings will itself come under judgment. Not, it should be stressed, my own judgment, but the judgment of the ethical, a universal judgment, a judgment beyond my control. It may be that my action may be judged mistaken, but this is the risk that is necessarily involved in all ethical decisions and actions.

Again in the context of a discussion of Rose's understanding of the equivocation of the ethical, Williams says that "the action we inaugurate is not in advance specified as successful, well-formed or orderly. It is involved with 'violence.' But, in turn, that violence is rendered recognizable, capable of being criticised, by the fact that the ethical is not abolished; the act of inauguration does not establish an anti-order of arbitrary free-for-all. The action taken in the moment of suspending the ethical is an act not of self-assertion but of self-dispossession or even self-*gift*."[17] So to recognize the equivocation of the ethical is to recognize that the ethical cannot be formulated and specified in advance. The ethical is enacted through the equivocal

---

14. Ibid.
15. Rose, *Broken Middle*, 148.
16. Derrida, *Gift of Death*, 66.
17. Williams, "Between Politics and Metaphysics," 12.

Part I: The Ethical

interplay between the universal and the particular in each singular moment. Furthermore, the ethical status of such an enactment cannot be predicted; it may turn out that such an act ends in ethical failure. Consequently a certain risk is unavoidable, and the possibility of failure has to be acknowledged. But the success or failure of our ethical acts is determined by a judgment to which we are subject rather than a judgment that we ourselves make: "to act in the equivocation of the ethical is to renounce the finality of my judgement on myself—which is, of course, what I do when I initiate any kind of communication, any speech."[18]

Thus, to make ethical decisions and take ethical actions is to engage in a constantly negotiated and delicate process of discernment, in which there is as much acknowledgment of ignorance as of knowledge, and which is open to the possibility of error. Indeed, the possibility of error may be said to be a necessary precondition of intelligible ethical action. Equivocation, risk, error, judgment—the very stuff of ethics, and yet the very things from which so much of modern ethical thinking has sought to flee.

The equivocation of the ethical is perhaps given its ultimate articulation in the Western ethical formulation *par excellence*, namely, in the Judeo-Christian commandment to love your neighbor as yourself. For all that this has been commonly accepted as constituting the ethical kernel of Judaism and Christianity, it has also to be said that the commandment itself is an expression of the equivocal character of the ethical as such. Furthermore, the form that this equivocation takes is itself multiple.

For one thing and as is well known, Kierkegaard drew attention to the disjunction between the commandment's status *as* a commandment on the one hand, and the content of that which it commands on the other. This was to draw attention to the fact that love itself is precisely that which cannot be commanded. Love is, by definition, free, which is to say that it is spontaneous and unforced. Love that is commanded thereby destroys its own status as love and becomes instead the enactment of legality, and the triumph of legality over morality. Another way of stating this is to understand the commandment to love as having "at its heart the collision of autonomy and heteronomy."[19] Indeed, it is this collision of autonomy and heteronomy that we have suggested constitutes the equivocation of the ethical. When Gillian Rose says that "the silence of the paradox is the witness of participation in the command to love and in the love which commands,"[20] she testifies to the equivocation at the heart of the commandment itself. It performatively

---

18. Ibid.
19. Reinhard, "Toward a Political Theology of the Neighbor," 12.
20. Rose, *Broken Middle*, 148.

embodies a certain enigmatic conflict between its status as a command and the content of that which is commanded. So as a command, it bears the trace of heteronomy, but in that which is commanded, actual love for the neighbor, we find the trace of autonomy. The commandment itself appears to crystallize the equivocal nature of the ethical itself.

But the antinomies do not stop there; on the contrary, they proliferate. This has been well expressed by Slavoj Žižek, Eric Santner, and Kenneth Reinhard in a lengthy passage that is worth quoting in full:

> the commandment to love the neighbor has seemed far from rational and has, in fact, appeared deeply enigmatic—indeed, as an enigma that calls us to rethink the very nature of subjectivity, responsibility and community. We might even say that neighbor-love is not a law that can be obeyed literally, nor a theory that can be definitively exemplified, but a rule that can be proved only by its exception. That is, neighbor-love functions more as an obstacle to its own theorization than as a roadmap for ethical life: whereas all ethical imperatives involve some ambiguity and hence require some degree of interpretation (e.g., What constitutes honoring one's parents? Is there a difference between "killing" and "murdering"?), the injunction to "love your neighbor as yourself" involves interpretive and practical aporias in *all* its individual terms, and even more so as an utterance. One cannot attempt to fulfil it without taking the risk of transgressing it. Despite its seemingly universal dissemination, despite its appropriation in various moral and political agendas, something in the call to neighbor-love remains opaque and does not give itself up willingly to univocal interpretation. And yet it remains always in the imperative and presses on us with an urgency that seems to go beyond both its religious origins and its modern appropriations as universal Reason.[21]

Žižek, Santner, and Reinhard then go on to raise specific questions arising from this aporia. First, we are confronted with the question of who is my neighbor. For Judaism, this takes the form of asking whether the commandment compels Jews to love non-Jews as well other Jews, and before modernity, this question took an even more circumscribed form, namely, whether one was commanded only to love strictly observant fellow Jews. But even on the most strictly exclusivist interpretation, they point out, the question is not easily resolved, given that to love any one particular neighbor is surely to fail to love another. In Christianity, the commandment is universalized so that it includes both Jew and Gentile, as in the parable of

---

21. Žižek, Santner, and Reinhard, *Neighbor*, 5.

the Good Samaritan. But we may extend Žižek, Santner, and Reinhard's questioning at this point and ask whether such a universalized love is itself coherent. Is love not, by its nature, particular? Just as it is impossible to command love, is it not also impossible to universalize it? Is a universalized love still love? These are questions to which we shall return more than once in what follows.

Second, they ask what precisely it is that constitutes the "love" that we are commanded to extend to our neighbor, a question that is all the more pertinent when it is pointed out, as they do, that the Hebrew word for love, *ahavah*, includes both romantic and sexual love. If this is so, does the commandment not constitute an excessive overstatement? The medieval Rabbi Nachmanides thought that it did, and argued that it should be interpreted as enjoining love of one's neighbor's welfare, rather than his or her person.

Third, they ask what the commandment implies about self-love and subjectivity. More specifically, does it enjoin us to love those *like* me, those to whom I am obliged to extend preferential treatment—the familial, the friend, and so forth? Or does it, on the contrary, extend to those who are quite *unlike* me—the other, the stranger, the enemy? Fourth, "does the commandment call us to expand the range of our identifications or does it urge us to come closer, become answerable to, an alterity that remains radically inassimilable?"[22]

For Žižek, Santner, and Reinhard, this last aporia is the one they particularly wish to explore, but at this point, I want to look more closely at the third of their aporias and, indeed, expand its scope. For in raising the question of what the commandment implies for self-love and subjectivity, this is not only to raise the question of whether this entails love of our "nearest and dearest" as opposed to love for the "other." This is certainly an important question, one to which we shall return, but it is an aspect of and bound up with a larger question of the apparent antinomy between love of self and love of other (whether that other is the friend or the stranger). As this question has been cast in much modern ethical theory, the commandment comes to be seen as strictly impossible. Self and neighbor are often conceived as being in "competition" such that love of neighbor is always at the expense of love of self. But even if we resist the temptation of thinking in this damaging way—even if we accept that loving your neighbor is actually a way of loving yourself, in that it enhances rather than compromises one's own being—the equivocation at the heart of the commandment cannot be so easily overcome. For the fact is that there remains an irreducible tension between loving yourself and loving your neighbor. In countless situations, it

---

22. Ibid., 7.

seems impossible to do both simultaneously, particularly when it is recalled that we are enjoined to love our neighbors "as" ourselves. So much pivots around this word "as." This is, certainly, a question of whether this "as" designates those neighbors "like" yourself. Much more critically, it involves the question of whether the command is in fact to love your neighbor "as much as," or "in the same way as," yourself. And once this question is formulated, the equivocations again proliferate. In particular, it is to highlight the tension between interestedness and disinterestedness, between an "interested" love of self and a "disinterested" love of neighbor.

So at the heart of the Judeo-Christian commandment, we have the expression of a tension: between legality and morality, between autonomy and heteronomy, between interestedness and disinterestedness. In the rest of this chapter, I want to consider the ways in which these tensions have been addressed in modern and postmodern philosophy, and I shall do this by examining the thought of Immanuel Kant and Emmanuel Levinas. Albeit in very different ways, I shall argue that they each "resolve" these tensions rather than tarrying with and negotiating them, and that the respective outcomes are alike problematic, resulting in disabling anxiety. In Kant's case, it is striking that the ethical tensions we have identified are the very antinomies that structure his ethical system. It seems that he was alert to the paradoxical equivocation that lies at the heart of the Judeo-Christian ethical tradition, but that he has expressed this by means of what Rose would call a "diremption"—by constructing a dualistic antinomy between legality and morality, autonomy and heteronomy, interestedness and disinterestedness.[23] Furthermore, these manifestations of diremption line up with and against each other: legality, heteronomy, and interestedness over against morality, autonomy, and disinterestedness. What the Judeo-Christian commandment insists should belong together in equivocation have here been pulled apart by Kantian duality. Having thus been pulled apart, however, they create a tension and anxiety that begs to be "overcome." For Kant, of course, as for his whole legacy of modern dualism, such antinomies are "resolved" by the elevation of one and the subordination of the other. Hence, Kant emerges as the champion of morality (over legality), of autonomy (over heteronomy), and of disinterestedness (over interestedness). In effect, this is to elevate the universal over the particular.

---

23. Rose speaks of "the diremption presupposed in Kant's priority of practical reason, of the categorical imperative, between inner morality and outer legality," *Broken Middle*, 276. She also says that "comprehension breaks into its Kantian elements, where cognition is modelled on law and separated from it, so that the laws of apprehension are both compressed into and separated from the ethical imperative, the law of freedom." Ibid., 308.

Part I: The Ethical

But such resolutions will always be unsuccessful. The ethical, which demands that we tarry with its equivocation, is always resistant to attempts to divide and separate it out, and especially to attempts to "overcome" it by elevating one side of the resulting antinomy over the other. This resistance is manifested in a number of ways. First, in pursuit of the ideal that stands as the prioritized side of the dualism in question, that ideal itself becomes increasingly incoherent. Indeed, as the incoherence of the ideal makes its appearance and as the ideal itself is pursued still further, this ultimately leads to it being inverted. This inversion is intimately linked to the second manifestation of resistance here, namely, that the banished side of the dualism can never be overcome; it makes its reappearance in the inversion of its other. So, for instance, in the Kantian pursuit of disinterestedness over interestedness, we see that the more the ideal of disinterestedness is pursued, interrogated, and probed the more it turns into an incoherent will-o'-the wisp, a conceptual impossibility that seems to collapse under the weight of its own contradictions. Furthermore, as this chimera is pursued still further, it ultimately becomes inverted, so that far from denying self-interest for the sake of the other, it actually ends up by promoting self-interest at the expense of the other.

I now want to explore in more depth these manifestations of resistance that appear in Kant's quest for disinterestedness in order to illustrate the actual operation of these general structural mechanisms. I shall look at disinterestedness in particular because it brings into sharp relief the paradoxical enigma we find at the heart of the commandment to love your neighbor as yourself. This is to return us to the third of the questions arising from this commandment, as formulated by Žižek, Santner, and Reinhard. What does it mean to love your neighbor "as" yourself? What is the relationship between love of neighbor on the one hand and love of self on the other? Kant's quest for disinterestedness constitutes an attempt to dirempt this paradox into a dualistic antinomy between disinterestedness and interestedness, and then not to negotiate this through the invocation of a third, but to "resolve" it by establishing the priority of the former over the latter. It is an attempt, unequivocally, to elevate the universal over the particular.

Disinterestedness: The Idol of Modernity

What is particularly distinctive about Kant's approach to disinterestedness is that while he was developing a theme that had long been a part of the historical theological tradition, he was at the same time making explicit the ways in which the notion had been adapted and reinterpreted during the early modern period. Hans Urs von Balthasar, for instance, is aware of this ambivalence, considering, as he does, the ways in which Kant was inaugurating a distinctively modern reinterpretation of disinterestedness, but recognizing also that he was radicalizing a theme that was by no means new: "Just as in Plato and Plotinus the eros must raise and purify itself until it loves and strives for the good only for the sake of the good, and as in the 'metaphysics of the saints' from Eckhart and Tauler to Ignatius and Fénelon the detachment and indifference of *amour pur* becomes perfect as love solely for the Beloved, in the same way Kant demands the performance of good for the sake of the good, without a primary consideration for happiness or goal or reward."[24]

But if there is a certain continuity here, there are also significant differences. As is well known, Kant radicalized and intensified this emphasis on disinterestedness in his account of ethics or practical reason. For Kant, the morality of an action depended not upon whether God's will was being fulfilled (a recourse that was in any case ruled out by his insistence on the autonomy of morality), but rather upon the motives of the individual subject who was performing the action in question. He says that everything must remain "disinterested and based only on duty, without being based on fear or hope as incentives, which, if they become principles, would destroy the entire moral worth of the actions."[25] Thus, if an act was in accordance with the Law and yet was performed with some motive, rather than purely and simply for the sake of the Law, such an act could be regarded as "legal," but not as in any sense "moral." As Balthasar succinctly puts it, "It is not the material coincidence of commandment and deed ('legality') which serves as the measure here, but only the formal acting from duty ('morality')."[26] Kant's distinction between "legal" and "moral" acts was highly instructive for making explicit the way in which his prizing of disinterestedness diverged from those of earlier accounts. For now, it is not the content or character of the act itself that is morally important, but the motive (or lack thereof) that gives rise to its performance. The fact that the same act could be legal but not moral in one instance and both legal *and* moral in another is an explicit indication of the way in which act and motive have here been separated out. It is this radical *separation* of act from motive that is characteristic of Kant's conception of disinterestedness and clearly distinguishes it from earlier accounts.[27]

24. Balthasar, *Glory of the Lord*, 497.
25. Kant, *Critique of Practical Reason*, 134.
26. Balthasar, *Glory of the Lord*, 497.
27. This is made clear by Kant when he says, "And thereon rests the distinction

Part I: The Ethical

Having said this, however, it must immediately be recognized that although Kant makes this separation much more explicit than any of his immediate (i.e., modern) predecessors, it was nonetheless a separation that was already well established by this time. Indeed, Michel de Certeau argues that the separation was already in place by the early 1600s: "if the distinction between 'intent' and 'act' is traditional in spirituality, during this period [i.e., the early 1600s] it takes on a new and dangerous weight. It permits a spiritual discernment: faith is no longer identifiable with its works, though indissociable from them; the good intent cannot go without the good deed, though the former is not guaranteed by the latter."[28] So the traditional *distinction* between "act" and "intent" gave way to a much more radical *separation*. Why had this occurred? The answer is suggested when de Certeau says that "faith is no longer identifiable with its works," an obvious echo of the slogan of the Reformation. And this separation is confirmed by Antónia Szabari when she traces it back to Martin Luther, pointing out that for him, "because the transcendental consciousness called 'God' makes the recognition of it called 'faith' into an obligation, [it is] not external formal characteristics of speech and action but the individual's conviction [which] determine[s] whether they are pious or blasphemous."[29] Thus, piety and redemption are determined not by the public, objective performance of "works," but rather by the inner, subjective state of the soul or the self. In other words, the subject has become foundational and preeminent. (It is also worth pointing out

---

between consciousness of having acted according to duty and from duty, i.e., from respect for the law. The former, legality, is possible even if inclinations alone are the determining grounds of the will, but the latter, morality or moral worth, can be conceded only where the action occurs from duty, i.e. merely for the sake of the law." Kant, *Critique of Practical Reason*, 84. Compare this with Thomas Aquinas's account. While Aquinas certainly makes a distinction between outer acts and the inner will and insists that the latter is not irrelevant to the moral worth of an action, the important point for Aquinas is the goodness of the inner motive, not that the action should be performed without motive. As a consequence, there is a much more organic connection between the outer act and the inner will than Kant will permit. See Thomas Aquinas, *Summa Theologiae*, 1a2ae, questions 19 and 20. For commentary, see McInerney, *Ethica Thomistica*, especially chapter 5, and Bowlin, *Contingency and Fortune in Aquinas's Ethics*. It is also worth noting that Kant's harsh separation of outer act and inner will is also alien to Judaism. As Michael Wyschogrod has pointed out, "The rabbis taught that it is better to fulfil a *mitzvah* (divine commandment) 'not for the sake of heaven' than not to fulfil it at all because 'from fulfilling it not for the sake of heaven he will come to fulfil it for the sake of heaven' (BSanh. 105b). The holiness of Torah obedience is such that even when it is done from the wrong motive, it brings the Jew closer to God and, in time, the wrong motive will become the right one." Wyschogrod, "Response to the Respondents," 233.

28. Certeau, *Possession at Loudun*, 99.
29. Szabari, "Scandal of Religion," 128.

that de Certeau's comments here are made in the context of a discussion of Roman Catholic religious orders in the early seventeenth century, so this "subjective foundationalism" is seen to characterize Roman Catholicism as well as Protestantism even if it is made more explicit by the latter.)

If there was indeed a general epistemic shift toward a subject-centered view of the world, one can understand why, in ethical terms, one's "intent" came increasingly to be separated out from one's "act." For an "act" is something communal depending on a certain degree of reciprocity. In a subject-centred episteme, it therefore becomes uncertain and unreliable precisely because of this and thus needs to be separated out from the more purely subject-based and therefore more trustworthy "intent." This sense of the "intent" being more trustworthy than the "act" is again suggested by de Certeau when he says that "*the former* [i.e., the intent] *is not guaranteed by the latter* [i.e., the act]"; a good deed cannot guarantee that a good intent lies behind or beneath it. In other words, the public, the observable, the communal, the objective is not to be trusted; it is deceptive. Instead, the moral guarantee can only be derived from the private, the hidden, the individual, the subjective. Thus, the act and the motive are not only more severely separated than ever before, but the motive is itself prized high above the act to which it gives rise. If this is indeed the case, one can conclude that the seeds for a high and pure conception of disinterestedness had been sown long before Kant was around to reap the harvest.

This, however, gives rise to an interesting paradox. We have seen that Kant's strenuous and "pure" conception of disinterestedness, whereby the presence of any motive (other than that of consciousness of fulfilling the Law)[30] invalidates the morality of any particular act, is only intelligible within an epistemic framework within which the individual subject is foundational and determinative. In other words, a subject-centered framework has given rise to a much more stringently self-denying form of disinterestedness. This paradox is not only evident between Kant's concept of disinterestedness and the epistemological framework in which it gets its sense; it is a paradox that is also evident within Kant's concept of disinterestedness itself. That is to say, modern disinterestedness is itself internally fissured by this paradox which makes it inherently unstable. For what we see is that the ideal of disinterestedness is pursued to such an extent that it ultimately becomes incoherent, giving rise to an impulse of self-annihilation such that death

---

30. As Kant puts it, "Since the law itself must be the incentive in a morally good will, the moral interest must be a pure nonsensuous interest of the practical reason alone. Now on the concept of an interest rests that of a maxim. The latter is thus morally genuine only when it rests on the mere interest in obedience to the law." *Critique of Practical Reason*, 82.

Part I: The Ethical

becomes a necessary precondition for its realization. At the same time, as this increasingly incoherent goal is pursued, the goal is itself inverted and gives rise to an impulse of self-promotion.[31] I now want to consider this internal paradox in more detail.

In what sense can it be said that the modern form of disinterestedness leads ultimately to a form of self-annihilation? Modern disinterestedness imposes upon the subject an impossible ideal; it is, in effect, an impossibility. For it insists that every moral act must be performed unilaterally, without any form of "interest" whatsoever. But to what extent is such moral unilateralism really possible? The argument that it is not, in fact, possible on logical and philosophical grounds has been famously articulated by Jacques Derrida in his discussion of the "gift." For Derrida, the gift is defined in terms that make it contiguous with the modern idol of disinterestedness. That is to say, in order to distinguish a gift from a mere contractual exchange it is necessary to understand the gift as being given "freely" (without any form of motive whatsoever) and without return. If, contrariwise, the gift is given on the basis of some hidden motive and/or with the hope of some form of return, then the free purity of the gift would be destroyed, which is, in effect, the destruction of the gift itself. As Derrida puts it, "for there to be a gift, there must be no reciprocity, return, exchange, countergift, or debt. If the other gives me back or owes me or has to give me back what I give him or her, there will not have been a gift, whether this restitution is immediate or whether it is programmed by a complex calculation of a long-term deferral or difference."[32] The logical contiguity of the gift with disinterestedness here is clear. But for Derrida, the gift is always an impossibility; its logical conditions are never met. For the gift is annulled not only by some form of "giving back" on the part of the recipient, but also by the latter's gratitude for and even recognition of the gift. This is because recognition of the gift gives back to the donor a "symbolic equivalent" in place of the thing itself.

Further still, the donor herself cannot even recognize the gift as gift, for this would inevitably entail the donor being "paid back" symbolically with the value of what is perceived to have been given. Such self-congratulation

---

31. Hans Urs von Balthasar, in the context of a discussion of Charles de Condren, Fénelon, and Caussade, has detected in their writings a simultaneous self-annihilation and self-promotion in their quest for a disinterested spirituality: "God, in His being all is so inexpressibly glorious that beside Him everything else not only is as nothing, but, truly speaking, wants to be as nothing." He also discerns a "disdain for human finitude in the interests of an all-embracing Whole in which the little 'I' disappears." And yet, he also comments that "the search for selflessness is far too self-concerned." *Glory of the Lord*, 125, 130, 132. For commentary on Balthasar here, see Milbank, "Sublimity," 265.

32. Derrida, *Given Time*, 12.

itself annuls the "free" character of the gift. Consequently, "At the limit, the gift as gift ought not to appear as gift: either to the donee or to the donor. It cannot be gift as gift except by not being present as gift. . . . the gift can certainly keep its phenomenality or, if one prefers, its appearance as gift. But its very appearance, the simple phenomenon of the gift annuls it as gift, transforming the apparition into a phantom and the operation into a simulacrum."[33] In other words, the impurity of the gift can never be escaped and therefore the gift is always an impossibility, even though the desire for the gift is constitutive of humanity and so the gift will always appear. When this analysis is transposed to that of modern disinterestedness, it may be said that a certain "interest" in our activities can never be escaped and, therefore, that disinterestedness is always an impossibility. In other words, Kant's morality is an impossible morality. If our acts are only moral in so far as they are completely disinterested, Derrida has argued that such disinterestedness is always impossible. The Kantian notion of "morality" thus becomes a conceptual chimera—something sought but never attained.

But there is an important corollary to be drawn out here. The conditions that render disinterestedness an impossibility are those that are constitutive of life itself. The desire for gratitude from the other, for a relationality with the other that involves a necessary give and take, as well as the very self-affirmation that is necessarily entailed in such desires, are inescapable—perhaps even transcendental—conditions of human life. In so far as disinterestedness demands that we lay such desire aside, it in fact demands that we lay down our affirmation of life itself. The result of this is a zero-sum game in which an increase of disinterestedness leads to a corresponding decrease in our affirmation of life and, conversely, an increase in our affirmation of life leads to a corresponding decrease in disinterestedness. In fact, this way of stating the problem is misleading, for we have seen that according to the logic of disinterestedness itself, there is no spectrum, hierarchy, or "degrees" of disinterestedness. One is either disinterested (in the complete absence of rewards, exchange, and reciprocity), or—if rewards, exchange, and reciprocity make an appearance, even to the smallest possible degree—one is not. But this, of course, only makes our zero-sum game with life and death even more severe. For in so far as one affirms (one's own) life, one sacrifices disinterestedness, and in so far as one affirms disinterestedness, one sacrifices (one's own) life. Death, it seems, is a necessary precondition for a realization of true disinterestedness.

Furthermore, if, as disinterestedness demands, the subject is always and everywhere to sacrifice all interest in its own existence for the sake of

33. Ibid., 14.

the other, it will find itself always and everywhere confronted with this suicidal demand. For the command of disinterestedness, as we have seen, is far more intense and severe than the command to feed the hungry and clothe the naked. It demands that whenever the needs and desires of others are compromised by our own needs and desires, priority must always be given to the needs and desires of others over our own in which we are commanded to have no interest. But where to stop? How far should this be taken? The problem with modern disinterestedness is that it provides no criteria for such discrimination. In place of such discrimination, there is simply a universal imperative: sacrifice oneself. This command to sacrifice oneself for the sake of the other resounds repeatedly and ever more loudly, even unto death. Consequently, the human subject finds itself every day and at each moment tormented by a suicidal impulse. For at all times and in all places, one is repeatedly confronted by instances of the needs and desires of others being compromised not only by our own needs and desires but also by our very existence. Taken to its logical conclusion, therefore, disinterestedness may only be achieved by means of our own self-annihilation.[34] Indeed, we shall return to this question below, for it is a conundrum that reappears in the very different work of Emmanuel Levinas.

But how does it come about that this impulse toward self-annihilation actually ends up by effecting its inversion? How does this pathological self-denial give rise also and simultaneously to an unprecedented self-promotion? The two phenomena are, in fact, closely related, for it is precisely this stringent self-denial that both arises out of and unwittingly gives rise to this impulse of self-promotion. Ostensibly (and, in premodern times, actually, one might venture), the denial of self that disinterestedness demands is pursued *for the sake of* and out of a love for others (whether God, neighbors, or both). One is commanded to deny oneself *in order to* give oneself up to God, and in so doing, one paradoxically affirms oneself. In this sense, disinterestedness is merely instrumental; it is cultivated in order to bring one closer to God or else it is a by-product emerging from one saturated by love. But the primacy here is all too easily reversed such that one gives oneself up to God or to other subjects *in order to* become truly disinterested. It is a conundrum that was expressed in slightly different terms (though

---

34. As John Milbank has observed: "Extreme 'disinterest' in one's own activity, though it can only be exercised by a subject, tends also to a suicidally sacrificial will against oneself. That is to say, it tends ineradicably to depersonalize or devolve into a will to be a fully usable object." "Can a Gift Be Given?" 132. Connected to this is his comment that "an absolutely pure giving, outside all motivations of self-pleasing, all return of self to self, and all expectation of any sort of return from the other, is more radically and coherently conceived in terms of an impersonal nihil. And any experience of self, even as willing, would seem to violate the purity of such imperatives." Ibid., 143.

directly related to the question of disinterestedness) by Archbishop Fénelon. "Granted that we wish to be happy," he says, "can we ever wish to be happy in order to glorify God; or do we invariably wish to glorify God in order to be happy?"[35] In which direction does the primacy operate here? What is done for the sake of what? Kant's answer is unambiguous; disinterestedness is our primary and ultimate goal, for it alone secures our morality. This has to be the case for Kant because morality gives rise to but does not require the "idea" (in Kant's sense) of God. Integral to Kant's understanding of the autonomy of morality is the notion that humans do not need the idea of an objective lawgiver in order to live a moral life. Indeed, the idea of God could potentially be positively harmful if it becomes a motive for living a moral life, thus destroying disinterestedness and, with it, morality itself.[36] For Kant, therefore, the answer is clear; far from being instrumental, the pursuit of disinterestedness is primary, the ultimate goal to which all else is subordinated.

Once again, this shift is perfectly intelligible in the context of a subject-centered epistemic framework. For in a framework where the subject is central, foundational, and determinative of all else, it is not difficult to see that when the notion of disinterestedness is introduced into it, the central imperative becomes to negate or deny this subject, an imperative to which all else is subordinated. So whether the subject is being affirmed or negated, the subject remains the central preoccupation in relation to which everything else is secondary. In so far as others do make an appearance here, they do so not in their own right as "others" to which we submit ourselves out of love and for their own sakes, but rather as secondary "tools" that we "use" (by ostensibly submitting ourselves to them) for the sake of our own primary purification and the cultivation of our own disinterestedness. This point is well made by Rowan Williams when he says that according to the modern logic of disinterestedness, "all ostensibly external ends (feeding a hungry person, attempting to change a government by some sort of political action, sexual fidelity, or what have you) are instrumental to the development of 'higher consciousness' . . . if disinterestedness is itself the goal, if there are not goals beyond the self, how do we distinguish this from

---

35. Quoted in Kirk, *Vision of God*, 459.

36. This is why, for Kant, God does not appear in the phenomenal world and why God allows us "only to conjecture His existence." For if God and eternity "would stand unceasingly before our eyes," then "most actions conforming to the law would be done from fear, few would be done from hope, none from duty. The moral worth of actions, on which alone the worth of the person and even of the world depends in the eyes of supreme wisdom, would not exist at all." *Critique of Practical Reason*, 152–53.

an ultimate narcissism . . . ?"[37] One way of articulating what is happening here is to say that the modern form of disinterestedness is a response to the problem of the subject-centered framework of modernity, but it is a misguided response. For what is really needed is a disruption and a breaking up of this very framework. Instead, what the modern form of disinterestedness attempts is a correction of the problem by working within this problematic framework by means of a strenuous and stringent effort to negate the still central subject. The paradox is, however, that the more strenuously and stringently one applies oneself to the denial of self, the more self-obsessed one actually becomes.

There is another but related way in which the modern quest for disinterestedness ends up by being paradoxically self-promoting. As we have seen, pure disinterestedness can only be achieved by renouncing all "interest" in one's actions—all possible rewards, returns, even acts of gratitude. If this is the case, however, then one's paramount concern becomes the avoidance of any form of return on one's actions. Although this is ostensibly other-regarding and self-denying, what actually happens here is that it becomes imperative to deny any form of exchange with the other, and thus necessary to repudiate any reciprocal acts, whether a return of the gift, a gesture of thanks, or a smile of gratitude. One must remain impervious to them all, in a stone-like state of impassibility. In effect, of course, this constitutes a denial of reciprocity, of exchange, of relationality, and as such it is a denial of community itself. In so far as there is a community envisaged here, it is a conglomeration of monadic, self-sufficient, impassive subjects, all taking care to repudiate any exchange, lest it contaminate their prized disinterest, and all narcissistically attending to the cultivation of their disinterested selfhoods.

If the logic of the modern idol of disinterestedness gives rise to this denial of relatedness, to the downgrading of others to the status of props or tools, it should come as little surprise to find that God is similarly downgraded. Although it was initially the case that disinterestedness was pursued out of a pure love for God alone, the modern intensification of the disinterested quest actually ends up by turning the subject away from God. For if, as we have seen, any form of return or reward for our actions is disallowed as "canceling out" our pure love for God, then an enjoyment of God's love for the subject—or of eternal life, or of salvation, or, indeed, of any reciprocal return by God of the subject's love for God—is ruled out; at the very least, the subject is to remain indifferent to these returns or rewards. The result of this is that God becomes increasingly detached from the again self-obsessed

---

37. Williams, "Religious Realism," 11.

subject and, as a result, becomes more and more distant.[38] In order to be truly disinterested, it seems, God must fade further and further into the distant horizon. Indeed, this implication was later fully explicated by Don Cupitt, who, committed to a Kantian disinterestedness, realized that this must ultimately culminate in a nonrealist conception of God.[39] God must be sacrificed, in effect, for the sake of the higher god of disinterestedness. God, like other subjects, thus becomes a prop or a part of the supporting cast, playing a secondary role in a drama in which the cultivation of the disinterested subject takes center stage.

If this is the case, then the traditional relationship between God and the self has been reversed. For the self has now become foundational, and God has become secondary. Indeed, this is a reversal that is made explicit by Kant. He rejects the theological model whereby God reveals to humanity what is good, true, and moral and replaces it with one whereby one begins with what one knows to be moral, and then forms an image of God on the basis of it. Indeed, he goes so far as to say that "we create a God for ourselves" on the basis of moral concepts: "For in whatever manner a being has been made known to him by another and described as God, yea even if such a being had appeared to him (if this is possible), he must first of all compare this representation with his ideal in order to judge whether he is entitled to regard it and to honor it as a divinity."[40] Humanity, in other words, has become the judge of God. The relationship between God and humanity has been reversed; man has become godlike.

This divinization of the human is particularly evident in the way in which the idol of disinterestedness demands that we love as God loves, that is, universally and indiscriminately. And this, of course, takes us back to one of the enigmas intrinsic to the commandment to love our neighbors as ourselves, as identified by Žižek, Santner, and Reinhard. If we are to exercise a pure love that is uncontaminated by any "interests" of our own, then there can be no grounds for loving family, friends, and immediate neighbors over and above all others. On the contrary, all others have an equal claim over our love, in much the same way that God loves all indiscriminately and "carest for no man." Once again, however, disinterestedness seems to give rise to an unprecedented self-promotion, as the finitude of the subject—with all its constraints—is apparently being denied, and it is instead being endowed with godlike capabilities and responsibilities. This has recently been

38. Thus, we can see why John Milbank has suggested that the modern intensification of the disinterested impulse gives rise to a conception of God as a "mere cipher," to the point of disappearing altogether. See Milbank, "Sublimity," 265.

39. See Cupitt, *Taking Leave of God*.

40. Kant, *Religion within the Limits of Reason Alone*, 157.

discussed by John Milbank, who, drawing on the work of Bernard Williams, endorses our impulse always to discriminate in favor of our nearest and dearest in the event of a common catastrophe, for instance: "To take any other position is . . . to deny our finitude, and our limited range of intense capacity for affection and attention. One can see this by asking the question, suppose the neglected nearest and dearest survive, despite our neglect? With the best intentions or respect for our altruism, how will they, as warm-blooded animals, really read our pious neutrality?"[41] The phrase "warm-blooded animals" is crucial here. For the modern idol of disinterestedness seems to presuppose not only that we are or are capable of being godlike in our capacities and responsibilities, but also that our ideal state should be, as we have seen, some kind of impassible, emotion-renouncing, and lifeless stasis. This, in turn, raises the question of whether, in human terms, such an indiscriminate, abstract, and universalized love can indeed be regarded as love at all. For Milbank, this quest for an indiscriminate ethic stands in contrast to that of Christianity. He says that "the entire Christian tradition at least up to the time of the Angelic doctor interpreted agape as 'neighbour love' to mean precisely a preferential love for those nearest to us, those with the most inherited, realized and developed affinity with us, as well as those strangers with whom suddenly we are bonded whether we like it or not, by instances of distress, shared experience or preferred comfort."[42] This is another point to which we shall return, for there are questions as to whether the equivocal tension between the imperative toward universal love on the one hand and the imperative to love our nearest and dearest on the other, can be quite as easily and complacently "resolved" in the way that Milbank seems to think it can be. Nonetheless, we can observe that there is a sense in which Christianity recognizes our finitude in relation to God and our relatedness with regard to our fellow human beings, in a way that contrasts with the model of modern disinterestedness.

And it is precisely at this point that the incoherent apotheosis and the antithetical inversion of the ideal coincide. For in discussing the specific ways in which disinterestedness leads unwittingly to a form of self-promotion, I have also noted that the particular self that is being promoted is one that is impassible, emotion-renouncing, and ultimately life-less. The self that is unwittingly being promoted is ultimately a self that is dead. If there is self-promotion here, therefore, it is a self-promotion that is ultimately self-annihilating. Furthermore, if we see the modern ideal of disinterestedness as an explication and development of the commandment to love your

---

41. Milbank, *Being Reconciled*, 39.
42. Ibid.

neighbor as yourself (as Kant himself did), then we see that the very thing that has been unwittingly expunged in this process is the concept of love itself. We have seen that the motivating force that fuels the Kantian system is that of the imperative for purity of motive rather than a suffusion of love. One sacrifices oneself to the other not out of an overwhelming love for the other, but out of an obligation to act in accordance with the dictates of the categorical imperative, and this legal act becomes a moral act if it is performed with no motive other than obedience to the law itself. But love does not enter into the equation here. Indeed, love is squeezed out of the system and drained away by the repudiation of reciprocity and exchange, phenomena that must be repudiated in order to protect disinterestedness but phenomena that, equally, serve as the preconditions for and as the expressions of love. So the subject that finds itself fractured by its being torn between self-affirmation and self-annihilation also finds itself deposited in a loveless world. How has this come about? How has an ancient and orthodox Christian teaching and practice gotten into such difficulties?

Part of the answer has been evident in much of what has already been said. These unsustainable paradoxes and contradictions arise out of the subject-centered framework within which Kant is located. Such a framework was by no means the invention of Kant, although a case may be made that he represents its culmination. Working with a foundationalism of the ego, with which he was philosophically bequeathed, he brings out the implications of this unremittingly—in the arenas of both pure and practical reason. In a framework that isolates and sets apart the subject from the world within which it is situated, the result is a dualism wherein the "I" is set over against all that is not-I. This gives rise to a whole series of consequent dualisms—of subject and object, of noumenon and phenomenon, and so forth. And the boundary between them is strictly nonnegotiable, precisely because there is no third through which they might be mediated.

The same dualistic diremption is carried over into the realm of practical reason, so that, as we have already observed, the ethical realm is sundered between morality and legality, autonomy and heteronomy, and disinterestedness and interestedness. These antinomies do bear witness to a certain irresolvable aporia at the heart of the ethical, and Kant therefore does at least bring the equivocation of the ethical into sharp focus in this respect. But, again, because there is no third through which these antinomies might be negotiated, they become fixed into absolute and nonnegotiable dualisms with the result that the tension between them reaches a sclerotic impasse. Aware that he cannot rest content with such an impasse, however, Kant seeks to overcome it not through the invocation of a third, but by means of the unequivocal subordination of one side of the dualism to the other. The tension between these antinomies, which should be constantly negotiated and renegotiated, is thereby "overcome," with the result that the aporia at the heart of the ethical is destroyed. Kant attempts to disfigure, forget, or repress equivocation by means of this unequivocal resolution.

The preeminent manifestation of this is Kant's unequivocal prioritizing of the universal over the particular. In the course of our discussion, we identified all those things that Kant downplays, represses, or indeed banishes—love, sympathy, fellow-feeling, contingency and, indeed, all those characteristics that were said to be transcendental conditions of life itself. In other words, what Kant repeatedly represses is the domain of *particularity*. In each and every instance, he subordinates the particular to the universal. For Kant, it is clearly the case that the effective realization of the ethical is hindered by the stubborn contaminating persistence of particularity. At each stage, the stain of particularity must be wiped away so that the universal purity of the ethical can shine through.

So the difficulties to which Kant falls prey may be explained in terms of his elevation of the subject on the one hand and his prioritizing of the domain of the universal on the other. But it would be a mistake, of course, to see these as two separate streams that flow together into the Kantian ethical problematic. On the contrary, the two are already intermingled, for the subjectivity in question is precisely a *universal* subjectivity, that defining feature of the entire modern episteme, as we noted at the outset. Not only do foundational subjectivity and the domain of the universal reach their apotheosis in Kant's philosophy, but they also realize their most perfect synthesis. It is this notion of universal subjectivity that ultimately destroys the ethical by overcoming the necessary equivocation between the universal, the particular, and the singular, just as it also overcomes the necessary equivocation between self and other, which is one of the ways through which the former is played out. Not only is such a model destructive of the ethical, but it is also destructive of subjectivity itself. We have seen how the elevation of subjectivity gives rise ultimately to its negation; how hubristic and suicidal impulses go hand in hand. Caught between these contrary drives, the subject finds itself tortured by *anxiety*, which can itself be understood as a symptom of the attempt to repress its irreducible particularity.

Having examined the specific example of Kantian disinterestedness, we thereby come to see the anxiety that is induced by the diremption of the ethical. The Kantian subject faces a choice between interested self-affirmation (life) and disinterested self-annihilation (death). It thus finds itself torn between this impossible choice, unable to take either of the alternatives available to it, and yet also unable to find a way through them simply because, as we have seen, no such way exists within the Kantian scheme. As a result, the subject oscillates pathologically between these two extremes, never resting and becoming increasingly fractured. The psychological—as well as the logical—difficulties inherent to such a quest are obvious. Incapable of a resolution, the subject is destined to err endlessly between these two extremes.

Where might one look for a rescue from this impasse? What comes after the modernity that reaches its ethical apotheosis in Kant? In asking these questions, it is necessary to turn to the work of Emmanuel Levinas, for few thinkers are more associated than he with the effort to rescue the ethical from the depredations to which it had been subjected in modernity. In the final part of this chapter, therefore, I want to consider the extent to which Levinas is able to deliver us from the Kantian anxiety we have been elucidating. Is Levinas able to restore a sense of the ethical equivocation that Kant did so much to exorcise?

Anxiety Perpetuated: The Levinasian Inversion

As is well known, central to Levinas's project is a critique of ontology as first philosophy, the science of Being, which, according to Levinas, has stood at the heart of the Western metaphysical tradition from Plato to Heidegger. But his critique of metaphysics sprang first and foremost from his re-conceptualization of ethics, his account of which is fundamentally phenomenological. That is to say, Levinas was not concerned to develop a prescriptive ethical schema (which would be yet another instance of the ethics as idolatry that he was repudiating), but, rather, to provide a phenomenological description of what *happens* in the ethical relationship. This description contrasts markedly with the phenomenology assumed, if not always explicitly stated, by the ethical theories of modernity.

As we have seen, the founding assumption of the ethics of modernity is the notion of the universal human subject. The assumption is that this subject is not ethically "prejudiced," but stands neutrally in an imaginary ethical vacuum, in need of a philosophical and ethical system that, when demonstrated to be rationally valid, will inform that subject of what is right and wrong, good and evil, and of how it should act in all possible circumstances. Alternatively, the subject is viewed as being "naturally" selfish and egotistical and therefore standing in need of a rationally established philosophical and ethical system that, because of its universal validity, can be relied upon to "restrain," "rein in," or even alchemically convert the subject's "natural" impulses. These conceptions of the ethical are entirely rejected by Levinas, who rejects the ethically "neutral" subject and also the naturally self-interested subject as fictions, and dangerous fictions at that. Rather, for Levinas, the subject is, from the very first, in a pre-reflective and pre-philosophical way, "called" by and "responsible" to the "other." In other words, the subject in no way "determines" or "decides," by a process of rational reflection, that it *ought to be* responsible to the other; it simply finds itself irresistibly subject to this call, a call that is prior to reflection and, therefore, prior to ontology and, indeed, all philosophy. Furthermore, to be subject to this call is part of what it is to be human; it is what constitutes the human subject *as* a human subject. In so far as this call to responsibility constitutes a "genuine" and "authentic" ethics, then it can be seen why, for Levinas, ethics *precedes* all thought, reflection, and philosophy. Far from the human subject "deciding," by a process of reflection, to be "ethical," therefore, for Levinas, the phenomenological reality is precisely the other way around; it is the ethical that gives rise to and constitutes the human subject.

It should be noted that Levinas's conception of the other here is not simply reducible to "other subjects" like myself. If this were all the other signified, then the other would be other in the sense of being the further away of two terms that are connected by virtue of a specific differential linguistic relationship—"that" as opposed to "this," "you" as opposed to "me." Understood in this sense, the other would not designate any intrinsically heteronomous phenomenon, but would simply identify one of two terms in a dyadic relationship by specifying its spatial and temporal proximity to the designating subject. For Levinas, however, the other is absolutely heteronomous (*tout autre*), not simply an other in relation to the designating subject. As wholly other, it resists all linguistic attempts to designate and contain it and exceeds the controlling human gaze. If the other were to be "captured" by the human gaze or by subjective conceptuality, then it would ultimately be destroyed because its defining characteristic, namely, its intrinsic heteronomy, would thereby be transgressed. This means also that the other is not reducible to the "neighbor" on the one hand, nor is it to be equated with God on the other. Beyond both characterizations, the other that calls us and to which we are responsible is absolutely unspecifiable, wholly other, *tout autre*.

But how can we be called by that which is unknown? And how can we feel responsible to that which is unspecifiable? Levinas's answer here is that the other "appears" to us and "calls" us through the *face*: "the face of a neighbor signifies for me an unexceptional responsibility, preceding every free consent, every pact, every contract. It escapes representation; it is the very collapse of phenomenality."[43] It should be noted, however, that the other

---

43. Levinas, *Otherwise than Being*, 88.

is not reducible to a specific face or to faces in a general sense. Rather, the face bears witness to an irreducible alterity. In the face of the other, we see an alterity that exceeds our controlling gaze. No matter how familiar a face may be to us, and no matter how close we may come to the bearer of a face emotionally, physically, and sexually, it bears witness to a fundamental and inherent otherness that we can never penetrate. Thus, the face bears witness to the other, though it does not exhaust and capture the other. The other "appears" in the face, though it is not contained by that face. In this sense, the face serves a similar purpose to that served by Jean-Luc Marion's icon; the face is, in effect, an icon of the other.[44] Or, to write in more specifically Levinasian terminology, in the face we find the trace of the other: "The trace of a past in a face is not the absence of a yet non-revealed, but the anarchy of what has never been present, of an infinite which commands in the face of the other, and which, like an excluded middle, could not be aimed at."[45]

From this account, it is clear that the other and the ethical are inseparable for Levinas, for the ethical is constituted by the subject's response to the other. Without this relationship to the other, there can be no ethical relationship at all. Once this is understood, it can be seen why Levinas's criticism of philosophy as ontology is so ethically charged. His objection to ontology is not simply philosophical, but primarily ethical. To some extent, Levinas's critique here illuminates some of the points made in relation to Kant. There we saw what happens when ethics are controlled and defined by the human gaze, when ethics becomes an idol. This situation came about when the subject was no longer "seized" by the other, but was, on the contrary, "seizing hold of" and controlling the other (and thereby destroying it). We saw that when ethics was reconceived in this way, it was ultimately destroyed, collapsing under the weight of its own internal contradictions. For Levinas, this would be an illustration of what happens when the other is "forgotten"—domesticated or devoured by the all-consuming subject. But Levinas's critique goes further than just pointing out the contradictions and paradoxes into which ethics falls when it is conceived in the manner of an idol. For him, the final outcome of a forgetting of the other is much more sinister. For when the human subject is no longer constituted by its being "seized" by the other, by its finding itself in a relationship of responsibility toward the other, and is instead constituted by its being foundational, constitutive, controlling, and imposing in its relationship to reality and the other, then the ultimate destiny of such a totalizing subject is to become totalitarian. As J. Hillis Miller has observed, the modern notion of

44. See Marion, *God without Being*.
45. Levinas, *Otherwise than Being*, 97.

Part I: The Ethical

subjectivity that was founded by Descartes "leads to the assumption that things exist, for me at least, only because I think them. When everything exists, only as reflected in the ego, then man has drunk up the sea. If man is defined as subject, everything else turns into object."[46] When the subject becomes the measure of all things, it ceases to be held responsible to that which is genuinely other and finds itself in a position of totalizing mastery. Although it may attempt to "check" or "rein in" this mastery by constructing an ethics to which it is held accountable, this ethics is itself founded upon an ontology of mastery, so that even this ethical system is itself little more than self-projection seeking a simultaneous and paradoxical self-negation. This paradoxicality installs an inherent instability into the ethical system itself, so that it eventually collapses, leaving nothing in its wake but a totalizing and mastering subjectivity, as Nietzsche saw all too clearly. Thus it is that the secret truth of all Western metaphysics and Western ontology is totalitarianism and its political counterpart is that of fascism. It is for this reason that the overcoming of metaphysics is fundamentally, for Levinas, an ethical task. If we are to overcome mastery and domination by approaching the ethical freed from philosophical shackles, then our task is to remember the other that modern philosophy repressed.

It is important to note at this point that what Levinas is enacting here is not only a reconfiguration of subjectivity, but also, and directly connected with it, a reconfiguration of the relationship between the universal, the particular, and the singular. Indeed, the shift from the preexistent universal subject to a subject that is constituted as such by its experience of the call of the other, is itself an enactment of the shift from the universal to the singular. The universal subject and its universal law is displaced by the irreducibly singular call evinced by the face, which itself constitutes the emergence of the singular subject. Just as the foundational subject and its self-representation carries a threat of a violent totalitarianism, so too an unequivocal prioritizing of the "universal" domain carries precisely the same threat. Consequently, any approach to the ethical that privileges the universal must, for Levinas, ultimately be ethically destructive. So just as it is ethically necessary to reconfigure subjectivity, so too it is ethically necessary to reconfigure the relationship between the universal, the particular, and the singular. The sovereignty of the universal must be displaced by the sovereignty of the singular if the ethical is genuinely to manifest and perpetuate itself.

There is, of course, an inherent paradox here in that Levinas's account of the sovereignty of the singular would appear to involve him in a

---

46. Miller, *Poets of Reality*, 3, quoted in Taylor, *Erring*, 22.

performative enactment of the sovereignty of the universal. That is to say, his account of the singular character of the ethical experience is one that claims for itself a universal validity, in which it is a singular experience to which all are subjected. Levinas is by no means unaware of this paradox. Indeed, his explicit recognition of it may be seen as an instance of his acknowledgment of the equivocation of the ethical, such that the singular can never *unequivocally* be prioritized over the universal and the particular. We shall discuss this paradox in more detail in chapter 3. But for the moment, it is sufficient to note that in the midst of this equivocation, Levinas does seek to displace the sovereignty of the universal with the priority of the singular—both so as to avoid violence and totalitarianism, which would constitute the destruction of the ethical, and also so as to escape the ethical impasses wrought by modernity of the kind we illuminated in relation to Kant.

But to what extent does Levinas really effect an escape from the disabling anxiety that we saw to have paralyzed the Kantian ethical subject? Has he effectively escaped the diremption that separates out and hypostatizes the enigma that lies at the heart of the commandment to love one's neighbor as oneself? Although Levinas does effect a critically important transformation of the ethical subject from a nominative to an accusative mode of being, and although he does reverse the priority of the universal over the singular and particular, I want to suggest that this inversion leaves much of the structural problematic of the Kantian inheritance intact. What we have, it seems, is an inversion of the relationship between self and other, between universal and singular, which nonetheless preserves the antinomy between them. The whole Levinasian ethical edifice is still structured by the question of the relationship between self and other, wherein the two are dirempted and separated out, and where the assertion and claims of one are always at the expense of the other. The subject is thus still exposed to an anxiety arising from the apparent incompatibility of loving self and other simultaneously. The enigma of the commandment is again turned into a paralyzing impasse. Furthermore, although Levinas is most sharply distinguished from Kant by his displacement of the latter's subjective foundationalism by a conception of the subject as "addressee," we find that this decentering of the subject turns out to be a movement more in the manner of an inversion rather than that of a structural overcoming. As we would expect of a such an inversion, we find that this actually ends up tipping into its opposite, so that the Levinasian self-denial actually ends up by being a covert form of self-promotion. Thus it is that we find that Levinas repeats the Kantian oscillation between self-denial and self-promotion that we saw to lie fatally at the heart of the Kantian system.

Part I: The Ethical

A second way in which Levinas only apparently overcomes the Kantian impasse lies in his reconfiguration of the relationship between the universal, the particular, and the singular. Once again, we see here almost a straight inversion. Whereas we observed Kant determinedly repressing the dangerous lure represented by the domain of the particular, we see in Levinas the enactment of a phobia toward the universal. Levinas's antipathy toward the domain of universality is motivated by his overwhelming fear of totalitarianism, a fear that recurs throughout his texts. As we shall see in chapter 3, some believe that Levinas's downplaying of the role of the universal has fatal implications for any conception of a Levinasian politics. But it also has significant implications for the ethical. Once again, we shall see the equivocation of the ethical being skewed in favor of one of the triadic modes—the singular, as manifested in the "face." This skewing may not be as extreme as that enacted by Kant, but the implications are again destructive. Indeed, we see hovering in the margins of Levinas's texts several Kantian ghosts, which it seems almost impossible to exorcise and which subject them to the same, if more spectral, processes of anxiety.

In explicating these claims, however, it should also be noted that Levinas's thought does undoubtedly represent an advance on the Kantian problematic. He goes some considerable way toward exposing its difficulties, albeit without entirely escaping them. One experiences, therefore, a certain degree of ambivalence when confronted by Levinas's texts. Indeed, we may modify one of Levinas's own comments and say that if Levinas represents an advance on Kant, this is so only in the sense that Levinas "bears a sense of what is beyond the Kantian essence."[47] Thus, he reconceives the subject in an accusative mode, but an antinomy between self and other remains fatally in place. Likewise, he seems to recognize the indispensible roles to be played by the universal, the particular, and the singular in the ethical, but fatally continues to prioritize one over the others. In this respect, it is interesting to note as well that Gillian Rose shares this sense of ambivalence when confronted with Levinas's text, although, for her, this is expressed in somewhat other terms. She speaks of Levinas "simultaneously acknowledging and refusing to know the inversions of love and the state" and suggests that "Levinas keeps inviolate a holy middle just as he reveals that it is broken."[48] We shall see, then, that our assessment of Levinas is not entirely critical; he represents an advance even as he fails to see that advance through; he

47. This is a modification of a comment of Levinas in *Otherwise than Being*, 5. Here he says that reason, the regulation of conflict, is not the enactment of the otherwise than being. "Commerce is better than war," but only in the sense that commerce "bears[s] a sense of what is beyond the essence."
48. Rose, *Broken Middle*, 248.

exposes the nature of the ethical enigma even as he dirempts and attempts to "overcome" it.

Let us now examine this in more detail. For Levinas, the primordial character of the ethical calling is such that we are subject to and, indeed, constituted by an irresistible obligation of responsibility to the other which comes to us and directly addresses us in the singularity of the "face." This experience is primordial—what Levinas calls a non-original or an-archic origin—because if it were a conventional origin, conceived within time, it would become the first within an immanent, temporal series rather than that which precedes this series.[49] An important aspect of this responsibility toward the other, however, is the fact that it is without limit. For Levinas, we are "absolutely" responsible for and to the other. There can be no question of an "appropriate," rationally calculated "degree" of responsibility. Just as the other itself is infinite, so too its demand upon us and our responsibility to it are infinite. So, when confronted with a face that places a demand upon us, there can be no question of "deciding" what is an "appropriate" or "adequate" response; our response can only be simply to surrender ourselves to this other, or, as Levinas says, to make ourselves as nothing in the face of the other. Levinas himself comments that there is "no longer any limit or measure for this responsibility, which 'in the memory of man' has never been contracted, and is found to be at the mercy of the freedom and the fate, unverifiable by me, of the other man. It is to catch sight of an extreme passivity, a passivity that is not assumed, in the relationship with the other, and, paradoxically, in pure saying itself."[50]

It is the case, of course, according to Levinas's phenomenological description, that others are equally placed under the same absolute and infinite responsibility as I am. But this is of no relevance to the infinite responsibility under which I am placed: "the subject affected by the other cannot think that the affection is reciprocal."[51] The fact that others are responsible for and to me is in no way a precondition or justification for my own responsibility toward them. Once again, this would be to relapse into a conception of ethics as idolatry, wherein autonomous subjects rationally decide to make a contract to be responsible for each other. On the contrary, the responsibility of others toward me is of no concern or relevance here: "The knot of subjectivity consists in going to the other without concerning oneself with his movement toward me. Or, more exactly, it consists in approaching in such a way that, over and beyond all the reciprocal relations that do not fail

---

49. Levinas, *Otherwise than Being*, 10.
50. Ibid., 47.
51. Ibid., 84.

to get set up between me and the neighbor, I have always taken one step more toward him—which is possible only if this step is responsibility. In the responsibility which we have for one another, I have always one more response to give, I have to answer for this very responsibility."[52] The call of the other, precisely in so far as it is absolute, is quite unconditional, and the raising of the question of the responsibility of others toward me would be a dangerous distraction. My vocation as a human subject is simply to pour myself out to the other that calls me.

But in articulating all of this, we must ask whether Levinas's insistence that the "absolute" responsibility under which the ethical subject is placed is not a post-metaphysical rendering of Kant's "absolute" disinterestedness, with all of the problems that we have seen this to entail. For we may perceive here yet another recapitulation of a Kantian either-or. We saw above that Kant's conception of disinterestedness is framed by an uncompromising either-or choice between interestedness on the one hand and disinterestedness on the other. If there are any motives or interests whatsoever, disinterestedness is destroyed and interestedness prevails, while disinterestedness may only be preserved if it is absolutely pure, without any motive or interest whatsoever. In Levinas's conception of "absolute" responsibility, we see him yet again working within a structurally similar either-or, and with a concomitant renunciation of any interestedness and promotion of a divestment of the self by itself. In this respect, David Wood has suggested that Levinas "makes the same mistake as Kant in supposing that any trace of self-interest is proof that what we are dealing with are those social arrangements for mutual benefit that masquerade under the name of morality, and not ethics. The former are characterized by some sort of symmetrical interaction. The latter by a fundamental asymmetry."[53] So for Wood, Kant and Levinas are complicit in their assumption that for ethics to be genuinely ethical, it must be uncontaminated by any trace of self-interest and, by implication, any mutuality and reciprocity. It is of the essence of the ethical to be asymmetrical and unilateral.

In his own discussion of Levinas's thought, John D. Caputo questions both the absoluteness of the other to which Levinas claims we are responsible as well as the absolute disinterestedness that this entails. As far as the absoluteness of the other is concerned, Caputo fears that this compromises the relationship between the other and the self which is central to Levinas's thought as well as to the ethical itself. He says that "if something were, properly speaking, absolutely Other, then it would not be a matter of concern

---

52. Ibid.
53. Wood, *Step Back*, 67.

for us and we would simply ignore it, being quite oblivious of it."[54] Clearly, this is inimical to the whole Levinasian project, the central claim of which is that the absolutely Other is our ultimate and indeed constituting concern. But Caputo goes on to say that if this is the case, it "means that the Other is related to us after all, viz., in a very powerful, unconditionally commanding way. We, in turn, should acknowledge this relation by responding to it, by answering it and taking it up, decisively and unequivocally. So in fact the absolutely Other is only relatively absolute, almost absolute, not quite absolute."[55] What Caputo is questioning here is the absolute separation between the other and the subject that talk of the "absolutely other" seems to imply. I shall return to this question in due course. But more relevant to our immediate concerns is Caputo's questioning of the very possibility of the absolute disinterestedness that Levinas commends.

Caputo makes the point that the subject can never quite shake off its own self-concern, no matter how disinterested it may attempt to be and no matter how "absolutely" it may feel itself to be responsible:

> When it comes to the absolutely Other and absolute heteronomy (altruism) I remain, as always, forcefully and decisively, to an almost excessive degree, inside/outside. I subscribe to the absolutely Other—almost, so long as we all understand that this is a hyperbolic expression for something that is very important *quoad me* (for me). . . . I cannot get absolutely outside to an absolute *alter*. I cannot shake off this little tag end, rag-tail ("for me") and make a clean cut. I do want to be absolutely altruistic—*inter alia*. I want to. But if that is what I want, then if I am altruistic I end up doing what I want.[56]

There are clearly echoes here of the Derridean deconstruction of the gift, as was discussed earlier in the chapter, and we may well see Caputo's comments as the articulation of a Derridean response to Levinas. Indeed, this appears to be confirmed when Caputo goes on to say that we should take Levinas with a "twist of deconstruction." Thus, Caputo thinks that Levinas displays some hyperbolic excess here, that he advocates a "powerful" and "fabulous tale," a beautiful but impossible dream.

But this point against Levinas may well be more telling than Caputo is willing to allow. For one thing, it is far from clear whether Levinas's dream is fabulous and beautiful (but unfortunately excessive and impossible). On the contrary, the either-or in which it appears to be ensnared, namely,

54. Caputo, *Against Ethics*, 80.
55. Ibid., 80–81.
56. Ibid., 83.

the choice between self-assertion and self-annihilation, is in many ways a frightening and, ultimately, destructive one. Furthermore and following on from this, far from being an excessively exuberant articulation of a basically sound ethical insight, we should rather view Levinas's insistence on an "absolute" responsibility as an inevitable outcome of a problematic Kantian inheritance from which Levinas has not ultimately escaped. To endorse the basic ethical structure, while at the same time expressing reservations with regard to Levinas's hyperbole, as Caputo does, does not in fact help us out here. For we would then be left with the problematic quasi-Kantian either-or antinomies, of which Levinas's excesses are the natural and inevitable outcome. Caputo has correctly identified the difficulty with Levinas's position, but I should argue that the implications are more far-reaching than he suggests. The challenge, as we have already intimated, is to attempt to find some way of being true to the enigma that promotes love of neighbor *and* love of self in a way that does not insist on giving an ultimate priority to one, which results in the inevitable destruction of the other, as we saw to have happened with Kant, and which, I am suggesting, happens also with Levinas.

For it seems that the fulfilling of our responsibility to the other in an absolute way, that is to say, without limit, can only end ultimately in our own self-negation, in a sacrifice of oneself for the other. We thus have a reinscription of the Kantian diremption between love of self and love of other; the affirmation of one is always at the expense of the other, so that absolute responsibility for the other seems to compromise one's own right to exist. This is made explicit when Levinas asks, "What is an individual, a solitary individual, if not a tree that grows without regard for everything it suppresses and breaks, grabbing all the nourishment, air and sun, a being that is fully justified in its nature and its being? What is an individual, if not a usurper? What is signified by the advent of conscience, and even the first spark of spirit, if not the discovery of corpses beside me and my horror of existing by assassination?"[57] Thus, my very existence, my very being, is at the expense of the other, and my own response to this can only be the sacrifice of myself to the other. It would therefore appear that Levinas has sundered the enigma that lies at the heart of the commandment to love my neighbor as myself. Interpreting the commandment as embodying not an enigma but an impossibility, Levinas "overcomes" this impossibility by sacrificing the self to the other. On Levinas's own grounds, it is difficult to see how this could lead logically to anything other than a suicidal self-negation. There are two insights here, which, when put together, seem to

---

57. Levinas, *Difficult Freedom*, 100. Quoted in Žižek, "Neighbors and Other Monsters," 150.

Anxiety

move ineluctably in this direction. The first is the insight, embodied in the passage just quoted, that the self's own being is sustained at the expense of and by constantly threatening the being of others. For Levinas, it seems that this agonistic conception is an inescapable, and presumably therefore tragic, aspect of the human condition. It might be said that this is a tragedy that can be overcome only by means of Levinas's second insight, namely, that we are constituted by a persecution, the only response to which is an absolute and unlimited substitution of myself for the other. My responsibility for the other is absolute, that is to say, without limit. As Adriaan Peperzak observes, "By giving food or time to others, one creates a lack for oneself. Giving the 'work' of a life yields death for the giver."[58]

Not that Levinas, of course, explicitly commends such a suicidal self-negation. For if one were to negate oneself, one would not be able to give oneself, to be for another. Levinas says that "to give, to-be-for-another, despite oneself, but in interrupting the for-oneself, is to take the bread out of one's own mouth, to nourish the hunger of another with one's own fasting."[59] Thus far, Levinas would seem to confirm the logic of self-denial (without limit) for the other. But he later speaks of "the passivity of being-for-another, which is possible only in the form of giving the very bread I eat. But for this one first has to enjoy one's bread, not in order to have the merit of giving it, but in order to give it with one's heart, to give oneself in giving it. Enjoyment is an ineluctable moment of sensibility."[60] Here, it seems that self-affirmation (the enjoyment of one's bread) is a necessary precondition of self-denial (tearing the bread from one's own mouth to give to the other). It appears that self-denial is only realized by means of a necessary self-affirmation, and that perhaps Levinas does thereby affect a reconciliation of love of self and love of neighbor.

But is this reconciliation real or is it merely apparent? In so far as self-affirmation is valorized here, it is so only in order to sustain and perpetuate self-negation. In other words, self-affirmation is always penultimate; the only intrinsic affirmation here is that of self-negation. The paradox at play here is that a fully consummated self-negation would only serve to bring an end to the desired perpetuation of self-negation. In order for self-negation to save itself from annihilation, it must invoke a self-affirmation, but this is valorized only in so far as it fulfils precisely the function of self-negation. In this way, of course, Levinas is able to remain true to his prohibition on there being any "limit" to absolute responsibility. The self-affirmation that

58. Peperzak, "Giving," 162.
59. Levinas, *Otherwise than Being*, 56.
60. Ibid., 72.

is involved here is not really a "limit" to self-negation because the former allows for the "limitless" perpetuation of the latter. Thus it is that the apparent reconciliation between love of self and love of neighbor in Levinas is only epiphenomenal. At the heart of Levinas's project, there remains a suicidal impulse toward self-negation that is only protected from such a suicide by an infinite deferral that allows for the perpetual return of its own self-negation.

But this state of affairs only follows from a model wherein the self is set over and against the other. A further comment of Caputo's is telling here. He observes that Levinas posits the absolutely Other on one side and the same on the other side.[61] Certainly, as Caputo himself goes on to comment, these two are not conceived as opposites or as symmetrical, but this fundamental structuring division sets up an absolute split between the self and not-self, between the same on the one side and the unfathomable abyss on the other (the Kantian echoes here of the relationship between the subject and the noumenon are again obvious). But when one is confronted with this absolute split, it is difficult to see how one could avoid the either-or antinomy between self-affirmation or self-negation. Levinas rightly rejects one way of traversing this antinomy, namely, that of rational calculation. But other possible negotiations—for instance, one that would invoke the tropes of mutual reciprocity, exchange and give and take—are ruled out because they would only be possible in a situation in which the subject-other structure is dissolved. Given such a structure, the antinomy between egoistic self-affirmation and nihilistic self-denial seems unavoidable. Faced with this absolute antinomy, Levinas, like Kant before him, pursues the course of self-negation. When Levinas speaks of the need to become as nothing in the face of the other, the Kantian echoes here are again unmistakable.

But as we did with Kant, we may well wonder whether such pathological self-denial does not tip over only too easily into its opposite. Is not a phenomenological structure that is constituted by an absolute opposition between the other on one side and the self on the other far too self-centered? Is this nihilistic self-denial not produced in response to a situation in which the self is affirmed and inflated as that which *alone* is answerable to and responsible for the other? Indeed, this is the suggestion that has been made recently by Slavoj Žižek. He asks, "is there not something inherently *false* in such a link between the responsibility for/to the other and questioning one's own right to exist? Although Levinas asserts this asymmetry as universal (*every one* of us is in the position of primordial responsibility toward others), does this asymmetry not effectively end up in privileging *one* particular

---

61. Caputo, *Against Ethics*, 80.

group that assumes responsibility for all others, that embodies in a privileged way this responsibility, directly stands for it—in this case, of course, Jews, so that, again, one is ironically tempted to speak of the 'Jewish man's (ethical) burden.'"[62] In other words, Levinas makes the subject a privileged and centered site that is itself responsible for all others. In spite of all the talk of absolute responsibility and self-denial, there seems to be here an inflation of the subject as that which *alone* bears the burden of ethical responsibility. The subject is constituted by its being called to responsibility for all that which is not itself. In a way that betokens a remarkable self-promotion, the individual ethical subject is seen to bear the weight of the whole world.

But do not Žižek's remarks in parenthesis—where he notes that, for Levinas, every one of us is constituted by the same call of responsibility—serve to qualify this self-promotion? Does the very fact of this *shared* responsibility not dilute and "limit" the self-promotion that we are detecting here? This would seem to be suggested when Levinas says, "my responsibility for all can and has to manifest itself also in limiting itself. The ego can, in the name of this unlimited responsibility, be called upon to concern itself also with itself. The fact that the other, my neighbor, is also a third party with respect to another, who is also a neighbor, is the birth of thought, consciousness, justice and philosophy. The unlimited initial responsibility, which justifies this concern for justice, for oneself, and for philosophy can be forgotten. In this forgetting consciousness is a pure egoism. But egoism is neither first nor last."[63] Thus, there is a qualification. The initial "unlimited" responsibility "for all" can indeed be "limited." Indeed, such qualification is intrinsic to the constitution of justice and politics. But it seems that we cannot avoid the conclusion that such a limitation of one's absolute responsibility "for all" whereby "I am approached as an other by the others" is always secondary, always epiphenomenal.[64] As far as the ethical relationship itself is concerned (which is first and last), one must recognize that it does not at all depend on reciprocity and, indeed, that it is necessary to remain oblivious to any such secondary reciprocity. Thus it is that just as we have seen that Levinas's "limitation" on self-negation is only apparent and secondary rather than real and primary, so too Levinas's "limitation" on self-promotion, which would see the subject's responsibility "for all" shared by means of reciprocity, is likewise only apparent and secondary.

It has to be acknowledged here that, for Levinas, an entering into mutual recognition and reciprocity is ultimately a betrayal rather than a perfecting

---

62. Žižek, "Neighbors and Other Monsters," 155.
63. Levinas, *Otherwise than Being*, 128.
64. Ibid., 158.

of the ethical. Just as we saw that for Kant, the ethical subject must protect itself from contamination in the form of reciprocal ethical relationships, lest this destroy the subject's ultimate goal of disinterestedness, so too the Levinasian subject must protect itself from any thoughts of reciprocal responsibility, lest the purity of "absolute" responsibility be sullied. In both cases, the other for or to whom we are obliged to sacrifice ourselves must ultimately be kept at a distance so that the ethical purity of the subject is preserved. All of this, of course, is contrary to all of Levinas's stated objectives. But this does seem to be the ineluctable impasse to which his thought leads. We thus have here an extreme and nihilistic self-annihilation tipping over into an extreme and inflated self-promotion. One ostensible goal tips over and is inverted into its opposite. As Žižek again asks, "and is this not the 'truth' of such an ethical stance, thereby confirming the old Hegelian suspicion that every self-denigration secretly asserts its contrary? Self-questioning is always by definition the obverse of self-privileging; there is always something false about respect for others which is based upon questioning one's own right to exist."[65] A number of other commentators seem to agree. David Wood, for instance, refers to Levinas's "fundamental solipsism" with its attendant dissolution of the other. He points out that "the idea that the obligation is all mine (and mine more than others) may only be meant to define clearly the nature and purity of obligation. But does this not deprive the other of all capacity for moral agency? Or magnanimity? Or generosity?"[66] So too Terry Eagleton has said, "One might wonder whether there is not a certain strain of inverted megalomania in this supreme self-abnegation. To be responsible for everyone sounds more like a neurosis than an ethics."[67]

Furthermore, Wood suggests that there is an inflation of the self in Levinas's thought that connects up with one of the criticisms we made of Kant in the last chapter. There we saw that the disinterested love that Kant commended was such that it was only appropriate to and realizable by God. The particularity, finitude, and limitations of human subjects appeared to drop from view, and humanity was being expected to love as God loves, namely, indiscriminately, and to exercise responsibility as God exercises it, namely, absolutely on behalf of all, and without reserve. Wood detects a similar abstraction of the self from its finite situatedness and a divinization of the subject in Levinas:

> Often, but not always, when I do something for my own benefit, I could instead be doing something that would benefit someone

---

65. Žižek, "Neighbors and Other Monsters," 155.
66. Wood, *Step Back*, 60, 68.
67. Eagleton, *Trouble with Strangers*, 228.

else more needy than I. But it is ethical incontinence to suppose that what follows from this is that I always should so act. That would involve me in the same kind of distance from the care of myself, a neutralizing abstraction from my own situatedness, that characterizes certain kinds of hysterical utilitarianism. Levinas is confusing the fact that there are no a priori limits to my ethical exposure to the other, the powerful grain of truth here, with the claim of infinite obligation or responsibility.... I am not a divine being.[68]

As we saw was the case with Kant, Wood thinks that the absolute responsibility demanded by Levinas is, in effect, a demand that we cease to be finite and situated and that we exercise that responsibility as God is believed to do. Once again, therefore, we see a repetition of the Kantian pursuit of an impossible self-annihilation, which itself conceals and promotes a simultaneous impossible self-promotion.

Indeed, this should not surprise us. For in his phenomenology of ethics, Levinas has not subverted the Kantian diremption, but has merely inverted it, and every inversion will always remain complicit with its opposite. The complicity of Levinas with Kant (and the ethical destructiveness of both) has been recognized by John Milbank when he says, initially of consequentialist ethics, that "this subject is liable to limitless persecution by the needs of others who are regarded contradictorily as not subject to this persecution, but as somehow already in the endlessly postponed *telos* of 'enjoyment.' And just the same bad infinite haunts the seemingly greater refinement of Kantian and Levinasian ethics. Both exhibit a similar obliteration of the living self in the form of the circular pointlessness of a subjectivity constituted through its respect for the (free or suffering) subjectivity of the other which is only subjective in returning that respect."[69] Thus, this Levinasian inversion perpetuates the same Kantian anxiety, the anxiety of "limitless persecution" and the simultaneous pursuit of two contrary goals that are in themselves incapable of being realized. Indeed, not only are they incapable of being realized in themselves, but they actually oppose each other, pulling the subject in two opposite directions simultaneously. Thus it is that the anxiety is not only perpetuated but enhanced because this Kantian-Levinasian trajectory is "pathological in its degree of obliteration of the possibility of consummation."[70]

---

68. Wood, *Step Back*, 145, 146.
69. Milbank, *Being Reconciled*, 144.
70. Ibid.

Part I: The Ethical

But there is also another important effect of this Kantian complicity. We have already noted the asymmetrical diremption that lies at the heart of the Levinasian phenomenology, namely, that between the self on one side and the "all" (the not-self) for which it is responsible on the other. This, of course, derives from the Kantian divide between the knowing subject on the one side and the world on the other, a divide that produces, epistemologically, the unknowable abyss of the noumenon. Apart from what is filtered through the human categories of the understanding to produce the phenomena, there can be no mediation between the subject and the noumenon, so that the latter remains forever inaccessible to the former. There is an infinite distance between them. There "appears" something of the same infinite distance in Levinas's conception of the ethical "other," a distance that Gillian Rose has identified as being one of the most problematical aspects of Levinas's thought.

Although Rose emphasizes the necessity of the suspension of the ethical understood in a particular sense, she suggests that Levinas suspends the ethical in a negative way. Just as Milbank sees in Levinas a "bad infinite," so too Rose sees a "bad suspension." This is so because the ethical is said to be "transcendent," which means that the ethical is suspended in the sense of being "kept apart and obscured in the institutions of 'being'—logic, politics, 'the said,' or discourse itself."[71] This, of course, raises the important question of the relationship between the ethical "happening" on the one hand and the philosophical expression of it on the other. It is Rose's contention that for Levinas, there can be no meaningful relationship between the two, which is what reinforces the sense of anxious paralysis. For Levinas, there is a certain impropriety in attempting to give philosophical expression to the ethical which, by its very nature, both precedes and exceeds the philosophical. Such expression inevitably entails bringing under the reign of the logos that which escapes the rule of the logocentric. So any attempt to "express" the ethical will unavoidably entail a certain betrayal—a betrayal of the ethical itself. This is something recognized by Levinas and which he expresses by means of his distinction between "saying" and the "said."

For Levinas, there is a "saying" involved in the occurrence or happening of the ethical relationship that, once it is given linguistic expression, becomes the "said." But the relationship between the "saying" and the "said" is not one of simple linguistic translation. When the "saying" becomes the "said," the "saying" is inevitably distorted and betrayed. And yet, as linguistic, reflexive, and, ultimately, philosophical beings, it is not possible to rest content with the "saying": the "saying" must be given expression as the "said." In other

---

71. Rose, *Broken Middle*, 258.

Anxiety

words, the expression of the "saying" as the "said" is both unavoidable and impossible. Therefore, in the case of Levinas's own work, for instance, there is a recognition that the call of the ethical itself compels him to speak and to write, and yet in that speaking and writing, he has betrayed the character of the ethical itself as well as one of the fundamental presuppositions of his own work. As he says of the ethical "saying": "It is non-thematizable, and even here is a theme only because in a said everything is conveyed before us, even the ineffable, at the price of a betrayal which philosophy is called upon to reduce."[72] From this, at least two conclusions ought to be clear. First, as linguistic and reflexive beings, it is not possible to rest content with the "saying," with the ethical as such; there is the need to move beyond this to the "said," though the question of what form the "said" should take remains a pertinent one. As Levinas says, "this reduction always has to be attempted, because of the trace of sincerity which the words themselves bear and which they are to saying as witness, even when the said dissimulates the saying in the correlation set up between the saying and the said. Saying always seeks to unsay that dissimulation, and this is its very veracity."[73] Secondly, the movement form the ethical "saying" to the philosophical "said" is never unproblematic, and the said itself can never be adequate or proper, simply because the ethical "saying" can never be captured as such.

It is this impossibility of the saying being conveyed without betrayal that is problematic for Rose. She speaks of "the supra-historicized opposition between 'law' *and* 'law,' divine law [the saying] and human law [the said], which is presented as divine 'anarchy' [the saying] opposed to positive 'law' [the said], or as ethics [the saying] opposed to politics and history [the said]. In effect, commandment is separated from representation, from any aesthetic, from any struggle or relation between universal and singular—the aporia, configured and reconfigured in institutions. Instead, divine law and positive law are alienated from each other and fixed."[74] So for Rose, at the heart of Levinas's project is an alienation that is impossible to overcome. There appears to be a sundering between the universal and the singular, and it is difficult to see what passage might effect a substantive relationship between the two. It is not that there is disagreement here on the necessity of a certain ethical aporia, but for Rose, this aporia must be capable of being "configured and reconfigured" in a dialectical process that does not reach final closure. This process must be one that is irreducibly triune, constituted by the interplay of universal, particular, and singular, without any one being

72. Levinas, *Otherwise than Being*, 162.
73. Ibid., 152.
74. Rose, *Broken Middle*, 260.

unequivocally prioritized over the other two. This contrasts with what she believes to be Levinas's fixing and stabilizing this aporia by a separating it out into two and by giving a clear priority to the singular. These elements, she believes, must be allowed to interact on the terrain of the third in order that something of the nature of the aporia may be revealed.

In our discussion of Levinas, however, we have seen that he is sensitive to the extreme impasses to which his thought seems inevitably to lead. For instance, we saw that the impulse toward self-annihilation is "reined in" by his insistence that in order to give oneself, one must first affirm oneself; in order to tear the bread from one's mouth for the other, one must first enjoy the bread oneself. Likewise, we saw that the contrary impulse toward self-promotion is itself "reined in" and qualified by the recognition that "by the grace of God," the self becomes an other for the others, and thereby becomes the recipient of the others' giving of themselves. At the same time, however, we saw that such sensitivity and recognition is always secondary and is never allowed to subvert the problematic primary structure that such observations are intended to address. As a result, the anxiety inherited from the Kantian diremption is perpetuated in spite of these hints of dissatisfaction with it.

Rose too detects that there are hints in Levinas that he recognizes what she presents as the diremption between ethics and *halakah*, ethics and law, and she enumerates some of these hints: that the meaning of confession and forgiveness may be inverted in their unintended consequences; that there is a potential violence in the exclusivity of love; that there is possible inversion in even acute responsibility for the other; and that general and generous principles can be inverted in the course of their application.[75] And yet, it seems that these hints of recognition are not sufficiently carried through so as to enable them to effect a subversion:

> For such a trajectory cannot protect itself from the very inversions against which it would warn, since it is invested in the diremption it posits between "the order of being" and "the disorder of the ethical" which disqualifies any "knowledge" or recognition or representation of precisely "what has already occurred," of the history and repetition of the inversion of universal and particular. Without legitimate knowledge or representation, this wisdom, which would alert us to the incipient "Stalinism" of our principled generosity and teach us instead a perfect equity, can only appear itself as a "disengaged" prescription—holy and without any purchase on "the real world."

75. See ibid., 261–62.

> A *fortiori*, it cannot undertake any reconstruction of "what has already occurred" to fulfil the aspirations of this perfect yet dirempted jurisprudence.[76]

So Levinas is correct to draw our attention to the inversions that are incipient in all ethical discourse and with respect to which we must always be on our guard. And we may add to these inversions the ones we have been highlighting in this chapter, namely, that between self-annihilation and self-promotion. But these inversions are precisely the effects of an ethical aporia between the universal and the singular. They can be negotiated only through the experience of laboring to know the equivocation between the universal and the singular by invoking a third. Levinas, however, has fixed and stabilized this diremption between the universal and the singular, with the result that he is unable to avoid the very inversions against which he warns. Furthermore, Levinas's rendering of the relationship between the universal and the singular has important ramifications for his understanding of the relationship between the ethical and political. We shall return to consider this in more detail in chapter 3.

We have seen that such alienation or diremption is a direct result of a certain Kantian legacy. We have been suggesting that Levinas inherits and perpetuates this Kantian structure even as he inverts it. In the Levinasian inversion, the more the ethical is conveyed, the more it is betrayed, so that we have a simultaneous coming into view and slipping away that forever preserves and ossifies this nonnegotiable distance. He is therefore stuck in an impasse of alienation, without any prospect of mediation or dialectical resolution. In this sense, we may see Rose's criticism of Levinas here as a transposed repetition of Hegel's critique of Kant.

Thus, Kant and Levinas are complicit in their assumption of a certain antinomy, namely, that *either* the subject is primary and it grasps and controls the world and everything in it, *or else* the other is primary and it "calls," "positions," and "founds" the subject. At the same time, either the universal is prioritized and it positions and subordinates the singular, or else the singular is prioritized, thus positioning and subordinating the universal. These either-or antinomies are constituted by a simple reversal of the primacy of "subject" and "other," of the universal and the singular. As we have seen, intrinsic to Levinas's philosophy is the conviction that the structure of epistemology in modern metaphysics is ultimately destructive with respect to the ethical. Modernity's foundational, totalizing, all-consuming subject, its explicit universalism, blocks any genuine encounter with the other and, therefore, blocks any genuine encounter with the ethical. But in reacting

---

76. Ibid., 263.

against this modern framework, Levinas has seemed to move to the opposite extreme. Now the *tout autre* becomes primary and all-consuming while the subject becomes secondary, is "positioned" and ultimately engulfed; now the singular becomes prior. So the basic structure remains the same; it is simply that the direction of primacy has been reversed. We have seen that such a structure does not allow for a more equivocal understanding of the relationship between self and other, between universal and singular, that would play itself out through the invocation of a third. The self either actively "positions" or it is passively "positioned," but mutuality and reciprocity seem to be *a priori* excluded. Furthermore, if the subject is not itself to be in a position of domination and mastery, then it seems that the only alternative for the self is for it to be passively subject to a process of negation. And, as we have seen, when the goal of the subject becomes precisely this kind of self-negation, the result is the paradoxical operation of two contrary impulses simultaneously: an inflated self-centeredness on the one hand and a suicidal annihilationsim on the other. The pathological anxiety arising from the Kantian diremption is thus perpetuated by Levinas, an anxiety arising from the impossibility of consummation. So our response here should not be to *reverse* the problematic structure of modern metaphysics but, rather, to *subvert* it. Such subversion can only be realized through the displacement of the dyadic structure shared by Kant and Levinas by a triune one. A simple movement from thesis to antithesis will always be insufficient.

2

COMPLACENCY

How might we move beyond the disabling paralysis to which both Kant and Levinas seem to lead? I have been suggesting that the ethical is itself constituted by an irresolvable enigma or aporia, manifested as, among other things, a tension between self and other. We have seen that Kant and Levinas, in their different ways, attempt to overcome this tension by subordinating one element to the other, and that this subordination ultimately produces a disabling ethical blockage. If this is so, then we might expect an alternative approach to consist not in the subordination of one element to the other, but in a "reconciliation" between them. In other words, the task might well be conceived as being to move away from a framework wherein self and other are set over and against each other in the manner of a zero-sum game to a new framework wherein self and other are reconciled such that there is no agonistic opposition between them.

We do indeed find precisely such attempts to "resolve" and "overcome" the Kantian-Levinasian ethical diremptions in contemporary ethical theory. Two in particular may be identified, operating from what might be thought of as antithetical starting points but with a remarkably complicit methodological structure. In both cases, we see the invocation of a *mediating third term* that in effect serves two functions. First, it does indeed "mediate" between self and other, so that they are no longer in direct competition in the manner of a zero-sum game. Self and other both *participate* in the mediating third, and a mechanism is thereby instantiated whereby to affirm one is at the same time a manner of affirming the other. Second, it provides a means of maintaining the universal-particular-singular triad (in contrast to Kant and Levinas), *but* a resolution now comes through the effective arrogation of one of the three domains by the mediating third itself. This means that while the universal, particular, and singular are all acknowledged, one of them is effectively "suspended" or "bracketed out" by being arrogated by the mediating third. The effect of this bracketing, I shall suggest, is to "mend" what should remain "broken" (as Gillian Rose would put it) and therefore to overcome what should be the irreducible equivocation of the ethical. The result is that a certain ethical complacency is induced. Consequently, this mediating third term serves not only as the ontologically privileged "first principle" of the framework as a whole, but also as the transcendental precondition for the reconciliation of what would otherwise be left broken and aporetically open.

In what follows, I shall look at two instances of such a mediating third term. In one case, the third is the excessive, transcendent plenitude of God, while in the other, it is the empty, immanent nothingness of the nihil. Thus it is that we find the ethical brokenness of modernity being mended by theology on the one hand and by nihilism on the other. That which modernity and postmodernity attempted to fix by means of the prioritizing of the universal or the prioritizing of the singular is now to be mended by the suspension of conflict through the mediation of a third. This third is transcendence or immanence, God or the nihil, theology or nihilism, the either-or choices with which we now seem inevitably to be faced.

The Mediating Third: God or the Nihil?

Let us now examine these two alternatives. I turn first to a contemporary articulation of the transcendental necessity of God as the mediating third term, which comes not directly from theology as such, but from the realms of psychoanalysis and linguistics and in the person of Julia Kristeva. This is an instructive example because it shows that it is not only explicitly theological discourse that is recognizing the necessity for this mediating "third term." But in articulating the nature of the logic that is at work here, Kristeva utilizes an explicitly theological source, namely, the writings of Thomas Aquinas. For Kristeva says that Aquinas has developed a theology wherein love of self is a necessary precondition for a genuine outpouring of love toward the other, thus allowing for that which the modern subject desperately needs, namely, the reconciliation of love of self with love of other.

The starting point for Kristeva is Aquinas's clarification of the hierarchy between three kinds of love. In her words, for Aquinas, our own proper good is found "in God as to its cause, in ourselves as to its effect, in our neighbor as in a similitude. Consequently the greatest good is God, but the first access to him comes from our immediate relation to ourselves; moreover, the similarity between others and ourselves permits us to have access to them. Self-love, in this logical concatenation to which Thomas subjects it, enjoys a historical or genetic primacy. But God remains the absolute proper, the best of myself, more myself than me, the absolute Self."[1] So the good is in the first instance accessible in oneself and only when this is firmly established can one communicate such goodness to others. Kristeva says that in order to extend this analysis, one should look at Aquinas's specific interpretation of the *sicut te ipsum* ("You shall love your neighbor as yourself"). Here again, love of others originates in love of self, primarily because in loving itself, the subject affirms the ontological good. Thus, to love one's neighbor as oneself is to be understood in terms of proximity and similarity rather than in terms of quantity. This means that for Aquinas, "*sicut te ipsum* does not mean '*as much* as yourself' but '*similarly* as yourself' . . . It is thus love of one's own self as one's own good that determines and directs other consecutive loves."[2] Kristeva immediately points out that this "love of oneself" is not understood in the sense of being set over and against the other or over and against God. Rather, it is understood as a participation in ontological good, which means a participation not only in God but also in the created species, which, being "of God," is preserved in love.

This analysis is of course entirely consistent with the old theological equation of being with goodness. If being is good, so too is my own being. As Kristeva paraphrases this, "I am, which means I am good, therefore I love myself—that is how one might sum up the praise of one's own, which includes what in contemporary terms would be called narcissism in an ontology of love."[3] The good is that which one "naturally" desires and it can be known only as good for oneself. I am a part of that good, which is also to say that I have a "natural" appetite for that good, and the consequence of this is that I love myself. Kristeva says of this model: "Beyond its psychological value for justifying and removing guilt from controlled narcissism, love of self thus presents itself, with Aquinas, as the logical go-between that internalizes the good at the same time as it ontologizes the Self as one's own always partaking of the good. A desiring subjectivity is in the process of being established, and nevertheless, conversely, the ontological immanence of each being to itself is at the heart of this theology."[4] Indeed, this is a relief

---

1. Kristeva, *Tales of Love*, 172. Kristeva is here drawing on Aquinas's *Commentary on Sentences*, distinction 29, article 5. Further on in the discussion she draws on the *Summa Theologiae*, 1a2ae, questions 19 and 20.
2. Ibid., 173–74.
3. Ibid., 174.
4. Ibid., 175.

that is much needed in light of the torture that modernity has inflicted on the subject, as was discussed in the last chapter.

What Kristeva emphasizes throughout her reading, however, is not simply that Aquinas expounds a theological justification for self-affirmation but that this self-affirmation is inseparable from and indeed is a necessary precondition for a genuine love for the other—both God and fellow subjects. If this were not the case, then love of self would indeed become unjustified and, further, sinful.[5] She points out that Aquinas's self-affirmation is only intelligible as a component (albeit a necessary one) within a larger "compromise" between love of self and love of the other. Love of self has no justification and no intelligibility outside of a larger framework that connects the goodness of the self to the goodness of the whole. Love of self is both made possible by and is a necessary precondition for love of the whole, which is to say, a love of the good.

Aquinas's analysis here also allows for a relationality and reciprocity, which we saw to be conspicuously lacking in the modern ethic of disinterestedness. Once again, his account of the way in which love unites the one who loves with the loved one may be understood in terms of a "compromise" between a meeting of two distinct substances on the one hand and the disappearance of individuality in union on the other. Acknowledging her debt to the work of Roger de Weiss, Kristeva notes that for Aquinas, loving union is to be understood again in light of the nature of the knowing subject: "By giving greater importance to the similarity and proximity of lovers in God, amatory union is not a dramatic union of substances but a merging of lives that were already God's. . . . In the final analysis, the Thomistic logic of love amounts to positing that because there is Unity and love for that Unity (of Self), there is also Union of the two (the loved one being identified with oneself)."[6] According to Kristeva, therefore, Aquinas enacts a skilful negotiation between self-love and love for the other such that self-love is a necessary precondition for its own dissolution. Self-love here requires exchange and reciprocity in order for it to be perfected.

Rendering this psychoanalytically, Kristeva says that "founding the participation of one's own in the universal good by way of love implied a normalization of narcissism—by removing guilt, thanks to an idealizing adjustment."[7] The crucial point here is the understanding that one is participating in the "supreme good," or what Kristeva calls "that absolute Third Party." Provided that this is indeed the case, then "love of self, far from being

---

5. Ibid., 178.
6. Ibid., 181.
7. Ibid., 183–84.

a deadly end or a disastrous snare, may turn out to be our way to salvation. To jouissance."[8] In other words, the Thomistic account allows for a justified self-love that modern disinterestedness could not countenance. More broadly, we can see how such an account represents an advance on many of the difficulties we have been identifying in the previous chapter. Here, love has displaced legality at the very heart of the system; love of self and love of other are no longer set over and against one another in an irreconcilable antinomy. Crucially, the self is affirmed without being made foundational.

As is well known, Kristeva is deeply—though not uncritically—influenced by the work of her fellow psychoanalyst, Jacques Lacan, and it is interesting to note a similar structural logic in operation in Lacan's own work. According to the model we have elaborated in Kristeva's reading of Aquinas, we see that love of self and love of other, the two poles in the injunction to "love your neighbor as yourself," can only be effected by means of what Kristeva calls "that absolute Third Party," and this is a point with which Lacan concurs. For Lacan, it is not that the injunction to "love your neighbor as yourself" involves a "third term" as a necessary but secondary supplement. On the contrary, the injunction is itself primordially an elaboration of the three terms, out of which the two poles subsequently emerge. As Lacan comments, "it's only because we count to three that we can count to two": "If I have said that religion is that of which one can make the most true . . . I'm going to draw your attention to what I've yakked on about for quite a while, right? that you shall love your neighbor as yourself—does that mean you will be three, yes or no? Yeah. The Borromean knot can only be made of three. The imaginary and the symbolic are not enough, a third element is needed, and I designate it the real."[9] So for Lacan, the injunction in itself implies three loves rather than just two as might initially be thought. Kenneth Reinhard explains why this is so in Lacan's analysis:

> Love of myself is *imaginary*, the specular reflection on myself that constitutes the narcissistic ego in the mirror stage; and love of the neighbor is *real*, insofar as the neighbor harbors the strange kernel of enjoyment Freud and Lacan call the Thing. However, this twoness cannot be reached directly and does not subsist on its own, Lacan argues, except by passing by way of the third love, never superseded, the *love of God*, which is the model of symbolic love, the love of the father that sustains the symbolic order. Hence, love of the neighbor *includes within it*

---

8. Ibid., 184.

9. Lacan, *Le séminaire, livre 21*. Translated by and quoted in Reinhard, "Toward a Political Theology of the Neighbor," 71.

the love of God, and together they constitute the Borromean knot of political theology.[10]

But this also raises the question of whether the concept of the mediating third and the role that it plays is in itself more important than the particular content embodied by that third. In other words, is the role that God plays in this model more important than the fact that it happens to be God who plays it? This question becomes all the more pertinent when we recall that, for Augustine, creatures and indeed all of creation are constituted by the fact that we are recipients of the divine gift of "being" which, as such, is "good." But we are equally, for Augustine, created *ex nihilo*, and the fact that this is so means that we have a natural tendency toward nothingness. So it is only God's sustaining work of conservation that preserves us in being and that prevents us from falling back into nothingness, which we undoubtedly would do if we were to be left to our own devices. This intriguing account raises a whole host of questions. But for our purposes here, the important point to note is that according to Augustine, we are constituted, as creatures, by God's gift of being, but also by our being created out of nothing. Stepping beyond the parameters of Augustinian orthodoxy, we may go so far as to say that the very existence of creation is the manifestation of an uneasy truce or, alternatively, the perpetuation of an ongoing tension between God and the nihil. In this sense, the continued existence of the creaturely world may itself be seen as a deferral of any final mending of this tension between God and the nihil.[11] But if we, as creatures, are as much constituted by our being created *ex nihilo* as by our being created by the divine gift of being, this raises the question of whether the work of the mediating third term between self and neighbor might as well be played by the nihil as by God. To what extent could the nihil serve as the mediating third term?

A suggestion along these lines, although not quite in these terms, has been made by Žižek, and he does so in the context of a discussion of an either-or antinomy between love of self and love of other. In particular, he addresses Levinas's point—as discusssed in the last chapter—that unconditional responsibility toward the other necessarily leads us into a questioning of one's own right to exist. We saw there that Žižek exposed a false humility in Levinas's logic and that, as with Kant before him, such self-questioning turned out to be the obverse of an equally real self-privileging. Faced with this irresolvable antinomy, Žižek turns for a resolution not to Aquinas but to Spinoza. Whereas for Kristeva, a resolution was to be found in the

---

10. Reinhard, "Toward a Political Theology of the Neighbor," 71–72.
11. I discuss these ideas in more detail in Hyman, "Augustine and the Nihil."

Complacency

invocation of the ultimate purveyor of transcendence, Žižek looks instead to the exemplary purveyor of immanence. As Žižek himself puts it:

> A Spinozistic answer to Levinas would have been that our existence is not at the expense of others, but a part of the network of reality. For Spinoza there is no Hobbesian "Self" as extracted from and opposed to reality. Spinoza's ontology is one of full immanence to the world; in other words, I "am" just the network of my relations with the world, I am totally "externalized" in it. My *conatus*, my tendency to assert myself, is thus not my exertion at the expense of the world, but my full acceptance of being part of the world, my assertion of the wider reality only within which I can thrive. The opposition between egotism and altruism is thus overcome: I fully am, not as an isolated Self, but in the thriving reality, part of which I am.[12]

As with Aquinas, therefore, Spinoza rejects the notion of a primary and foundational "self" set against a secondary and separate "other" (whether my neighbor or reality in general). For both Aquinas and Spinoza, that monadic conception of selfhood is rejected in favor of a model of subjectivity that understands the self as being constituted by its participation in a wider network of reality. This reality is not set apart from and divided from the subject, but is part and parcel of its own very being. The difference between them comes, of course, in their conceptions of the nature of this reality: for Aquinas its character is fundamentally transcendent, whereas for Spinoza its nature is radically immanent.

But this also has implications for the characters of the respective selfhoods that are here being affirmed. For Aquinas, the self participates in the divine gift of being and goodness, and there is therefore a sense in which the self bears a trace of the divine and shares in this transcendence. For Spinoza, on the other hand, the self participates in the monistic immanent oneness of reality, and there is therefore a sense in which the self becomes nothing, becomes itself an instance of the nihil. That Žižek himself develops this implication is evident when he says that the answer to the Levinasian problematic

> should not be an assertion of my right to exist in harmony with and tolerance of others, but a more radical claim: Do I exist in the first place? Am I not, rather, a *hole in the order of being*? This brings us to the ultimate paradox on account of which Levinas's answer is not sufficient: I am a threat to the entire order of being not insofar as I positively exist as part of this order, but precisely

---

12. Žižek, "Neighbors and Other Monsters," 155–56.

> insofar as I am a hole in the order of being. As such, as nothing, I "am" a striving to reach out and appropriate all (only a Nothing can desire to become Everything).[13]

So for Žižek, the command to love your neighbor "as" yourself is to be understood, as it was for Kristeva, following Aquinas, as emphasizing that to love the self and to love the neighbor is not to do two radically disparate things. Rather, there is a sense in which, in doing one, I am thereby also doing the other. For Aquinas, loving the self and loving the neighbor are two instantiations of what is fundamentally the unified act of loving God. For Žižek, the neighbor is not a manifestation of the divine gift of being but is, rather, inextricably a part of that wider network of reality of which I too am a part. Further, the neighbor is a monstrous abyss, a lack, just as I too am radically unknown, a lack, Nothing. So again, in loving the self and in loving the neighbor, we have two instances of what is fundamentally the unified act of affirming reality, from which neither the self nor the neighbor is ultimately separable.

In juxtaposing here the respective models of Kristeva-Aquinas and Žižek-Spinoza, we see the relationship between them as being constituted of both an antithetical inversion and a convergent unity. The inversion is, of course, most obvious at the ontological level, where we are presented with a straight antithesis between transcendence and immanence, between God and the nihil, and, as we have seen, this has implications also for our understanding of selfhood: do we bear the trace of God or are we finally Nothing? But in terms of the dynamics both models put to work in the command to love one's neighbor as oneself, we have seen that there is a remarkable convergence. Indeed, I want to suggest that this convergence is of more significance than the opposition. It could well be argued that the ontological difference here has all sorts of ramifications and that there is more at stake in this opposition than mere terminology. This is undoubtedly the case, but I shall suggest that there is more at stake in that upon which they converge than in that upon which they differ. If this is so, then I shall also suggest that the point at issue is not that of choosing between them, or making a case for one over against the other; it is rather a case of questioning both at the point of their convergence, and, in particular, of asking what is being excluded in this very convergence.

Of what, then, does this convergence consist? We have already discussed the primary feature of this convergence, namely, their respective invocations of a "mediating third term" that serves to overcome the disabling Kantian-Levinasian opposition between self and other. The two models of

---

13. Ibid., 156.

theology and nihilism discussed here both rightly seek to overcome this blockage, but they do so by attempting to "mend" and "reconcile" the ethical aporia rather than seeking to put it back into play. This "mending" and "reconciliation," I suggest, rescues us from ethical paralysis, but it does so at the price of inducing an ethical "complacency." It is the nature of this complacency that I here want to raise.

Complacency: The "Resolutions" of Theology and Nihilism

In speaking of complacency here, I am not of course suggesting that those who adopt the Thomist or Spinozist ontologies with their respective "mediating third terms" are thereby personally complacent about the phenomena of evil, suffering, and injustice, whether of a personal or political kind. Rather, what I have in mind here is a complacency with respect to the difficult, broken, and aporetic character of the ethical endeavor as such. The practical effect of the invocation of a "mediating third term" is to "resolve" and "overcome" this difficult and broken aporia. But why and in what manner do the "resolutions" of the mediating third terms induce complacency? I want to suggest that they do so in two main ways. The first is a complacency with respect to the tension or equivocation between love of self and love of neighbor. The second is a complacency with respect to the equivocation between the universal, particular, and singular, which, I am suggesting, lies at the heart of the ethical. Let us look at each of these in turn.

The first point to note is that the practical effect of invoking God or the nihil as a mediating third term between the self and the neighbor is to dissolve, or at least weaken considerably, the oppositional difference between them. This is, in fact, a phenomenon on which we have already commented, and this becomes particularly evident when Kristeva speaks of the "merging of lives" and the "Union of the two." In affirming self and other, we are, in effect, affirming the same thing. In some ways, of course, such a dissolution or weakening may well be regarded as desirable, particularly when we recall that many of the difficulties with the Kantian-Levinasian trajectory were seen to derive from an absolute separation between self and other (whether my neighbor or reality in general). Given that this is the case, it may well be thought that a solution is to be found in an ontology that decenters the self and its accompanying antinomy between self and other. But we may well wonder whether the invocation of the mediating third enacts an inversion of this difficulty simply by dissolving a distinction that had previously been hypostatized, and we may well question whether this provides an adequate solution. By making love of self and love of neighbor almost equivalent (and admittedly, the importance of this "almost" should not be underestimated for these thinkers), the enigma and the tension between them comes to be dissolved or at least weakened.

Does this matter ethically? I would suggest that it does because at the heart of the ethical is a *tension* between love of self and love of neighbor. The tension is difficult to negotiate, and this very difficulty goes some way toward explaining why, historically, the tension has often been evaded. One way of evading it is to suppose that love of self and love of neighbor are somehow *in competition*, so that love of one is always at the expense of the other. This is the kind of approach we observed in the last chapter. Where the two are in competition, it seems that the self must be *denied* in order to love one's neighbor. But as we saw, this gives rise to both a suicidal self-negation and a hubristic self-promotion, which is ultimately destructive. But another way of evading the tension is by minimizing it, by seeing love of self and love of neighbor as being essentially continuous or functionally equivalent, so that there is no real tension between them at all. This is what I am suggesting we see in the invocation of the "mediating thirds." But the challenge is to avoid both of these evasions and to live in the midst of this irreducible tension, which, I am arguing, is to live in the midst of the equivocation of the ethical. Even if we accept that loving one's neighbor does not compromise love of self, but is a way of enhancing one's own life, of living more fully and more joyfully, this may serve to correct the model of self and neighbor being in "competition," but it by no means completely eradicates the tension. For it is not possible, always and everywhere, to love myself and to love my neighbor fully and simultaneously. Rather, the attempt to do both constantly gives rise to difficult dilemmas, the answers to which are by no means self-evident.

As we saw David Wood to observe in the last chapter, "Often, but not always, when I do something for my own benefit, I could instead be doing something that would benefit someone else more needy than I. But it is ethical incontinence to suppose that what follows from this is that I always should so act."[14] If this is so, then decisions must constantly be made as to how I should act in specific situations, when I should "do something for my own benefit" and when I should instead "be doing something that would benefit someone else more needy than I." Often we may make such judgments unthinkingly and unreflectively. Indeed, our finitude perhaps makes it inevitable that we should do so if we are to avoid the kind of anxious paralysis that could potentially arise from an obsessive concern with the tension as such. But this should not blind us to the fact that when we do act

14. Wood, *Step Back*, 145.

unreflectively in this way, we are engaging in a (perhaps inevitable) "forgetting" of a very real ethical tension that is forever present. While in our everyday life, our finitude is such that this "forgetting" may be necessary to maintain our sanity (perhaps in the way that psychoanalysis has insisted that the mechanism of repression is necessary for mental equilibrium), it would be a mistake to extend this pragmatic necessity to the levels of ethical reflection and meta-reflection. The *tension* between loving oneself and loving one's neighbor is constitutive of the ethical and is articulated in the command to love your neighbor as yourself.

This is why, I suggest, susceptibility to the commandment is experienced not as an "easy" and "natural" requirement, but, on the contrary, as a forceful and difficult intervention. It is experienced as an external interruption that breaks up our self-satisfied complacency. It calls us to pursue a path that is difficult, both in terms of the deliberative judgments that it entails and the execution of those judgments in practice. But for all the difficulty and discipline that it entails, it is nonetheless still an intervention that irresistibly summons us. As we saw Žižek, Santner, and Reinhard to observe, again in the last chapter, the command "remains always in the imperative and presses on us with an urgency that seems to go beyond both its religious origins and its modern appropriations as universal Reason."[15] It seems that the commandment is experienced as difficult (perhaps strictly impossible) *and* it is also one to which we seem to be universally summoned. We therefore have to make sense of *both* these features of our phenomenological relationship to it.

So it would seem that there is a fundamental ambivalence at the heart of subjectivity between the impulse to love ourselves and our susceptibility to the imperative to love our neighbor. This experience of ambivalent tension stands in need of verbal expression, which is precisely the function that the commandment serves. As we have noted, this tension is expressed in the realization that the commandment is strictly impossible to fulfil. The commandment is thus not a means of overcoming the tension but, rather, a way of perpetuating it.

Set against this, the Thomistic model of "amatory union" wherein love of self and love of neighbor appear to be qualitatively equivalent seems not to do justice to this tension, ambivalence, and difficulty. When love of self and love of neighbor come to be seen as continuous, or as functionally equivalent, when the commonality between them becomes more important than and obscures the difference between them, it is difficult to see why the commandment would come to be experienced as such a forceful and

---

15. Žižek, Santner, and Reinhard, *Neighbor*, 5.

difficult ethical intervention in the first place. The Thomistic model seems to smooth away the tension that lies at the heart of the commandment. It has to be acknowledged, of course, as we have seen Kristeva to do, that the "amatory union" of which Aquinas speaks does not entail, as she puts it, "a dramatic union of substances." Aquinas and Kristeva are clearly not envisaging some kind of mystical undifferentiated unity between self and neighbor. Nonetheless, they seem to be emphasizing similarity and proximity to such an extent as to move in the direction of a porous intermingling that does not do justice to the kind of ambivalence to which we have been alluding. If we are to avoid a model of monadic subjects in competition, so too we should avoid a model that too readily blurs the differences between subjects, between self and neighbor. In this respect, the Thomistic model of "amatory union" comes to appear as an "idealized" version of love, a love wherein the sense of dissolution between self and neighbor overcomes the sense of alienation between them. In other words, this appears to be a model of love more appropriate to a "redeemed" world rather than to a "fallen" one. It appears to be a model of love that prematurely "mends" our "broken" world in anticipation of eschatological redemption. It appears as another instance of what Kathleen Sands has called "the deadening distance that has grown up between theology and . . . experience," a theology framed by "the assumption that fundamental contradictions or conflicting orders do not really exist."[16]

Furthermore, the Thomistic model of "amatory union" does not appear to do justice, phenomenologically, to our experience of subjectivity. If not simply mistaken in this respect, it is nonetheless partial. If there is a sense in which I do feel united with my neighbor in a "merging of lives" and in a "Union of the two," there is also simultaneously a sense in which I feel cut off from my neighbor, a sense in which my neighbor is unknown to me, or, as Žižek would have it, a sense in which my neighbor is an unfathomable abyss. This too is only an aspect of my experience of my neighbor, but it is a real one nonetheless and one that cannot and should not be ignored. This is, of course, to do no more than acknowledge the reality of the psychoanalytic notion of ambivalence.

Terry Eagleton has made some pertinent comments in this respect and has drawn attention to the way in which our senses of "oneness" or "union" with our neighbors and of "separation" or "alienation" from them are in a constant state of ambivalence; they are always in tension or interplay. For one thing, he notes that it would be a mistake to suppose that our neighbors appear opaque to us in contrast to our experience of ourselves

---

16. Sands, *Escape from Paradise*, 2, 3.

Complacency

as being wholly transparent to us. It is by no means the case that the other is hidden from us while our own selves are completely accessible to us. On the contrary, the interplay between transparency and opacity is as much a part of our experience of ourselves as it is of our experience of others. As Eagleton puts it, "Others are bound to appear opaque if we are deluded enough to believe that we are wholly transparent to ourselves."[17] Eagleton's language here has unmistakable psychoanalytic resonances, and elsewhere he explicitly invokes the name of Jacques Lacan as well as that of Walter Benjamin. He says that for Lacan, "the imaginary enclosure of glances is fractured by a lack: the fact that I can never look at her from the place where she sees me. The gaze thus becomes an interplay of light and opacity, in which the translucent imaginary is stained by the intrusion of the symbolic, with its non-reciprocities and anonymous relations. It betrays the ambiguity of Baudelaire's urban crowd, in which, as Benjamin comments, 'no one is either quite transparent or quite opaque to all the others.'"[18]

It would seem that the ambiguities here are multiple. The other—the neighbor or the stranger—is both close at hand, in union with us, and also set apart, opaque and strange to us. And yet, this experience of ambiguity does not simply set the neighbor apart from us because it is also the manner of our experiencing ourselves. Our own subjectivity is simultaneously close to us and irreducibly strange and opaque to us (as the experience of psychoanalysis repeatedly attests). And yet, even this structural similarity between our experience of the other and our experience of ourselves serves not *only* to bring self and other together; for this ambivalence in our experience of others is at the same time qualitatively different from the ambivalence in our experience of ourselves. That is to say, the way in which the other is transparent to us is qualitatively different from the way in which we are transparent to ourselves. Likewise, the way in which the other is opaque to us is qualitatively different from the way in which we are opaque to ourselves. It seems that this interplay between transparency and opacity, between light and shade, union and alienation, is one that plays itself out interminably. This is what it means to be one among others.

It would be tempting to say that any ethics adequate to life would have to take account of this interminable interplay. But even this would be to understate the case. It would perhaps be better to say that this tension, ambivalence, and equivocation is precisely what gives rise to and is creative of the ethical. It is precisely the labor of attempting to negotiate this tension that actually constitutes the ethical as such; it is what gives rise to

17. Eagleton, *Trouble with Strangers*, 44.
18. Ibid., 73.

that formulation of equivocation *par excellence*: the command to love your neighbor as yourself.

In this context, we can begin to see why the invocation of a mediating third might induce complacency. For now, the irreducible ambivalence gives way to an "amatory union" wherein the boundary between self and other has become porous because of their common participation in the mediating third. Now, in loving and affirming myself, I am thereby also loving and affirming that which is not myself—the "good" or the "nothingness" by which both I and my neighbor are constituted. In loving myself, I am therefore indirectly also loving my neighbor, and in loving my neighbor, I am thereby also loving myself. But for all the advantages of this model over one wherein there are monadic selves in competition, does this not make things too easy? If, as I have been suggesting, the ethical is actually constituted by a tension or equivocation between self and other, then does this weakening of this tension or "mending" of this equivocation not give rise to an ease that induces complacency? I am suggesting that it does, and to this end, I now want to look at how this ethical complacency is actually manifested in practice.

In order to do this, we also need to invoke the second major role played by the mediating third. If the first function was to overcome the equivocation between self and other, the second function (which is perhaps another manifestation of the first) is to overcome the equivocation beteween the universal, the particular, and the singular. Whereas we saw that Kant and Levinas overcame this equivocation by elevating one domain of this triad, the invocation of the mediating third overcomes this equivocation in a rather different way. While the necessity of all three domains is acknowledged, the influence and role of one of them is minimized in practical terms by it being effectively arrogated by the mediating third itself. Where the mediating third is God, it is the domain of the universal that is deemed to be God's domain, with the result that the finite, human realm is left to enact the interplay of the particular with the singular, the universal having thereby been "suspended" in the sense of being delegated to God. Where the mediating third is the nihil, it is the domain of the particular that is delegated to it, with the result that the realm of practical action is left to enact singular instantiations of the universal. In both cases, the practical outcome is the "suspension" of one of the three domains, which is ultimately to the detriment of the ethical itself. Let us look in more detail at how these mechanisms actually operate in practice.

The Aquinas-Kristeva strategy of invoking God as the mediating third is one that has been taken up explicitly by John Milbank. Indeed, in chapter 1, we noted the ethical implications of this. In the face of Kant's elevation of the universal law and his warning against the lure engendered by attention to particularities (as in feelings of sympathy, for instance), we saw that Milbank interprets the Christian tradition as offering a reversal of this state of affairs. More specifically, we saw that he understands the Augustinian-Thomistic tradition to interpret neighbor love as an exhortation to love our "nearest and dearest" over the universal faceless multitude. For Milbank, such universal neighbor love is impossible for finite created beings. Our duty as such is to love those to whom we are closest in the knowledge that others are doing similarly and that our collective efforts in this regard are gathered up into the universal love of God. In terms of the analysis I am developing here, we might say that there is an effective division of labor being instantiated in the interplay between the universal, the particular, and the singular. In Milbank's thought, the enactment of the domain of the universal is the preserve of God, leaving us to enact the domains of the particular and the singular; thus God loves all equally and impartially, leaving us to love our particular neighbors in singular situations. This, however, leads us to ask whether such a division of labor is in fact too neat. Does it not too clearly parcel out the domain of the universal to God and to the eschaton, leaving this world with its stubborn particularity and singularity? In other words, just as we have seen this approach to *anticipate* the eschaton by means of its "idealized" model of love, so too it simultaneously and paradoxically suspends the universal precisely through its recognition of the *deferral* of the eschaton. But should we not see much more interpenetration between these domains, so as to do justice to the world as itself an arena of equivocation between the universal, the particular, and the singular, between divine creativity and the nothingness out of which it comes?

It should be said that Milbank himself acknowledges a degree of equivocation here and that the division of labor he commends is not absolute. For one thing, he acknowledges that there is a "tension" between the ethical perspectives of "unilateralism" on the one hand and "reciprocity" on the other in the New Testament itself, where

> in Luke's Gospel "benefactors," or those who wield power by giving are regarded with suspicion; where one is adjoined to love one's enemies and also . . . *not* to invite to feasts those who can invite you back (Luke 6: 32–35). . . . This is Derrida's favoured focus for the Christian essence, and yet it is surely to be contrasted with St John's Gospel, where there is no mention of loving enemies, where love seems to ceaselessly circulate among friends—I in you, and you in me—where there are erotic gestures (between Jesus and Mary of Bethany) and where the

Part I: The Ethical

> disciples are described as the Father's "gift" to the Son, just as his Son is his gift to the disciples.[19]

So Milbank here recognizes the possibility of reading the Christian tradition as itself embodying equivocation, an equivocation between unilateralism on the one hand and reciprocity on the other. But he then goes on to "resolve" this equivocation by prioritizing one dimension over the other, reciprocity over unilateralism, a prioritizing that he sees to be justified by the doctrine of the Trinity. As he puts it, "it may very well be argued that Christianity has combined both perspectives on giving, but if it has done so it is surely more fundamentally under the *aegis* of reciprocity, even though the eschatological character of this goal requires 'an absolutely unilateral' moment for the gift in our fallen present time. The sovereign gift from the divine height (to 'widows and orphans') is received only as a gift also returned from below, in the incarnation of the *Logos*, as the return of humanity to the Father."[20]

If the acknowledged equivocation between "unilateralism" and "reciprocity" is ultimately overcome by the prioritizing of reciprocity, so too we see the same mechanism at work in his analysis of the tension between "universal" love and "neighbor" love. When, as we saw in chapter 1, Milbank says that we should love our nearest and dearest *and also* those with whom we are unexpectedly brought into contact, he is thereby acknowledging the ongoing claim upon us of the universal—acknowledging that "love of neighbor" is not restricted *solely* to love of our "nearest and dearest." He has amplified this point further in his recent acknowledgment that the Augustinian-Thomistic exhortation to love our "nearest and dearest" is qualified by another strain in the tradition that is manifested in Eckhart's exhortation to love all equally. Just as Eckhart's perspective of a "mystical identity" between humans and God blurs the absolute distinction between God and his creatures, so too it likewise blurs the absolute division of labor between God loving all and creatures loving those to whom they are closest. As Milbank himself puts it, "perhaps in qualification rather than rebuttal of the Augustinian *ordo amoris* (according to which there is hierarchy in the loving imperative, based on the Gospel principle of loving most the closest, who is 'the neighbour'), Eckhart suggests that, from the mystical perspective of identity with God, one should love all equally. Such a principle of equal concern for all—which can only be socially realized, since it is unattainable for the isolated individual working by himself—implies a radical extension of social welfare. And this implication accords with Eckhart's double stress

---

19. Milbank, *Being Reconciled*, 160.
20. Ibid.

on the practical and on justice."²¹ What we see here is both a minimal acknowledgment of equivocation, but also a further minimizing of it by yet another division of labor—this time between the ethical and the political. The principle of "equal concern for all" is relegated to the political realm (it can "only be socially realized") while the ethical realm remains resolutely particularist (preserving the principle of the *ordo amoris*). The effect of this is to minimize equivocation within the ethical, minimize equivocation within the political, and minimize equivocation *between* the ethical and the political. Indeed, I shall return to this point in much more detail in chapter 3 and, indeed, in subsequent chapters.

In some ways, of course, Milbank is effecting an important correction of the anxious paralysis of the Kantian universalism we analyzed in chapter 1. Milbank is quite right to criticize this universalism and to develop a theological justification for particularist, partisan approach to "neighbor love." We have seen that he defended our instinct to discriminate in favor of our nearest and dearest in the case of a common catastrophe, for instance, asking how our neighbors would regard our "pious neutrality" if we failed to give priority to our "nearet and dearest." There is, of course, an important insight that Milbank brings to light here. In specific circumstances, we may well make a judgment in favor of our nearest and dearest, perhaps unthinkingly and without hesitation, and without any retrospective doubts about whether this was the right thing to do. But the mistake Milbank makes, I suggest, is to turn a judgment that may well be made in a specific circumstance into a generalized principle *in advance of* those specific circumstances. However much we may feel justified in prioritizing our nearest and dearest in a singular situation, we cannot ignore the fact that this involves us in a certain betrayal of the universal dimension of ethical life by which we are equally called. We cannot avoid the stubborn contingent fact that the prioritizing of the nearest is at the expense of others, however much we may comfort ourselves that these neglected others are in turn being prioritized by their own neighbors (and, of course, this may not always necessarily be so). It may well be that such prioritizing is an unavoidable feature of our finite and constrained existence, but this does not make it any less tragic, and neither should it blind us to the betrayal of the universal demand that it entails.

This is, of course, the point that Derrida has made in drawing attention to the *aporias* involved in all ethical decisions that entail the elevation of one over others. How can I justify assisting one starving person when to do so entails the neglect of another starving person a street away? As he puts it,

21. Milbank in Žižek and Milbank, *Monstrosity of Christ*, 207.

Part I: The Ethical

> I am responsible to any one (that is to say to any other) only by failing in my responsibilities to all the others, to the ethical or political generality. And I can never justify this sacrifice, I must always hold my peace about it. Whether I want to or not, I can never justify the fact that I prefer or sacrifice any one (any other) to the other. I will always be secretive, held to secrecy in respect of this, for I have nothing to say about it. What binds me to singularities, to this one or that one, male or female, rather than that one over this one, remains finally unjustifiable (this is Abraham's hyper-ethical sacrifice), as unjustifiable as the infinite sacrifice I make at each moment. These singularities represent others, a wholly other form of alterity: one other or some other persons, but also places, animals, languages. How would you ever justify the fact that you sacrifice all the cats in the world to the cat that you feed at home every morning for years, whereas other cats die of hunger at every instant? Not to mention other people? How would you justify your presence here speaking one particular language, rather than speaking to others in another language? And yet we also do our duty by behaving thus.[22]

In other words, by discharging my ethical responsibility toward singularities, I seem to be betraying my ethical responsibility to the universal. Milbank has been dismissive of such ruminations, characterizing them as being held captive by "over precious *aporias* about the treatment of some being also the neglect of others,"[23] and indeed his reading of what he takes to be the Augustinian-Thomist model is his way of responding to this. Milbank is thereby making an important point insofar as he is warning of the dangers of ethical sclerosis here. Whatever Derrida's own position, his reflections should not be carried to the extent of inducing anxious paralysis. At the same time, however, Derrida's point is not to be so hastily dismissed. For it does serve to remind us of the inevitable betrayal of the universal that occurs whenever we make a judgment—however necessary—in favor of the singular or particular. Whenever we make a judgment in favor of our "nearest and dearest," for example, however justified we may feel this to be, our doing so should be haunted by an awareness of those we are thereby neglecting. This is nothing other than a haunting awareness of the universal dimension of the ethical that we are temporarily suspending.

Does this matter? I should argue that it does because this haunting awareness of our suspension of the universal may assert itself so strongly at times that it may lead us to suspend this very suspension. For we should

---

22. Derrida, *Gift of Death*, 70–71.
23. Milbank, *Being Reconciled*, 39.

not prejudge the ethical by assuming that we will *always* or even in general make the decision to elect the singular and suspend the universal. However often we may make ethical judgments in favor of those close to us in the way Milbank suggests, there *may* be specific circumstances in which we judge that the right thing is to do otherwise—to suspend the call of the singular, close-at-hand neighbor in favor of the universal call of the nameless others. In certain circumstances, we may judge this the right thing to do. By transposing what ought to be a singular judgment into a generalized principle made *in advance* of specific situations, Milbank has dissolved the thoroughgoing equivocation at the heart of the ethical. By delegating the universal dimension of responsibility to God, the mediating third, he allows for the suspension of the universal in the creaturely world in the knowledge that it will be enacted by God in the divine world. But this, I suggest, is to make things too easy. It is to become complacent about the ethical judgments that have to be made anew in each singular instance.

Much of what I have said above would apply, albeit in inverted form, to Žižek's invocation of the nihil as his own mediating third. I shall refrain from spelling this out at similar length because I shall return to it in more detail in the context of our impending discussions of the political. But at this point it will suffice to note some of the ways in which the most salient features of my analysis of Milbank's approach could be applied also to Žižek's thought. Thus, whereas Milbank gives ontological priority to God, the domain of the universal, Žižek gives ontological priority to the nihil, to the domain of the particular. That the nihil belongs to the domain of particularity in this context may not immediately be evident, and more will need to be said here. We have already noted something of the nature of Žižek's nihilism in his account of subjectivity, in which he asserted that the subject is ultimately Nothing. But, we also noted, the subject is not Nothing *as distinct from* the wider material reality of which it is a part; on the contrary, the subject is at one with that wider reality precisely in the fact that they both share in a common Nothingness. For Žižek, such nihilism is the true formula of materialism. Accepting the conclusion that, ultimately, "nothing exists," Žižek amplifies this by saying,

> The statement "material reality is all there is" can be negated in two ways: in the form of "material reality *isn't all there is*" and the form of "material reality *is non-all*." The first negation (of a predicate) leads to the standard metaphysics: material reality isn't everything, there is another, higher, spiritual reality.... As such, this negation is, in accordance with Lacan's formulas of sexuation, inherent to the positive statement "material reality is all there is": as its constitutive exception, it grounds its

universality. If, however, we assert a non-predicate and say "material reality *is non-all*," this merely asserts the non-all of reality without implying any exception—paradoxically, we should thus claim that "material reality *is non-all*," not "material reality is all there is," is the true formula of materialism.[24]

Following on from this, Žižek says that the materialism that he thus asserts is by no means "a fully existing external reality"; on the contrary, given that its premise is the "non-all" of reality, it rather asserts an ontological incompleteness: "We should thus not be afraid of the much decried 'dissolution of matter in a field of energies' in modern physics: a true materialist should fully embrace it. Materialism has nothing to do with the assertion of the inert density of matter; it is, on the contrary, a position which accepts the ultimate void of reality—the consequence of its central thesis on the primordial multiplicity is that there is no 'substantial reality,' that the only substance of the multiplicity is void."[25] Žižek's ontological *materialism* is therefore also an ontological *nihilism*, a materialism that asserts that there is ultimately only the void. This is, of course, a distinctive type of materialism, one that is refracted through his "parallax" lens, which means also that it is a materialism shot through with equivocation and incommensurability.

This in turn means, among other things, that there is an equivocation between necessity and contingency, but it is an equivocation that arises out of an ultimate prioritizing of the contingent. This can be seen, for instance, when Žižek says that "a process of formally inevitable unfolding must prevail" but this means that

> the conceptually determined "formally inevitable unfolding" is not there from the very beginning of the process, it gradually "prevails," and this "prevailing" is the (in itself contingent) process by means of which the conceptual necessity (I am almost tempted to say: in an autopoietic way) forms itself out of the initial contingency. In other words, there is no preexisting necessity that directs the dialectical process, since this necessity is precisely what arises through this process, i.e., what this process is about. . . . Yes, there is a necessity, but this necessity is *retroactive*, it arises as the (*contingent*) self-sublation of contingency.[26]

What we see here, then, is that the equivocation between necessity and contingency is lessened by the ultimate prioritizing of contingency. So too—and as we saw to be the case with Milbank—ethical equivocation is weakened by

24. Žižek in Žižek and Milbank, *Monstrosity of Christ*, 95.
25. Ibid., 97.
26. Ibid., 246.

the bracketing or suspension of one of the three domains of the ethical triad, paradoxically because it is the very domain that is ontologically privileged. Thus, Žižek's ontological privileging of the contingent, the finite, and the immanent means that that very domain, the domain of particularity, can, in a sense and in ethical terms, be allowed to take care of itself.

What does it mean to say this? We have seen that for Milbank, his ontological prioritzing of the universal (God) paradoxically gave rise to a creaturely and practical prioritizing of the particular and the singular. That is to say, the ontological prioritizing of God gave rise to an ethical prioritizing of the nearest and dearest. In Žižek's case, we find the same mechanism in operation, but in inverted form. Because the contingent, the particular, is all there really is, there is a sense in which it can be allowed to take care of itself. Thus, in Žižek's scheme, it seems that the universal has to be *produced*, as an ethical task. Practical attention thus gets shifted to the task of inaugurating *singular* instantiations of the *universal*. This means in turn that the ethical/political imperative gets shifted away from love of the nearest and dearest to the love of all, the nameless multitude, the universal third. As we shall see in more detail in chapter 3, this leads Žižek to prioritize the political over the ethical. The call of the neighbor who is close at hand serves only as a stumbling block to the realization of universal justice. Such universal justice can only be instantiated through the enactment of revolutionary violence, which Žižek frankly admits. However one responds to this, one can understand it as an inevitable result of a dilution of equivocation by the practical bracketing of the demands of the particular. It is only by this practical bracketing of the particular that the universal is given such virulent sway. Whereas on Milbank's model the task of the realization of universal justice was acknowledged to be God's prerogative, in Žižek's explicitly atheistic materialism, there is no God to undertake this task. It must therefore be assumed in its entirety by humanity itself; humanity must bring about the instantiation of the universal.

Understood thus, the criticisms we developed against Milbank may now be directed against Žižek, albeit in inverted form. Thus, in singular circumstances, it *may* be judged right to suspend the claim upon us of our "nearest and dearest" in favor of the nameless multitude. Under specific conditions, it may be thought right to suspend the claim upon us of the particular to give full vent to the claim of the universal. But this can only be done in each instance, by means of singular judgments in circumstances that are unique and nonrepeatable. It is a mistake to generalize this suspension of the particular and instantiation of the universal *in advance* of specific situations. This is to ignore or relegate the very real ethical claims upon us of the domain of the particular, a relegation that may be judged right in specific situations (with the tragic neglect of our nearest and dearest, perhaps, in the process) but that should never be elevated as a general rule. This is to prejudge every situation in favor of revolutionary violence, a prejudging that may well turn out to be ethically destructive. This is again to overcome thoroughgoing equivocation between the universal, the particular, and the singular; it is through the perpetuation of this equivocation that the ethical proceeds.

In light of these analyses, it would seem that there is perhaps something ethically problematic about unequivocal ontological resolutions. For we have seen that when there are such resolutions, the precarious equivocation between the universal, the particular, and the singular becomes skewed. Whichever of the three domains is ontologically privileged, it seems that the same domain is "bracketed out" or "suspended" in the practical ethical realm. This "bracketing" or "suspending" has the practical effect of skewing equivocation by prejudging ethical decisions in advance of specific situations, and this prejudging, we have seen, is ethically problematic. In which case, could it perhaps be said that the equivocation of the ethical depends upon an ontological equivocation? Are the interests of the ethical best served by the refusal of any ontological resolutions? I shall return to this question in more detail in chapter 6, but at this stage, our analysis does provisionally suggest that ontological equivocation is the best way of perpetuating the equivocation of the ethical.

In contrast, both Milbank and Žižek seem to cultivate a form of ethical complacency. Milbank too easily equates the ethical imperative with a love of our nearest and dearest, while Žižek too easily equates it with an instantiation of universal justice. There will be occasions when ethical decisions will be made in one direction or the other, but to endorse either direction in advance of singular situations is to be complacent about the intrinsic equivocation and difficulty of the ethical. Furthermore, this complacency is ethically dangerous. Milbank's approach makes ethics unduly partisan and obscures the extent to which the ethical sometimes calls for the suspension of such preferences. Žižek's approach makes ethics unduly impersonal and obscures the extent to which the ethical calls for us to be attentive to the particular neighbors who are at risk of being made expendable in the violent fight for universal justice. There is a tension here between neighbor-love and universal justice, and the interests of the ethical can be served not by resolving this tension, but by tarrying with it. Insofar as there is any resolution, it can only be momentary in the enactment of specific ethical decisions that have to be made anew in each singular instance. Thus, the response to the anxious ethical paralysis produced by Kant and Levinas is not to resolve the tension between self and neighbor through the invocation of a mediating third, not to be complacent about the tension between the universal, the particular, and the singular, but to embrace the equivocation of the ethical, precisely in the interests of the ethical. This is to undertake the necessary task of ethical *labor*.

Labor: The Enactment of the Ethical

At the conclusion of these reflections, it might be objected that our discussion has been unduly abstract. We have been discussing these processes of ethical judgment, action, and risk-taking in complete isolation from those judgments, actions, and risks themselves. In some ways, this is an inevitable outcome of the content of our analysis. For I have been arguing precisely that ethical judgments cannot be made in isolation from contingent circumstances, from the concrete realities of life. There cannot be an ethical "system"; there can only be ethical "practice," the taking on of the burden of ethical "labor." We have seen, of course, that such practice is informed, guided, and shaped by a universal vision or *telos*, but the instantiating of that universal in the particular is something that can only be practiced in singular situations and not something that can be prejudged or formulated into a system. Any theoretical discussion must therefore, of necessity, be in abstract terms, looking at the formal ("empty") structures of the ethical that are waiting to be filled by the concrete realities of life. Or better, we are, retrospectively and at a second-order or "meta" level, analyzing the shape and structure of the judgments that we do in practice make.

But as we reach the conclusion of this chapter, it will nevertheless be helpful to give some indication of how the abstract analysis developed above might be related to the labor of the ethical in practice. In order to do this, therefore, I shall briefly discuss what I take to be an example of the equivocation of the ethical in practice. This is therefore an attempt to articulate the ethical *between* the theoretical and the practical, and the most fertile ground on which to do this is that constituted by film and literature, for they occupy precisely that shifty terrain between theory and practice. Any number of possible examples might be chosen, but in what follows I shall discuss a particular Hollywood movie and its portrayal of the streets of New York.

The film, *Sleepers* (1996), has been the subject of mixed reviews. It is sometimes said to be one of director Barry Levinson's weaker films that pales in comparison with others such as *Rain Man* (1988) and *Disclosure* (1994). Nonetheless, in spite of this, the film is an instructive illustration of the complex and equivocal character of the ethical, manifesting some of the ambiguities inherent in ethical life, of the kind that we have thus far been

Part I: The Ethical

discussing. The film is based on a novel of the same title written by Lorenzo Carcaterra, who claims that it depicts, in disguised form, actual historical events. The first part of the film is set in Hell's Kitchen, in the West Side of Manhattan, during the mid-1960s; it depicts the childhood of four close friends, boys between the ages of about twelve and fourteen. Somewhat nostalgically, the world portrayed is one of relative poverty and less-than-ideal marriages, but nonetheless one also of safety and security, built around close relationships of family and friends. The Italian-American backdrop looms large, with small-time crime bosses and the Catholic church living peaceably if uneasily side by side, and with both casting their unmistakable shadows over the community's inhabitants. These twin pillars exercise their contrary allures over children growing up in their midst, making the transition to adulthood a precarious business. It is symbolized by one of the boy characters ("Shakes") spending some of his days as an altar boy in his local church, assisting the local priest, Father Bobby, a chain-smoking and streetwise mentor to whom the boys are in many ways closer than they are to their own parents. On other days Shakes works as an errand boy for the local mafia boss, King Benny, delivering payoffs to corrupt police officers.

The crucial turning point in the first half of the film is summarized by reviewer David Stratton: "These early scenes evoke carefree summer days in which the four friends fool around, play stupid pranks and generally enjoy life. But it all comes to an end one day in the summer of '67, when a thoughtless incident involving a quick-tempered Greek hot dog vendor results in a near-fatal accident. The boys are arrested and sentenced to nine to eighteen months at the Wilkinson Home for Boys, a Dickensian hellhole where chief guard Nokes (Kevin Bacon) proves to be a sadistic pedophile."[27] Their time at Wilkinson is portrayed as being one of relentless exposure to sexual, physical, and mental abuse.

The film then cuts to 1981, by which time two of the four boys have successful careers, one as a journalist and the other as a lawyer. The other two have fallen into a life of drug dealing and killing, which is of a different order to the petty crime that overshadowed their youth. Upon encountering Nokes, their former abuser, in a bar, the two criminals impulsively take their revenge by committing a point-blank killing in full view of witnesses. The two are quickly arrested and charged with murder, and at this point the community network of the boys' youth swings into action to save the murderers from their seemingly inevitable fate. Shakes and Michael—now journalist and lawyer—lead the whole operation, with Michael taking on the case of the prosecution, which he conducts in such a way as to ensure

---

27. Stratton, review of *Sleepers*, par. 7.

the acquittal of his two old friends. Meanwhile, Shakes virtually scripts the case of the defense, which is prosecuted by a pliable lawyer recruited by the mob boss King Benny. In the process of securing the acquittal of the two murderers, the whole scandal of the regime at Wilkinson Home for Boys is exposed, thus ensuring the downfall of the guardsmen who are still living. There is a sense in which justice—albeit outside the parameters of the law—is seen to have prevailed.

The underlying moral of the film has been much discussed. David Stratton again comments that "the moral dilemma posed by the film that taking the law into one's own hands is acceptable if the original crime was heinous enough is not as glibly presented here as it is in the John Grisham-Joel Schumacher hit *A Time to Kill*. Nevertheless, the theme can interestingly be contrasted with all those liberal, anti-revenge, anti-lynch-mob pics that Hollywood once produced. As in the Grisham film, the assumption here is that because the crimes against the four youths were truly terrible, the avenging of those crimes outside the legal system is perfectly in order."[28] But is the assumption underlying the film really as simple as this? At the very least, a neat narrative of "redemption" is avoided insofar as we learn that the two murderers subsequently return to their lives of crime and killing and themselves die in a state of degeneration before the age of thirty. What we certainly do see is the ultimate triumph of the internal values of community solidarity and mutual protection that we saw to have framed the world of the boys' youth. This world of internal justice, in which "revenge" is the primary principle, is seen to have formed and shaped the boys' childhood, and ultimately saves them when they are threatened by the twin forces of external crimes and the rule of law. Whether the moral of the film is that this is "perfectly in order" is far from obvious, and we may well question whether the film is making an explicit ethical pronouncement of this kind at all.

Where the film does much to illuminate the equivocal character of the ethical is in the critical role played by the priest, Father Bobby. As the court trial unfolds, it becomes clear that the success of the ploy hinges on the securing of a false witness who can testify to the "fact" that the two murderers were elsewhere at the time that the murder took place. Father Bobby seems to be the only person who can both be trusted with the secret of their undertaking and at the same time appear as a plausible witness. He is approached by Shakes, who is not unaware of the enormity of the "favor" for which he is asking. But however much it may conflict with the demands of the priest's faith, Shakes is simultaneously aware that this could in some sense be seen as the "right" thing to do, and in a way demanded by that faith

28. Ibid., par. 11.

Part I: The Ethical

itself. In other words, it could be said that Shakes is aware that intrinsic to faith is the notion of the "suspension of the ethical," though the question of what constitutes a legitimate "suspension" is not something that can be unequivocally determined in advance, nor even in retrospect. This theme is obviously prefigured, albeit at a more trivial level, earlier in the film when Father Bobby says farewell to Shakes as he is on the point of entering the prison house. Asking the priest to keep an eye on his parents, who Shakes fears are on the point of killing each other, he adds, "No matter what you hear, tell them [my parents] that I'm doing OK." "You mean you want me to lie?" "It"s a good lie, Father. You can do it."

When, years later, Shakes asks the priest to tell a lie for a second time, albeit one of a quite different magnitude, he again puts it in terms that suggest that the lie would not be a betrayal of his faith but a fulfilment of it. "It's not too late, Father. You still have a chance to bring home a couple of stray sheep. One more chance." "Is that chance legal?" "Last chances never are." "So you're asking me to lie? You're asking me to swear to God and then lie." "I'm asking you to save two of your boys." In this exchange, we see the labor of the ethical being put into play, as the respective theological imperatives toward truth (the domain of the universal) and salvation (in this case, the domain of the particular) manifest themselves contradictorily in the singularity of the dilemma being faced. Earlier in the film, Shakes serves Father Bobby as an altar boy one last time before his committal to the institution. As they prepare for the service in the church vestry, the priest glances at the liturgy for the day. "This is one of my favorites." "What is?" "Whatever you do to the least of my brethren, you do to me."

The fact that the priest eventually decides to tell the lie and "save" his boys should not be interpreted as an endorsement of the wider scheme of revenge in which he was now enmeshed. To see his decision as involving a simple connivance with or a condemnation of revenge would be as misleading as seeing his decision as being simply to commit perjury or to tell the truth. A complex web of theological impulses—involving love, redemption, justice, and salvation—impels him to make the decision he makes, and these impulses have to be set over against the revenge, the lies, and the deceit in which the same decision thereby involves him. He is all too aware that, whatever decision he makes, it will be ethically "contaminated." Ethical purity is only possible at the level of the universal, a level abstracted from the specificity of the particular and the singular. As the universal is "contaminated" by the particular and the singular, so every ethical decision is likewise "contaminated." And in the absence of ethical purity, there can be no guarantees. When Shakes leaves the priest to meditate on his request, the priest says, "I've got a decision to make. I only pray it's the right one." He knows that he can only pray that the decision he reaches will be the right one, that there can be no guarantee that it will be. To act ethically is to act in the domain of risk, which is to act in the domain of life. As King Benny observes, "Life is risk."

The risk that is taken is open to judgment, but a judgment that can only be passed from the vantage point of the Absolute, a vantage point inaccessible to humanity, what might be described as the judgment of God. As if to underscore this, the film avoids the temptation of ending with the conversion of the two murderers from their lives of crime and killing, thereby retrospectively justifying the priest's "suspension of the ethical." There is a scene in which it comes close to doing so. After the two accused men have been acquitted, the four friends—who have not been reunited for years and never will be again—spend one night together in a comradely alcoholic reverie that seems to affirm the ineradicable ties that still hold them together amidst all the ravages of time and the divisions of circumstance. The scene seems to imply that the priest has done the right thing, and in a sense he has. But the fact that the two acquitted men go on to kill, and the fact that they themselves die young in a state of degeneration, serves to underscore the equivocation. These subsequent developments do not "condemn" the priest's action any more than the four friends' night of salvation "justifies" it. For the "absolute" knowledge that would definitively "justify" or "condemn" the decision is once again lacking. The act was an ethical decision, a risk taken in good faith, open to judgment.

Such a risk could not be averted through Kant's elevation of the universal or Levinas's prioritization of the singular. Neither could it be averted through Milbank's focus on the "nearest and dearest" or Žižek's proclamation of universal justice. All approaches attempt somehow to anticipate and prejudge the singularity of the situation, and it is in that irreducible singularity that the decision must be made. As such the decision is a leap into the abyss, but this does not mean that it is made in a vacuum. On the contrary, the singular decision is made in the context of an ever-present universal, in this case constituted by the priest's religious faith. But that universal must be instantiated in the particular, and the manner of that instantiation cannot be prejudged by the universal itself. In light of this, it is apparent that decision, risk, faith, and judgment are inescapable. Herein lies the labor of the ethical.

That risk is constitutive of the ethical has to be acknowledged when it is recognized that in each ethical moment, we can never be sure of the full range of circumstantial factors at work. Just as the priest in *Sleepers* was unable to anticipate the full implications of his action, so too in any singular instance we can never be sure of the full range of the psychological factors at play, whether in myself or in another; we can never be sure of the full implications that our decision or action will have; we can never be sure whether our intentions and hopes will be inverted. In these and all sorts of other ways, every ethical judgment and every ethical action is the taking of a risk. Such risks are unsettling, which is why ethics itself is, or should be, unsettling. This unsettlement is what makes ethics an activity of difficult labor. Again as was the case with the priest, even at the end of this process (or of each process) of difficult labor, we are still left without any guarantee that the decision made or action taken will be judged aright. The most that we can do is to act in *faith* and in anticipation of a retrospective *judgment*.

The faith at work here is a faith that we are acting ethically, even in the absence of any objective guarantee that this is so, an understanding of faith that is, of course, entirely consistent with that of Kierkegaard. As he puts it, "Without risk there is no faith. Faith is precisely the contradiction between the infinite passion of the individual's inwardness and the objective uncertainty."[29] As for the judgment, as we observed at the outset of chapter 1, it cannot come from myself, for I shall never be in possession of all the elements of certain knowledge that would allow me to pass this judgment on myself. Just as there is an element of surrender to an other in the act of faith, so there is likewise a surrender to the other in the giving up of myself to judgment. This act of judgment can, logically, only be passed from a perspective of omniscience, which is why talk of the judgment of God makes an inevitable appearance here. As Don Cupitt has observed, "to be religious means that one's whole life is as it were subject to a constant scrutiny and under assessment from an absolute point of view that silently records everything and misses nothing. The religious requirement extends to one's whole life and to every detail of one's life. It does not allow one to keep any secret compartments or locked doors. It searches the heart. And it is of course this feature of the religious demand that has given rise to the traditional affirmation of the omniscience of God."[30]

All of which is to raise the question of the extent to which the ethical disposition outlined here leads to, or requires, or presupposes, religion. This is a complex question, a full discussion of which I am going to defer until chapter 6, by which point our discussion of the ethical will have been supplemented by a discussion of the political. But for the moment, it will suffice to note just two points. First, the account of the ethical that has been developed in these chapters clearly presupposes—and could not possibly operate without—a universal dimension. That is, a conception of the good, the true,

---

29. Kierkegaard, *Concluding Unscientific Postscript*, 182.
30. Cupitt, *Taking Leave of God*, 85.

and the beautiful that is not only an expression of the good, the true, and the beautiful *for me*, but one that is thought to have universal validity. The assertion of a universal itself constitutes a risk, for we do not make such an assertion from an Absolute standpoint, but from a standpoint of particularity. Such a standpoint "contaminates" universality but does not invalidate it. Indeed, we have seen that the risk of asserting a universal domain is one that must be taken, for without it the ethical would be unintelligible as such. I shall this discuss this in more detail in chapter 5.

Second, we have also seen that the ethical operates by means of a structure that involves a certain unknowing and therefore the necessity of risk-taking, which must be done in faith, in anticipation of judgment, a judgment that comes from elsewhere, from an absolute or omniscient perspective. Such a structure already appears remarkably theological. Without explicitly intending to do so, we seem irresistibly to have invoked a theological supplement. In our account of the equivocation of the ethical, therefore, we have borne witness to the necessity of a universal, and also raised the possibility that this universal might well be theological in character. At the same time, however, we have also raised the question of whether the invocation of theology might be problematic for the ethical. As we have seen earlier in this chapter, there is a danger that God, which the ethical seems indirectly to invoke, could serve to "mend" and "overcome" the necessary equivocation of the ethical. If there is a sense in which the ethical draws us irresistibly to theology, there is also simultaneously a sense in which the ethical seems to propel us away from it. There is, therefore, yet another form of equivocation at work here. What our account of the ethical bears witness to, I suggest, is a certain return of theology, but a return of theology that is itself equivocal.

But this is to anticipate a discussion that will be for now be deferred, as it will more profitably be unfolded after the ensuing discussion of the nature of the political. In the meantime, and by way of transition, it is necessary for us to consider the question of the relationship *between* the ethical and the political.

Part II

BETWEEN THE ETHICAL AND THE POLITICAL

3

BETWEEN

As we make the transition from the ethical to the political, we are immediately confronted by the contentious question of the relationship between them. How are we to conceive of the relationship between the ethical and the political? Are they complementary and is the relationship between them therefore continuous? Or are they in tension such that there is no easy reconciliation between them? In much recent work, the latter view has prevailed, and this may be seen in a particularly vivid way in the work of both Levinas and Žižek. Their analyses may be diametrically opposed, but they share a conviction that there is no easy continuity between the ethical and the political; on the contrary, both see the ethical and political as being inassimilable.

In the face of this disjunction, Levinas, as is well known, gives an unequivocal phenomenological priority to the ethical. The primary and founding moment is located in the encounter with the face of the other by which and to which we are called to assume a position of infinite responsibility. The ethical thereby constitutes or "founds" all else, including the subject itself. Consequently, the political emerges as a secondary supplement, through a process whereby the subject abstracts itself from its singular relationship with the face and brings into view the nameless third. Through the coming into view of this third emerges also the question of "justice" and thus also the political as such.

This whole model has been subject to radical criticism and, indeed, to *reversal* by Žižek. He argues that the relationship between the ethical and political should be configured precisely the other way around. For Žižek, the primordial experience is of others as an indifferent multitude, and it is against this primary background that love emerges as a secondary and violent gesture of cutting across this multitude in order to privilege the

Part II: Between the Ethical and the Political

neighbor. Justice, the realm of politics, is inaugurated when one refocuses on this primordial multitude against the imbalance and distortion that the focus on the neighbor has wrought. Thus, for Žižek, it is justice—politics—that is primary and foundational, with ethics—the particularity of love—emerging as a secondary supplement. In this chapter, it is not my intention to make a case for Levinas and against Žižek, or vice versa. Rather, I shall contest the very point at which they converge, namely, their shared conviction, albeit antithetically expressed, that the ethical and political are structurally incompatible. On the contrary, I shall argue that there is a continuous relationship between the ethical and political derived from their shared triune structure, wherein *both* are committed to the labor of negotiating the tension between the universal, the particular, and the singular. Before doing this, however, it is necessary for us to return to Levinas, and particularly to look at his understanding of the political in relation to the ethical.

Levinas and the Political

We have seen that, for Levinas, the ethical consists in the subject's primordial experience of subjection, a call of responsibility toward the singular other, which operates unilaterally and unconditionally, irrespective of the other's disposition toward me and irrespective of the existence of any third party. But it is the very appearance of this third party that interrupts this phenomenological structure and that gives rise to the *political*, to the question of justice. As Levinas comments, "the third party introduces a contradiction in the saying whose signification before the other until then went in one direction. It is of itself the limit of responsibility and the birth of the question: what do I have to do with justice? A question of consciousness. Justice is necessary, that is, comparison, coexistence, contemporaneousness, assembling, order, thematization, the visibility of faces, and thus intentionality and the intellect, the intelligibility of a system, and thence also a copresence on an equal footing as before a court of justice."[1] The appearance of the third party obviously gives rise to a great deal more than the question of justice and of the political. But what is also clear is that the political originates in a structure that is *contrary* to that of the ethical, that *limits* the ethical, is a *corrective* to it, and that operates according to a fundamentally different logic.

More particularly, the correction at issue here is that of the logic of asymmetry by that of symmetry and—a point to which I shall return—the correction of the logic of singularity by that of universality. "The relationship with the third party is an incessant corrective of the asymmetry of proximity

---

1. Levinas, *Otherwise than Being*, 157.

in which the face is looked at. There is weighing, thought, objectification, and thus a decree in which my anarchic relationship with illeity is *betrayed*, but in which it is conveyed before us."² The contrary nature of the relationship between that which is being corrected and that which is the agent of correction is well expressed when Levinas speaks of justice as inaugurating the "comparison of the incomparable." But the ambivalent character of the relationship is also expressed when Levinas says that the question of justice both betrays my relationship with illeity *and also* conveys it before us. Clearly, therefore, in spite of their contradictory logics, there is a sense in which the political can or should convey the ethical before us, and in that sense should be consistent with it. Where the "political" takes forms that do not convey my relationship with illeity before us, this cannot properly be spoken of as embodying "justice," nor can it properly be thought of as "political." Thus, Levinas says that "justice is not a legality regulating human masses, from which a technique of social equilibrium is drawn, harmonizing antagonistic forces. That would be a justification of the State delivered over to its own necessities. Justice is impossible without the one that renders it finding himself in proximity."³

On this basis, it is clear that Levinas's conception of the political is at odds with that of modern liberalism. This is brought out further by Howard Caygill when he says that

> war and the political assume a proximity in Levinas's thought that were it recognised would prove extremely uncomfortable for liberal readers accustomed to keeping war—as the alleged pathology of civility—separate from peace.... Levinas's emphasis on fraternity also diverges from the norms of liberal political theory. The dominant, liberal tradition of political thought since Kant and Hegel gives overwhelming primacy to the concept of freedom and then, to a lesser degree and under certain historical conditions, [to] the concept of equality. Yet, as Levinas constantly reminds us, the modern political has been trinitarian since the French Revolution, comprising not only freedom and equality but also fraternity. It is upon the third member of the trinity that Levinas focuses his attention. He seeks the promise of peace in an ethics of alterity that points toward the rethinking of fraternity.⁴

---

2. Ibid., 158.
3. Ibid., 159.
4. Caygill, *Levinas and the Political*, 3–4.

Part II: Between the Ethical and the Political

So for Levinas, what passes for the political in the discourse of modern liberalism is disqualified from being an instantiation of the genuinely political by its forgetting of the ethical, which should serve as its source and wellspring, a forgetting that results in it enshrining "liberty" at the expense of "fraternity." The Levinasian paradox is thus that the political must be consistent with the ethical, even though their respective logics are fundamentally inconsistent.

The logic here is rather like that which we saw to be manifested in the relationship between the "saying" and the "said"; the "said" manifests and conveys the ethical "saying" even if, in so doing, it betrays it. Indeed, the structural similarity between these two relationships is more than coincidental. There is a sense in which the ethical is of the order of the "saying," while the political is of the order of the "said." In terms of the relationship of the political to the ethical, Levinas says, "the contemporaneousness of the multiple is tied about the diachrony of the two: justice remains justice only, in a society where there is no distinction between those close and those far off, but in which there also remains the impossibility of passing by the closest. The equality of all is borne by my inequality, the surplus of my duties over my rights. The forgetting of self moves justice." The equality of all is borne by my inequality. In other words, the political is borne by the ethical, even though they are fundamentally inconsistent. In fact, only if the political is indeed borne by the ethical do we have a genuine instantiation of the political at all. As he goes on to say, it is important to know whether the "egalitarian and just state" "proceeds from a war of all against all, or from the irreducible responsibility of the one for all."[5] What is furthermore manifested here, of course, is that the primacy of the ethical is uncompromised; the political is subservient to it and always emerges as a secondary supplement.

It is clear, therefore, that for Levinas, the ethical and political operate according to fundamentally different, and indeed inconsistent, logics. But among subsequent commentators, there have been differences both as to the precise nature of this distinction and, also, as to what the implications of this distinction would be. In particular, there has been much discussion of the vexed question as to whether a Levinasian account of ethics can give rise to a corresponding Levinasian politics. Such thinkers as Howard Caygill and Simon Critchley have answered this question in the affirmative. For Caygill, Levinas's ethics requires a political supplement, but it is one that is answerable to and consistent with (even in the midst of a certain inconsistency) his account of the ethical. This political supplement gives rise to what

---

5. Levinas, *Otherwise than Being*, 159.

Caygill calls a "messianic eschatology" and the elaboration of a "prophetic politics."[6] I shall discuss Critchley's approach in more detail in chapter 4, in the context of which I shall question whether Levinas is in fact able to provide the resources for an effective political outlook. What is clear, however, is that both Caygill and Critchley are in no doubt that there is a "harmonious connection" between ethics and politics in Levinas's thought, and that the politics in question is a robust, concrete, and potentially effective one.[7]

Others have likewise endorsed the effectiveness of Levinas as a political thinker, while at the same time insisting on—and defending—the fundamental structural difference between the ethical and political, as well as the unequivocal priority of the ethical. Regina Schwarz, for instance, has defended Levinas from the charge that his ethics lacks a politics, saying that "by turning away from the understanding of the subject as solipsistic but as constituted by its responsibility for another, by justice, Levinas has delineated an understanding of the subject that is not only preemninently social but also political."[8] Or at least up to a point, for Schwarz is aware that there remains a suspicion of the political on the part of Levinas, particularly as manifested in his suspicion of the State. The question then becomes whether this suspicion of the political does condemn him, as some have argued, to the propagation of a pre-political ethics. Recognizing Levinas's ambivalence toward the political, but also believing that such ambivalence must be understood and properly appreciated, Schwarz suggests that rather than understanding his thought as being "pre-political," "if anything, his ethics is postpolitical, not only because he lived through and took account of the Nazi horror, but also because it is after explicitly engaging politics in his work that he embraces an ethics that goes beyond politics—not an alternative to politics, but an ethics he believes works when politics fails, and so an ethics that politics must answer to."[9] It is important that politics must be answerable to ethics in this way and it is important, thus, that the priority of the ethical is preserved because the political lies logically and structurally in close proximity to the "said," to ontology, to the attempt to compare the incomparable. As such, it is always prone to violence and totalitarianism, and this is why the ethical must always watch over it and preserve its preeminence. Levinas, sensitive to totality and its dangers of intolerance and

---

6. See, for instance, Caygill, *Levinas and the Political*, 149–50.

7. Kenneth Reinhard speaks for a number of others when he says that "Howard Caygill is more convinced of the harmonious connections between politics and ethics in Levinas's thought than I am." Reinhard, "Toward a Political Theology of the Neighbor," 48 n. 82.

8. Schwarz, "Revelation and Revolution," 118.

9. Ibid., 118–19.

Part II: Between the Ethical and the Political

fascism, would insist that the political as such must always be answerable to the ethical, must be open to questioning by the ethical, and, consequently, must always be secondary with respect to the ethical.

Schwarz's defense of Levinas's "postpolitical" status is provoked by yet another group of commentators, namely, those who would accuse Levinas of political impotence, of ushering in the "fakeries of liberalism." She is concerned with the criticisms of Alain Badiou, in particular, but she is also aware—and discusses the fact—that similar accusations have been made by Slavoj Žižek. For both Badiou and Žižek, an effective politics that does not relapse into liberal impotence must be underpinned by an unequivocal commitment to and proclamation of an unqualified universal. Once this unequivocal commitment to a universal is weakened or compromised, it cannot but lead to a weakening of the political itself and a betrayal of the quest for justice. This is why, for Badiou and Žižek, Levinas is held to be politically suspect: because his political commitment to the universality of justice is always subordinated to—and, for them, weakened by—the priority of the ethical. But, of course, for Levinas, as Schwarz points out, this weakening or undercutting of the logic of universalism is done with good reason: in order to outflank the totalitarianism and violence that always comes in its wake.

In light of all this, it seems tempting to say that what is at issue here is nothing less than a question of the preeminence of the universal over the singular. It would seem to be the case that such commentators as Badiou and Žižek believe that Levinas precludes a full commitment to the political because he precludes a full commitment to the universal; it seems that the universal domain of the political must always be subordinated to the singular domain of the ethical. For Levinas, it might be said, the universal is always secondary and always answerable to the singular. Such a characterization would not be wholly misleading, and yet, it would need to be hedged about with qualifications and equivocation. To say straightforwardly that Levinas subordinates the universal to the singular would be rather like saying straightforwardly that Levinas subordinates the "said" to the "saying." While there is a sense in which this is indeed the case, one cannot say that this is so without simultaneously being aware of the structural complexity that is involved in this process.

The complexities and equivocation involved here are well expressed by Adriaan Peperzak when he says that "insofar as we remain within philosophical reflection . . . we would not know how to escape from the *universalization of the asymmetrical relation*, separating and inseparably binding together every ego and every Other. Thus *asymmetry* shows itself to be a universal and universally *reciprocal* relation."[10] The paradox that Peperzak articulates here has been taken up and greatly developed by Fabio Ciaramelli, who has explored the complex interplay between individuation and universality in Levinas's discourse. Levinas's apparent phobia toward universalism is articulated by Ciaramelli when he says that the authority of my obligation "is grounded not in the universality of the *logos*, but in the immediacy of the transcendence of the other who places me under obligation. . . . In order to express this an-archy of subjective responsibility without resorting to the abstractions and generalizations of ontological language, *Otherwise than Being* states repeatedly that this situation concerns my own ipseity, my own privacy above and beyond any conceptualization in which the concept of the I arises *après coup*."[11] And yet, at the same time, it is clear, as Ciaramelli observes, that Levinas seeks to articulate and claim for the ethical an absolute and universal meaning. The paradox lying at the heart of Levinas's discourse on the ethical is that "even if there is a universality of the ethical by virtue of the fact that each subject is called to a responsibility as infinite as mine, it is only from the perspective of my own assignation and election that I can put it into words."[12] Levinas, it seems, is uncompromising in his insistence that the ethical origin lies in the uniquely singular experience of the "I" (in a nongeneralizable sense). And yet, at the same time, he wants to make a universal claim for the quality of this experience that in no way detracts from its irreducible singularity. The fact that this is not expressible in formal structures of logic would not be an insurmountable difficulty for Levinas, for the sovereignty of such structures is one of the very things he is questioning. As Ciaramelli points out and as we have already noted, there is a parallel here to the movements at play in Levinas's account of the interdependent, fluctuating, and ambiguous relationship between the saying and the said: "In the dimension of the Said the meaning of such a situation becomes universal while its unsayable origin preceded the Said and lies in the ipseity of the subject in the Saying. . . . In *Otherwise than Being* Levinas deliberately courts this ambiguity in order to preserve the particularity of the subject *alongside* its universal ethical significance."[13]

If it is the case, therefore, that Levinas wants to claim a universal significance for an ethical origin that would lose its significance if it were anything other than irreducibly singular, then we can see that the situation

---

10. Peperzak, "Autrui, Société, Peuple de Dieu," 314. Translated and quoted by Ciaramelli, "Levinas's Ethical Discourse," 84.

11. Ciaramelli, "Levinas's Ethical Discourse," 88.

12. Ibid., 92.

13. Ibid., 93.

at issue here is by no means as simple as a straightforward jettisoning of the universal in favor of the singular. There is a sense in which the two must necessarily coexist. We may see this as another manifestation of Levinas's acknowledgment of equivocation. But at the same time, there is, finally, a prioritization of the singular, even if this is not to dissolve the undoubted necessity of the universal. Whether Ciaramelli would agree with such a judgment, this seems to be suggested when he says that "it is no doubt paradoxical to ground the universal signification of the ethical on this extreme particularity, that is, on the facticity of my individuation. But Levinas's whole effort is precisely to show in a philosophical Said the universal signification of such a radical preoriginary Saying."[14] The universal is grounded in the singular, the "said" bears witness to the "saying," the political is answerable to the ethical. While it would undoubtedly be a mistake to see these distinctions as manifestations of hierarchical dualisms, it is nonetheless the case that there is a certain weighting at work here, a subordination and prioritization. Indeed, we saw that in Schwarz's defense of Levinas against his political detractors, the reality of such subordination and prioritization was defended rather than denied. If this is so, then are Badiou and Žižek right to call for an unequivocal prioritizing of the political over the ethical, which is, for them, a prioritizing of the universal over the singular?

Ethics versus Politics?

Žižek accepts that, for Levinas, there can be no easy grounding of politics in the ethics of the face; on the contrary, the two are incompatible. But for Žižek, even this is too neat. He now apparently agrees with Schwarz's characterization of Levinas's position as being "postpolitical," but unlike her, he believes that this entails an exclusion of the properly political dimension: "One is tempted to say that, far from being reducible to the symmetric domain of equality and distributive justice, politics is the very 'impossible' link between this domain and that of (theological) ethics, the way ethics cuts across the symmetry of equal relations, distorting and displacing them."[15] It can be seen, therefore, that Žižek's reconceiving of the relationship between ethics and politics is not simply a case of reversing Levinas's prioritizing of ethics over politics, but also entails a reconceptualization of the domain of the political itself. For Žižek, the political is not reducible to the domain of equality and distributive justice; it is something other than and more than

14. Ibid., 100.

15. Žižek, "Neighbors and Other Monsters," 149.

this, and we find that it also involves him in a reconceptualization of Levinas's understanding of the ethical as well.

Key to Žižek's analysis here is that Levinas's ethics, grounded as it is in a phenomenology of the "face," in fact embodies a domestication or gentrification of the other. For Žižek, drawing on Judeo-Freudian traditions, the other is inhuman, a monstrous, unfathomable abyss as well as the gentrified neighbor experienced in the face-to-face encounter. Taking into account both dimensions of the other, Žižek suspects that it embodies the coincidence of opposites, the place where innocent vulnerability overlaps with pure evil. He suggests that these two dimensions are perhaps the same thing viewed from different perspectives, another manifestation of the "parallax" gap. If this is so, then Levinas's grounding of the ethical in the singularity of the face is incomplete and unsustainable. He suggests that the "lure" presented by the singular face is a temptation to be avoided. Instead, we should give priority here to the Law, understood as an external and universal intervention that intervenes and guards against the "lure" of the face. The Law, thus understood, is that which protects us from the monstrous abyss of the neighbor. All of this prepares the way for Žižek's radical overturning of the Levinasian structure:

> We should therefore assume the risk of countering Levinas's position with a more radical one: others are primordially an (ethically) indifferent multitude, and love is a violent gesture of cutting into this multitude and privileging a One as the neighbor, thus introducing a radical imbalance into the whole. In contrast to love, justice begins when I remember the faceless many left in shadow in this privileging of the One. Justice and love are thus structurally incompatible: justice, not love, must be blind; it must disregard the privileged One whom I "really understand." What this means is that the Third is not secondary: it is always-already here, and the primordial ethical obligation is toward this Third who is *not* here in the face-to-face relationship, the one in shadow, like the absent child of a love-couple.[16]

In justifying this claim, Žižek follows Lacan in making the point that love and hatred are not symmetrical phenomena, and here a further distinction is made between "universal love" and "true love." He says that universal love only acquires actual existence if there is at least one whom I hate, and it is this hatred of the exception that is the "truth" of universal love. In contrast, true love can emerge only out of a background of universal indifference. The unique individual object of love stands out of this indifferent background.

16. Ibid., 182.

Part II: Between the Ethical and the Political

The consequence of this is that true love emerges out of universal indifference, while hatred emerges out of universal love. This therefore confirms Žižek's anti-Levinasian stance. Levinas's insistence on my unconditional responsibility for "all" (universal love) actually presupposes the existence of hatred. On the other hand, Žižek's insistence on the priority of the indifferent multitude is what creates the conditions for the emergence of true love. As Žižek puts it, "the true ethical step is the one *beyond* the face of the other, the one of *suspending* the hold of the face, the one of choosing *against* the face, for the *third*. This coldness *is* justice at its most elementary."[17] So the singularity of the face in front of me is a lure that must be resisted because it is in danger of blurring the gesture of justice that would focus on the faceless Thirds. That this move embodies a critique of Levinas's prioritizing of particularity (or singularity) in favor of the universality of justice is made explicit when Žižek goes on to say, "it is only such a shift of focus onto the third that *uproots* justice, liberating it from the contingent umbilical link that renders it 'embedded' in a particular situation. In other words, it is only such a shift onto the Third that grounds justice in the dimension of *universality* proper."[18]

In explicating this criticism of Levinas, Žižek makes clear that there are two distinct lines of analysis here. Although he is clearly drawing attention to the problematic sociopolitical consequences of this Levinasian approach in terms of its weakening of genuine justice, the arena of the political, Žižek is also at pains to point out that Levinas's rendering is phenomenologically problematic in its own terms. He says that prior to encountering the face of the other, the Third is always already here. The first relationship with the other is as faceless Third, in its status as a paradoxical background-face. The Third is what Žižek calls a "formal-transcendental fact." Žižek seems to allude to some of the criticisms we developed in chapter 1 when he says that our very finitude constitutes a limit to our ethical responsibility to the other. The limit that the Third embodies is therefore not a secondary supplement but a "positive condition of ethics," that which is a prior starting point necessitated by our status as finite beings.[19] But if this is so, it is clear that, for Žižek, to make the phenomenological descriptive error he believes Levinas to have made does have detrimental sociopolitical consequences. As we have observed, the singularity of the face represents a trap or bait, which can only detract us from the full and unequivocal force of the universality that is required for justice. Žižek's goal is to restore the full force of the political

17. Ibid., 183.
18. Ibid., 184.
19. Ibid.

and rescue it from the sovereignty of the ethical. For Žižek, the ethical is not the grounding of the political, nor is it even necessarily complementary to it. The ethical, in effect, represents a distraction. It finds its place only if it recognizes the full force and priority of the political, out of which "true" love, the ethical, may emerge.

What are we to make of this encounter between Levinas and Žižek, specifically as it relates to the vexed question of the relationship between the ethical and the political? Certainly, for both, there is no easy compatibility between the ethical and political; there is certainly a sense in which the ethical and political are incommensurable. And we have seen that both in a sense and to an extent acknowledge equivocation. But notwithstanding the complexities, nuances, and caveats we have identified, the crux of the disagreement between Levinas and Žižek does seem to be reducible to a question of *priority* in relation to the ethical and political. Both identify a certain structural incompatibility between the operation of ethical and political logics, and both respond to this incompatibility by asserting the ultimate priority of one over the other. But in what follows, I shall suggest that this is to misunderstand the nature of what is at issue in the disagreement between them. I want to consider whether the dispute between Levinas and Žižek is indeed best understood as a dispute between the ethical and the political at all, or whether we are in fact being confronted by a quite different kind of structural disagreement.

Singularity versus Universalism?

In the foregoing discussion, I several times voiced the suspicion that what is fundamentally at stake in the dispute between Levinas and Žižek is the question of the preeminence of the universal over the singular or vice versa. Indeed, I want to suggest that this constitutes the very core of the disagreement, and that it is only secondarily and contingently a question of the priority of the political over the ethical or vice versa. It only becomes fundamentally an ethical-political question if the ethical as such is understood as the operation of a "singular" logic (as Levinas, ultimately, does so understand it) and if the political is understood as the operation of a "universal" logic (as Žižek does so understand it), but there is no necessity for the ethical and political to be understood in these ways. It is perfectly possible, in fact, for the ethical to be transposed into a universal key and, simultaneously, for the political to be transposed into a singular key. Indeed, it will be worth enumerating some examples of these counter-conceptions.

Part II: Between the Ethical and the Political

We have already documented a classic example of a "universalist" rendering of the ethical in the approach of Kant. As we saw in chapter 1, Kant's response to the equivocation of the ethical was to separate out its component parts, including the universal and the particular, and thus overcome the equivocation by ascribing an unequivocal priority to one side of the resulting diremption over the other. In particular, Kant valorizes the universal Law in such a manner that it relegates the particular to a position of perpetual subordination. In this sense, there is a close structural similarity here to the approach of Žižek. Indeed, for all that Žižek is perceived as standing within the tradition of Hegelian-Marxist dialectics, there is also a very strong Kantian undercurrent in his thought, deriving from his perpetuation of Kant's valorizing of the universal. It is therefore not surprising that Žižek's cautionary injunction against being seduced by the "lure" embodied in the singular face carries with it more than just a faint echo of Kant's cautionary injunction against being seduced by feelings of sympathy in our direct and particular encounters with others. For Kant, such encounters are likely to lead us astray ethically, away from the proper universal domain of the ethical and the justice of its universal Law. As he puts it, "Even the feeling of sympathy and warmhearted fellow-feeling, when preceding the consideration of what is duty and serving as a determining good, is burdensome even to right-thinking persons, confusing their considered maxims and creating the wish to be free from them and subject only to law-giving reason."[20] For both Kant and Žižek, we must cultivate an "indifference" to the concrete other precisely in order to avoid contaminating the sovereignty of the universal. If Kant is commonly regarded as representing the apotheosis of the modern Enlightenment tradition, it is also that very tradition that has been condemned, not least by Levinas, for its totalitarian and violent outcomes. Žižek's complicity with this tradition is again illustrated by the fact that he does not deny these outcomes, but accepts them and positively endorses them, thus giving rise to his "plea for ethical violence," which he believes to be a necessary precondition for a realization of justice. An unequivocal renunciation of violence as such can only lead to passivity and what we have seen to be described as the "fakeries of liberalism."

Of course, Žižek also brings his Hegelian insights to bear on this Kantian heritage by insisting that violence and love are not simple opposites, separate realities connected by nothing but their opposition. Rather, such violence is the necessary obverse of love, the two being deeply complicit and ultimately inseparable, another manifestation of the parallax gap. It is this Hegelian insight that brings Žižek close to an acknowledgment of

---

20. Kant, *Critique of Practical Reason*, 123.

the equivocation and triune character of the ethical. And yet, he resists a thoroughgoing descent into equivocation by his apparent insistence on the priority of the universal. On the one hand, he insists that we have a parallax gap between the God of love and the God of wrath, or between the Jewish Law and the Levinasian neighbor, or between love and violence; he insists that each is really the obverse side of the other, and that the choice between them is a false one.[21] But on the other hand, he appears to make an unequivocal choice in favor of the universal, the Law, and violence. For all their mutual implication, Žižek appears to want to prioritize one over the other. To draw attention to the dangers of the "lure" presented by the face and its problematic Levinasian outcomes may be a necessary aspect of recognizing the equivocation of the ethical. But rather than dwelling within this equivocation and tarrying with it, Žižek seems to undo it by his clear espousal of a universal violence. In effect, what we are seeing here, I suggest, is Žižek's penultimate oscillation between Kantian and Hegelian impulses, but, insofar as we have a prioritizing of the universal, it is the Kantian impulse, in this respect at least, that ultimately prevails. For all their differences, Kant and Žižek are here as one in their ultimate valorization of the universal, although Kant understands the proper site of the universal to be the ethical, whereas Žižek understands its proper site to be the political.

But if this is so, then it has also to be said that the prioritization of the singular is likewise capable of being rendered both ethically and politically. We have seen in previous chapters, as well as in the foregoing discussion in this chapter, that for Levinas, the bedrock foundation of the ethical is the irreducibly singular encounter with the other, however much there may be a penultimate acknowledgment of equivocation. But we also saw that this resolute prioritization of the singular was nonetheless not exclusivist, in the sense that it was by no means at the expense of the universal. We saw, particularly in Ciaramelli's discussion, that Levinas enacts his own distinctive oscillation between the singular and the universal, and we may view this as Levinas's own way of hovering close to an acknowledgment of the equivocation of the ethical of the kind that we have similarly observed in Žižek.

It may be said that Levinas's valorization of the singular over the universal is bound up with what might be described as the immanentist and perhaps nihilistic aspects of Levinas's work. At first sight, this may appear to be a counterintuitive observation, for is Levinas not the thinker who, above so many others, emphasizes otherness and transcendence, particularly in his insistence on the heteronomy of the other and the transcendence to which the face gestures? While these elements are undoubtedly there,

---

21. See Žižek, "Neighbors and Other Monsters," 185–90.

Part II: Between the Ethical and the Political

they do flow within an undeniably immanentist stream. This aspect of Levinas's work is well brought out by John D. Caputo when he observes that, for Levinas, "'Being' means the brutal order of reality, the way things are done in the world (paganism), what he and Nietzsche following Spinoza called the *conatus essendi*. But what is 'otherwise than being' is the Good, *epekeinas tes ousias*, although definitely not in the strictly Platonic sense of an eternal transcendent metaphysical structure, in a world beyond this world, about which Levinas was as atheistic as Nietzsche."[22] The implication here is that Levinas's indebtedness to Spinoza and Nietzsche is more than one of mere terminology. Indeed, Caputo suggests that Levinas's thought comes very close to being a "death of God theology." He says that, for Levinas, "our being turned to God (*à-Dieu*) is our being returned to the neighbor, and that is all the God there is. God commands but God does not exist. About the separate and supreme being of classical theology, Levinas (the most theological resource of postmodern thinkers) is no less than Nietzsche (their most antitheological resource) an atheist."[23] This oscillation between transcendence and immanence, between the theological and the atheistic, again bears witness, perhaps, to Levinas's simultaneous acknowledgment and refusal of equivocation. But if Caputo is right, the refusal is instantiated by the fact that Levinas ultimately stills the oscillation, mends the equivocation, by his ultimate prioritizing of immanence and nihilism.

It is perhaps considerations such as these that have prompted some, more hostile, commentators to characterize Levinas's project as an "ethic for nihilists."[24] If there is an element of truth in such a characterization, then in looking for a political rendering of Levinas's valorization of the singular, we should perhaps expect to find it in a corresponding "politics for nihilists," and it may be suggested that this is what we find in the influential contemporary political writings of Michael Hardt and Antonio Negri. Indeed, in their espousal of a political anarchy, we find an unequivocal assertion of the priority of the singular over the universal, as well as an affirmation of a Spinozist-Nietzschean ontology of absolute immanence. As one might expect, their disposition toward the whole postmodern trajectory is ambivalent. Like Badiou and Žižek, they are philosophically and politically frustrated with the postmodern emphasis on the tropes of the fragmentary, the hybrid, the transitional, the flexible and so forth. For Hardt and Negri, as we shall explore in more detail in the following chapters, these features coincide with the very thing that is to be resisted, namely, the "Empire" of global

---

22. Caputo, "Atheism, A/Theology and the Postmodern Condition," 273.
23. Ibid., 273–74.
24. Pickstock, "Theology and Post-modernity," 75.

capitalism. The theory and rhetoric of postmodernism will therefore be of little use in the project of "overcoming" Empire, since it will do little more than reflect and reinforce the logic of Empire itself. In such an attitude, they are as one with Badiou and Žižek. But whereas Badiou and Žižek's response to this is to call for the unequivocal return and imposition of a "universal," Hardt and Negri have no such recourse. This is where their ambivalence towards postmodernism is made most explicit, for, as Negri has observed, they are seeking to develop an "ontology of the political subject outside of all teleology and within the postmodern conditions of absolute immanence."[25]

This means that, for them, political redemption comes not by means of a violent, external, universal intervention, but, rather, by means of a spontaneous, internally generated wellspring of power from below, from the unequivocal "singularities" that constitute the multitude. In his clarification of the use of the term "multitude" in Hardt and Negri's most well-known book, *Empire* (2000), Negri subsequently observed that it referred to "a set of *singularities* bearing inalienable rights" and in this sense is to be contrasted with notions of the "people" or "class" and the "masses." The quality of the multitude "consists in its expressing living labor" and the "valorization of production derives from the capacity of *singularities* to produce value."[26] Negri is well aware that such a conception has been found most vulnerable by critics at the point at which the multitude as a set of singularities expresses itself as subject, as force, as capacity for decision. Negri sets out to address this weakness more explicitly in subsequent work. But for our purposes at this juncture, the important point to note is that, for Hardt and Negri, political liberation comes not through the intervention of a "universal" but through unleashing the potentialities of "singularities."

In light of this, we begin to see that, for all the differences in their respective conceptions of the political, Levinas on the one hand, and Hardt and Negri on the other, are in fact deeply complicit. If it is fair to say of Levinas that he develops an "ethic for nihilists," then it is certainly fair to say of Hardt and Negri that they develop a "politics for nihilists." In both cases, they are working within conditions of immanence in the wake of the death of God. In both cases, they are suspicious of universal metanarratives. And we may see such characteristics either as a manifestation of or as the basis for their ultimate commitment to singularity. We have seen that for all of Levinas's equivocation, he ultimately "mends" the brokenness of the ethical by his insistence that the bedrock foundation of the ethical lies in my singular encounter with the face of the other. So too, for Hardt and Negri,

---

25. Negri, "Political Subject," 231.
26. Ibid. My emphasis.

teleological universals and collective conceptions of "class" or the "masses" are repudiated in favor of a conception of the multitude as a collective of irreducible singularities. It is only from these singularities that the power of emancipation can emerge. Thus, in a manner reminiscent of the relationship of complicity we exposed between Kant and Žižek, we see that for all their differences, Levinas and Hardt and Negri are here as one in their ultimate valorization of the singular, although Levinas understands the proper site of the singular to be the ethical, whereas Hardt and Negri understand its proper site to be the political.

From the foregoing juxtaposition of Kant with Žižek and of Levinas with Hardt and Negri, I want to suggest that two conclusions in particular may be drawn. First, it should be clear that the ethical is not, by definition, constituted by the domain of the singular; neither is the political, by definition, constituted by the domain of the universal. We have seen that the sphere of the ethical may be rendered in either a universal (Kant) or a singular (Levinas) key, just as the sphere of the political may be rendered in either a universal (Žižek) or a singular (Hardt and Negri) key. It is undoubtedly the case, of course, that some of these thinkers argue that the ethical *should* fundamentally operate according to a singular logic, just as others argue that the political *should* fundamentally operate according to a universal logic, and, indeed, vice versa on both counts. But nonetheless, as the very existence of the debate shows, these are matters of contention rather than of definition. Once this is accepted, then this leads us to see that the debate between Levinas and Žižek should not be seen, fundamentally, as a question of whether ultimate priority and valorization is to be accorded to the ethical or to the political. The debate between them becomes a matter of the ethical *versus* the political only because of the ways in which they each define the ethical and political (and on these definitions they broadly agree). But these definitions can be contested, as indeed I have contested them in the foregoing chapters, where I argued that the ethical is constituted by a tension between the universal, the particular, and the singular. I shall argue similarly with respect to the political in the chapters that follow.

In light of this, my suggestion is that there is no necessary *opposition* between the ethical and the political. Indeed, insofar as they are both constituted by the same equivocation between the universal, the particular, and the singular, we may say that there is a continuous rather than an incommensurable relationship between them. Nonetheless, the debate between Levinas and Žižek cannot be so easily dismissed. For even if we recast their disagreement as being one between whether singularity should be elevated over universalism or vice versa, their respective definitions and resulting prioritizations of the ethical and political are each grounded in contrasting accounts of the primordial origin of the ethical-political. If these definitions are to be contested, therefore, then so too must their accounts of the ethical-political origin.

We have already given some consideration to their respective phenomenological accounts of the ethical-political origin. We have seen that for Levinas, the primordial origin of subjectivity is the call that issues from the singular Face. The Third, the multitude, is secondary, supplementary, and appears to view only after the constitution of subjectivity, interrupting and disturbing the founding relationship between the singular Face and the thereby constituted subject. In contrast, for Žižek, the primordial origin of obligation derives from the indifferent multitude which is "always-already" here. The primary obligation is toward this Third, and it is the Face of the neighbor that secondarily and violently cuts into this primordial obligation, arbitrarily privileging the One and thereby introducing a radical imbalance into the whole.

But what if both of these accounts are inadequate and perhaps even unintelligible? To what extent is it coherent to see either the universal multitude or the singular Face as issuing a quite contextless call? To what extent would the call of either be intelligible, recognizable, and compelling if emerging out of an empty abyss? Would it not be more intelligible to see each appearing to us through its contrast with the other? What if the face of the Other approaches and calls us out of the "already there" abyss of the multitude? The face of the Other makes its call upon us precisely because it confronts us with its irreducible singularity in contrast with the universal background *out of which* it emerges; that universal background would be needed in order for the singular face to be brought into focus before us. The singular responsibility of love only becomes intelligible in contrast to the "cool indifference" of justice. Furthermore, what if, equally and simultaneously, the abyss of the multitude calls us to instantiate justice for it precisely because of the singular claim that the face *already makes* upon us? In other words, the abyss of the multitude only appears to us as such because of its character as a series of singularities of the kind that has already called us in the form of the singular face. The call to justice only manifests itself because of the call of responsibility to the singular face to which we are already subjected. Without the face, the third might only elicit a response to indifference rather than a call to justice.

So on this reading, the call to responsibility issued by the face and the call to justice issued by the third each constitutes and manifests itself in and through the other. There is an enigmatic interplay, an equivocation, between the call of the Face and the demand made by the faceless multitude. Each is intelligible to us, is manifested to us, through its contrast with the other.

Part II: Between the Ethical and the Political

The attempt to isolate either one as primordial and foundational appears doomed to fail and bears witness to a certain impossibility. The face and the third, it seems, come to us and exercise their hold upon us in a relationship of dependent co-origination. The notion of dependent co-origination, of course, derives from Buddhism, for which it is a central teaching. The second-century Buddhist philosopher Nagarjuna demonstrated that all things depend on other things for their existence. In the *Mūlamadhyamakakārikās*, he says, "A thing is different insofar as it presupposes a second different thing. One thing is not different from the other thing without the other thing." This dependence empties everything of inherent existence, and this is why dependent co-origination is equated with emptiness: "The 'originating dependently' we call 'emptiness'; this apprehension, i.e. taking into account [all other things], is the understanding of the middle way."[27] The fatal error, on this reading, is to isolate any one element as being primordial or foundational; each "thing" is manifested through its distinction from other "things." I am suggesting that the calls that issue from the singular Face and the universal multitude should be similarly understood in terms of this kind of dependent co-origination.

But in that case, we should expect the same phenomenological structure to apply also to the constitution of subjectivity itself. In this sense, I suggest that Levinas and Žižek are both right to say that the call to responsibility or to justice is not something that "happens" to a subject that is already formed. Rather, it is the fact of that being called that is actually constitutive of subjectivity itself. But what if we are constituted as subjects not only by a "persecution" that derives from the call of responsibility to the face but by a "persecution" that consists precisely in the contrary and simultaneous calls of responsibility from the other *and* the third? Contrary though they are, each issues its call in and through the other in the manner of the "dependent co-origination" just described. Understood thus, the particularity of the subject would be constituted by the singular call of the Other *and* the universal call of the Third. This is not to suggest that the subject is constituted by or represents an easy synthesis between the singular and the universal. On the contrary, the subject is constituted by and brought into being precisely as a site of tension between the demands of the singular and the demands of the universal in a way that is irreducible. The work of responding to the call of *both* the singular *and* the universal, which is itself constitutive of subjectivity, is a work of endless negotiation that is never finally "resolved." Indeed, any such "resolutions" will always be false and

---

27. Nagarjuna, *Mūlamadhyamakakārikās* 14:5, 24:18. Translated in Streng, *Emptiness*, 199, 213.

damaging because they will entail the inevitable negation or repression of an inescapable aspect of our subjectivity.

In this phenomenology, what we see being repeatedly performed are acts of negotiation between the universal, the particular, and the singular. We have seen that the potentially destructive opposition between the call of the face (the singular) and the call of the multitude (the universal) finds an "outlet" in the subject (the particular) in whom the tension is negotiated, not by means of an easy mediation, but by serving as the site on which the labor of the negotiation is fruitfully put into effect. Secondly, when confronted with the potentially destructive opposition between the call of the face (the singular) and subjectivity (the particular)—the destructive character of which we saw displayed in chapter 1—this tension is "relieved" by the appearance of the multitude (the universal) in the manner suggested by Žižek. When the Levinasian call threatens to become suicidally self-negating, it is the emergence of the third—the multitude—that affirms the finitude of the subject, that bears witness to the legitimate limits of the subject's self-sacrifice, thereby negotiating between love of self and love of neighbor, thus averting mutual destruction. Thirdly, when the call to justice (the universal) and the "cool indifference" it cultivates in the subject (the particular) threatens to turn into a totalitarian violence and an indifference to neighbors, it is the call of the face (the singular) that again averts mutual destruction; it is the singular face that qualifies and limits the unequivocal call to universal justice; the face is not so much a lure to be resisted, but is, on the contrary, a necessary corrective.

It should be noted that all three operations necessarily occur simultaneously and that, in each case, no one domain—universal, singular, or particular—is ontologically or phenomenologically prioritized over the other two. So there are no privileged ontological "mediating thirds" of the kind we observed in chapter 2, the result being that a complacent "resolution" of the tension is avoided. But if a complacent resolution is avoided, so too is a tension that is paralyzing or self-destructive, as it would be without the intervention of the "third" of the triad in each case. The third provides a "release" so as to avoid the other two domains becoming locked into a relationship of mutual destruction, but without that third being prioritized over the other two in such a manner as would induce complacency. In light of this, we begin to see the necessary and delicate balance (which is nonetheless always in tension) that must be maintained between the universal, the particular, and the singular, which, in this instance, we have here been characterizing as the call to justice, subjectivity, and the call of the face, respectively.

But let us end by returning to the question with which we began, namely, the question of the relationship between the ethical and political.

Part II: Between the Ethical and the Political

We have seen that both Levinas and Žižek posit a logical incommensurability between the ethical and political, even if their respective solutions are markedly different. But I have argued that this incommensurability only arises because of the way in which they define the ethical and political, whereby the former embodies a logic of singularity and the latter a logic of universality. Against both, however, I have been advocating a quite different conception of the ethical and political. As I have been arguing in the foregoing chapters, the ethical should be conceived as being constituted by a perpetual tension between the universal, the particular, and the singular. In the following chapters, I shall argue that this is also true of the political. There is therefore tension *within* the ethical and *within* the political, but there is no real tension *between* them. On the contrary, there is continuity between them deriving from the fact that they are both constituted by the same equivocation. As Terry Eagleton has said, "Ethics and politics are distinct modes of investigation in the sense that each scrutinises social existence from a different angle—in the case of ethics, the values and qualities of human conduct and relationships; and in the case of politics, public institutions and processes of power. Yet there is no clear ontological distinction at stake here. The difference is more methodological than real."[28] The call to justice and the call of the Face are alike at the heart of the ethical, just as they are both at the heart of the political. It is necessary now, therefore, to give some detailed attention to the nature of the political.

---

28. Eagleton, *Trouble with Strangers*, 306.

Part III
THE POLITICAL

4

PASSIVITY

The Tensions of the Political

As we make the transition to the more explicitly political part of our study, it will be necessary for us to give some attention to our definition of the political, especially in light of the arguments put forward in the last intermediate chapter. There I concluded that there is no inherent structural conflict between the ethical and the political. On the contrary, there is a relationship of direct continuity between them. In what, then, does the difference between the domains of the ethical and the political consist? This can be stated relatively simply. The ethical articulates and reflects upon the nature of my encounter with the other: the enigmatic encounter that we have seen to be articulated in the commandment to love my neighbor as myself, and that is enacted through an interplay between the universal, the particular, and the singular. The political extends this encounter in such a way that it articulates and reflects upon the way in which a common life is or should be structured in communion with others—in Levinas's terms, the third (the many thirds) "beyond" myself and the other. The question at the heart of the political is thus the question of how a common life may be structured in such a way that is consistent with and which extends the ethical injunction to love my neighbor as myself.

The understanding of the political I am advocating is deliberately broadly conceived. It is taken to encompass a community's norms, procedures, and customs (in a nation-state system, this would comprise a state's sovereign power, constitution, laws, and conventions) and all the activity pertaining to public life taking place within the legitimate parameters of these norms, as well as any thought and action that may serve to question or overturn these parameters. I am not therefore restricting the domain of the political in advance, as does Alain Badiou, for instance, when he insists that the political is the site of a Truth-Event, and therefore can only be that which disorientates a given situation of being. The reasons for this broad understanding of the domain of the political will hopefully become clear as these chapters proceed.

But in specifying further what I understand the political to be, it will be helpful to draw a structural parallel (rather than a structural contrast) with my understanding of the ethical, as was elaborated in the first part of this book. We saw that the ethical is constituted by an enigmatic tension that is expressed in the command to love my neighbor as myself. We saw that this expressed a tension in a very specific sense. It was not that a discrete preexisting subject found itself subject to this external command to do something that conflicts with that subject's "natural" tendency. Rather, it is the case that a subject finds itself internally "torn" between a love of self and love of neighbor in a way that is constitutive of subjectivity as such. There is thus a sense in which love of self and love of neighbor are in tension, but that subjectivity requires the perpetuation of this tension; it is the site on which this tension plays itself out. The subject must fully love itself *and* fully love its neighbor if it is fully to *be* as a subject. The necessary tension comes from the impossibility of doing both to the utmost simultaneously. As such, the ethical is the site of this necessary tension.

Likewise, I want to suggest that the political also emerges and is constituted by a site of tension. On the one hand, in envisaging a common life and the manner of a communal mode of being, the political generates customs, norms, and conventions that serve to regulate the conduct and practice of common life that takes place within it. In speaking of "regulation" here, it is important to emphasize that this does not at all entail a Hobbesian view of politics as the regulation of what would otherwise be a destructive war of all against all. Rather, we should understand "regulation" here as the observance of a "rule," that is, the operation of principles or precepts around which there is public consensus. But what is important here is that a distinction is to be made between "norms" and that over which the "norms" are thought to "rule" or "preside." Indeed, Vincent Lloyd has spoken of a necessary tension between "norms" and "practices," a tension that is irreducible and that must be preserved.[1] There is always a temptation to "mend" this tension, to imagine that "norms" can regulate and program "practices" without reserve, or, alternatively, to imagine that "practices" can proceed without the regulation of "norms." But either way, such temptations are false idealizations that are untrue to life. Not only are they false idealizations but

---

1. Lloyd, *Problem with Grace*.

they would also entail the death of the political. For the political actually depends upon—indeed is constituted by—this tension between "norms" and "practices."

Indeed, it is instructive here to note the specific way in which Marxism envisages the "end of politics" in precisely these terms. Alain Badiou has discussed this in terms of what he calls the "vulgar Marxist idea" that "the State is always the State of the ruling class." Badiou interprets this as meaning that "the State solely exercises its domination according to a law destined to form-one out of the *parts* of a situation; moreover, the role of the State is to qualify, one by one, each of the compositions of compositions of multiples whose general consistency, in respect of *terms*, is secured by the situation, that is, by a historical presentation which is 'already' structured."[2] In other words, the State does not *impose* its "norms" upon "practices"; it is not that the ruling class uses that State as an instrument of control. Rather, the State *reflects* an already established situation (this, we might say, is its *passive* function), while at the same time it forms a unified and coherent whole out of this situation (which we might say is its *active* function). In this sense, it is evident that "the State is both absolutely tied to historico-social presentation and yet also separated from it."[3] For Badiou, it is because the State re-presents the historico-social presentation of a situation that its administrative and management function is more "structural and permanent" than the coercive function. It is because of the structural continuity between the presentation of a situation and its re-presentation in the State that the latter (the "norms") is not primarily coercive in relation to that which it regulates (the "practices"). But if not primarily coercive, there is nonetheless a separation and, we might wish to say, a tension between them. Badiou goes on to articulate this separation as follows:

> because the parts of society exceed its terms on every side, because what is included in a historical situation cannot be reduced to what belongs to it, the State—conceived as operator of the count and guarantee of the universal reinforcement of the one—is necessarily a separate apparatus. Like the state of any situation whatsoever, the State of a historico-social situation is subject to the theorem of the point of excess.... What it deals with—the gigantic, infinite network of the situation's subsets—forces the State to not identify itself with the original structure which lays out the consistency of presentation, which is to say the immediate social bond.[4]

2. Badiou, *Being and Event*, 105.
3. Ibid., 106.
4. Ibid., 106–7.

Part III: The Political

But in what precisely does this separation consist? In the sense that the State produces a unified and coherent whole out of a situation, it does so according to a law that, as Badiou says, "comes from elsewhere," that is, from somewhere other than the situation that is itself being structured or re-presented. But this means that there is a sense in which this operation is alien to or in tension with the situation that is being structured. So an individual or a "voter" is not considered in his or herself, as would be the case in the situation, but rather as an abstraction, as a member of the class of "voters." This separation—of the State from the situation or of norms from practices—is what gives rise to the coercion that is necessary to this operation: "This coercion consists in not being held to be someone who belongs to society, but as someone who is *included* within society. The State is fundamentally indifferent to belonging yet it is constantly concerned with inclusion." The State must count and include everything, but it does so by erasing the significance of concrete individual lives. This is why, "despite the protestations and declarations to the contrary, it is always evident that in the end, when it is a matter of people's *lives*—which is to say, of the multiple whose one they have received—the State is not concerned. Such is the ultimate and ineluctable depth of its separation."[5]

Now, in speaking of that which "comes from elsewhere," that part of the State that does not *reflect* the situation over which it presides, but rather, that part which is *imposed* upon it, Badiou terms this an "excrescence." He defines this term as referring to that which is represented at the level of the State , but which is not presented at the level of the situation. In other words, it is that part of the State that is excessive to the situation. Badiou says that while this is obvious with respect to the State's bureaucratic and military machinery, the classic Marxist analysis goes further in regarding "the State *itself* [as] an excrescence. By consequence, as political programme, the Marxist proposes the revolutionary suppression of the State; thus the end of representation and the universality of simple presentation."[6] This derives from the Marxist understanding of the persistent antagonism between classes in all pre-communist societies. This antagonism is irreconcilable and the State emerges as a way of "dealing with" or "controlling" this. This means that once the antagonism between classes has been overcome, the rationale for the existence of the State disappears: "on the basis of a modification of these differences, it is possible to hope for the disappearance of the State. It would suffice for the singular to become universal; this is also called the

5. Ibid., 107–8.
6. Ibid., 108.

end of classes, which is to say the end of parts, and thus of any necessity to control their excess."[7]

On this classic Marxist reading, therefore, it would seem that the existence of "norms" and "practices" is itself an effect of antagonism and conflict between classes within the realm of practices. When this antagonism and conflict is overcome, then "norms" disappear and one is left with the singular domain of "practices." If, as I am suggesting, politics is located precisely in the tension between "norms" and "practices," then we may say that what the classic Marxist analysis envisages is precisely the *end of politics*. On the Marxist analysis, of course, this would not be a cause of regret precisely because with the end of class conflict, there is no longer any role for politics to serve. In historical terms, of course, in the so-called communist countries, the situation was markedly different. Far from dissolving or being abolished, the State in the Marxist regimes reached its apotheosis. As Badiou again has commented,

> if the government and even the material substance of the State can be overturned and destroyed; even if, in certain circumstances, it is politically useful to do so, one must not lose sight of the fact that the State as such—which is to say the re-securing of the one over the multiple of parts (or parties)—cannot be so easily attacked or destroyed. Scarcely five years after the October Revolution, Lenin, ready to die, despaired over the obscene permanence of the State. Mao himself, more phlegmatic and more adventurous, declared—after twenty-five years in power and ten years of the Cultural Revolution's ferocious tumult—that not much had changed after all.[8]

Indeed, and going beyond Badiou here, one might be tempted to say that the Russian and Chinese revolutionaries did indeed effect the end of politics but in precisely the opposite way to the classic Marxist analysis we have been considering. In other words, faced with the "obscene permanence of the State" and the stubborn persistence of "norms," the end of politics could only be effected by the complete subordination of the situation to the State, the total devouring of "practices" by imposed "norms." Consequently, what we see in the juxtaposition between classic Marxist predictions and the actual Marxist experience are two symmetrical experiences of the "end of politics." The first sees "norms," or in this case the State, dissolve into perfectly egalitarian, communal, and antagonism-free "practices." The second sees a forced attempt to realize the same end by the complete or

7. Ibid., 109.
8. Ibid., 110.

near-complete subordination of "practices" to "norms." It might be said that both approaches were doomed to fail because they were both idealized abstractions, the successful realization of which depended upon a utopian state of affairs that was something other than the finite, broken world we inhabit. It might be said that while the impossibility of the first strategy was quickly realized, the resort to the second soon resulted in totalitarian nightmares. The salutary lesson of these experiences is the necessity of living in the tension between "norms" and "practices" in such a way that there is never any a priori resolution of the conflict between them. Indeed, it is precisely in the midst of this tension that I am locating the political itself. As I have suggested, it is when attempts are made to reduce "norms" to "practices" or to subordinate "practices" to "norms" that we see the end of politics *per se*.

I perceive Rowan Williams to be saying something close to this when he says that

> a politics entirely based on "charity" in the sense of egalitarian transcendence, non-competitive communion, and so on, fails to be a politics at all, because it depends on not recognising the truth that the non-charitable world habitually deals with—conflicts of interest and desire, the unavoidability of loss, the obstinacy of others. It is simply not the case that we are able instantly to recognise and welcome an identity of interest in every other we come across. We are not transparent to each other in that way. We "learn" each other, we cope with each other, in the trials and errors, the contests and treaties of speech: which takes time and doesn't quickly or necessarily yield communion.[9]

Thus, any attempt to "impose" norms unequivocally on cultural practices that will always be in some measure resistant to such imposition will always lead to tragic outcomes. Politics, if it is genuinely to be politics, will always realize the futility of such idealized abstractions. Politics is thus located in—and acknowledges rather than erases—the broken, imperfect, and ultimately unyielding world that constitutes our reality.

In making these claims, however, it is important also to make some clarifications. For one thing, to say that politics is framed by an acknowledgment of the necessary tension between norms and practices does not mean that politics must reconcile itself to the necessity of the currently prevailing norms and practices, in our case the system of nation-states that we have inherited in the post-Enlightenment world. The analysis of Badiou that we were earlier invoking utilized the concept of the State as the re-presentation

---

9. Williams, *Lost Icons*, 70.

of a situation where the latter is itself of the order of presentation. Badiou's invocation of the terms "State" and "situation" I have been interpreting as analogous to the terms "norms" and "practices" respectively, terms derived from Vincent Lloyd and Gillian Rose. But it is important to remember that for Badiou, the "State" is only a contingent instantiation of what he calls the "state of the situation." For Badiou, the "state of the situation" is a metastructure or redoubling that is always entailed by and which necessarily supplements a "situation." But the "state of the situation" may take many forms; the nation "State" is in fact only one contingent manifestation of it. Indeed, the national "State" system might be seen as the *state* of the historico-social *situation* of modern capitalism. And of course, it is well known that commentators such as Michael Hardt and Antonio Negri would argue that we are mutating or have mutated into a new historico-social *situation* of global or advanced capitalism in which the *state of the situation* is a new regime of "Empire" in which nation-states have been superseded even if they have not entirely disappeared. Thus, in arguing that politics takes place in the space between "norms" and "practices," this is by no means to restrict the political to a sphere of action between the "norms" and "practices" that currently happen to prevail, as it might be argued that liberal democracy does. On the contrary, any form of radical politics, however much it may recognize the necessity of initiating action within the arenas of current norms and practices, will have as its long-term goal the displacement of these by quite other norms and practices, even if this displacement can never be guaranteed by the action or thought of political subjects.

While the displacement of one situation and its state by another is consistent with Badiou's conception of the political, it must, of course, be observed that my conception of the political as a practice that occurs within *current* norms and practices is certainly not. Indeed, this observation marks a major site of disagreement between Badiou's account of the political and the account that I am attempting to develop here. For Badiou, politics is to be found only in the irruption of the infinite into the finite, thus disorientating the field. In other words, politics is constituted by the subversion of current norms and practices in accordance with the operation of an infinite truth procedure. It follows from this that what might conventionally be called politics (operating within the currently prevailing norms and practices) is not in fact politics at all. This is made clear and amplified when Badiou says,

> In collective situations—in which the collective becomes interested in itself—politics (if it exists as *generic politics*: what was called, for a long time, revolutionary politics, and for which another word must be found today) is also a procedure of fidelity.

Part III: The Political

> Its events are the historical caesura in which the void of the social is summoned in default of the State; its operators are variable; its infinite productions are indiscernible (in particular, they do not coincide with *any part nameable according to the State*), being nothing more than "changes" of political subjectivity within the situation; and finally its enquiries consist of militant organized activity.[10]

But it is precisely this constriction of politics to "revolutionary politics" that I here want to contest. Politics equally, perhaps primarily, takes place in the here and now, in the norms and practices that we currently happen to inhabit, while being open to the possibility that—and indeed *hoping* that—these will themselves be subverted or overthrown.

There is a path of negotiation to be undertaken here, I want to suggest, the aim of which is to avoid two undue circumscriptions of what actually constitutes politics as such. On the one hand, there are those who accept with passive resignation the sway of current norms and practices and restrict political activity to the enactment of changes and modifications within them; those who seek to challenge or think beyond those norms and practices are dismissed as dreamers, poets, and philosophers, and thus as being not genuinely engaged in politics at all. On the other hand, there are those for whom politics is constituted solely by the overthrow of current norms and practices. In the revolutionary and total realignment of a situation, we see the enactment of politics; those who seek merely to work within current parameters are dismissed as mere tinkerers and rearrangers who are happy to modify without fundamentally rearranging current norms and practices.

In what follows, I shall argue that this is a false choice that must be refused, and that the true political challenge is to pursue both simultaneously. In this specific respect, one can agree with Hardt and Negri when they say that "there is no conflict here between reform and revolution. We say this not because we think that reform and revolution are the same thing, but that in today's conditions they cannot be separated. Today the historical processes of transformation are so radical that even reformist proposals can lead to revolutionary change. . . . It is useless to rack our brains over whether a proposal is reformist or revolutionary; what matters is that it enters into the constituent process."[11] While endorsing Hardt and Negri's refusal of a false choice between reformism and revolution, I do not assume that there is any easy continuity or any possibility of synthesis between them. Rather, I shall argue that the two are constantly in tension and that this is a ten-

10. Badiou, *Being and Event*, 340.
11. Hardt and Negri, *Multitude*, 289.

sion that must be preserved and within which we must labor. The pursuit of political goals within current norms and practices always risks falling into passivity and tragic resignation to injustice. The restriction of politics to revolutionary change always risks becoming blind to increasing injustice and the necessity of political acts of mercy *within* currently prevailing sociohistorical conditions. The path of negotiation I am advocating here is not one that eliminates these risks and mediates between these extremes. There can be no question of this tension being mended. On the contrary, these risks are perpetual and mediation is forever deferred. Rather, one must negotiate a path along which one acts on decisions aware of the risks that these decisions and those actions necessarily entail.

Such an approach is consistent with the one we have already outlined in our consideration of the relationship between norms and practices. We saw that there is a necessary tension between norms and practices, but that this tension is constitutive of the political as such. We must resist the temptation to reduce norms to practices (as that state of affairs which classical Marxism anticipated), as we must also resist the temptation to subordinate practices to norms (as actually happened within the twentieth-century Soviet states). To succumb to either of these temptations is, in effect, to inaugurate the end of politics. I am now suggesting that such a tension must similarly be perpetuated between *current* norms and practices on the one hand and *future* heterogeneous norms and practices on the other. Again, we must resist the temptation to reduce the future to the present (which is what our current regime of global capitalism evidently seems to do; in this specific respect, Francis Fukuyama would seem to have been correct), and we must also resist the temptation to reduce the present to the future (which is what Badiou and a number of other contemporary thinkers propose even if not quite in these terms). We would thus have the perpetuation of a tension both vertically (between current norms and current practices) and horizontally (between *current* norms and practices and *future* norms and practices). Furthermore, what the perpetuation of both these vertical and horizontal forms of tension means in practice is the keeping in play of the interaction in both spheres between the universal, the particular, and the singular, the importance of which we repeatedly emphasized in the first half of this book in our consideration of the ethical.

Indeed, we might understand all of these four political temptations as being constituted by an undue prioritizing of one of the three domains of the universal, the particular, or the singular. For instance, the classical Marxist anticipation of the end of the State might be viewed as the elevation of singularity, or, as Badiou puts it, "It would suffice for the singular to become universal."¹² Meanwhile, the communist state's subordination of practices to norms might be viewed as the elevation of universality over both the particular and the singular. Universal norms position, direct, and control particular and singular practices without reserve, or at least attempt to do so. Likewise, the subordination of the future to the present in which there is resignation to the sway of current norms and practices would seem to enact the elevation of particularity. That this is so is perhaps not immediately quite so evident. But a resignation to the prevailing is actually sustained by a casting of doubt on the possibility and efficacy of all universality as such. It is an exhortation to rest content with, and indeed to embrace stubborn particularity. As Badiou has pointed out, "It is commonly claimed nowadays that the only genuinely universal prescription consists in respecting particularity."¹³ (Although he goes on to note that he finds this thesis inconsistent in that it ends up doing no more than proclaiming the universality of universality, which is, he says, "fatally tautological."¹⁴) On the other hand, Badiou explicitly elevates the universal as the only site of politics proper. He insists that every universal is singular or a singularity, and that the "event," from which every universal originates, "is intransitive to the particularity of the situation."¹⁵ In this sense, therefore, the universal sets itself *against* the particular. The latter belongs to the order of being, while the former is infinite and, as such, disrupts the order of being. The universal, through its irruption in the form of the "event," overcomes the stubborn particularity of the order of being. In all four instances, therefore, we see an a priori decision being made for the elevation of one of the domains of the universal, the particular, and the singular over the other two. It is precisely this, I am suggesting, that is ultimately politically destructive. The perpetuation of the political actually depends upon the perpetuation of the necessary tension between the universal, the particular, and the singular, without this tension being prematurely resolved or mended by the a priori elevation of one over the others.

But much more needs to be said. It is one thing to propose an understanding of the political wherein it is defined by this ongoing tension between the universal, the particular, and the singular. If one rejects other configurations of the political simply because they do not meet this definition, one will fall into a vacuous circularity. What is necessary, of course, is to show why it is *desirable* to understand the political in this way, and

12. Badiou, *Being and Event*, 109.
13. Badiou in Badiou and Žižek, *Philosophy in the Present*, 29.
14. Ibid., 30.
15. Ibid., 29, 31.

concomitantly, to show why alternative configurations give rise to *undesirable* and perhaps even self-destructive political effects. This is, indeed, what I endeavored to do with respect to the ethical in the first part of this book. It is this task, with respect to the political, to which I now wish to address myself.

In proposing an understanding of the political that locates it precisely in the *tension* between the universal, the particular, and the singular, one is setting oneself against a certain tendency in recent philosophy, theology, and political theory, which has been to *subordinate* the domain of the universal to that of the particular or the singular. These voices have been concerned to repudiate what they perceive to be the debilitating effects of sovereignty, tyranny, and hierarchy that they believe to have disfigured all previous political configurations. For them, the main enemies of political transformation are not so much stasis and impotence as oppression and totalitarianism. Such things are inevitably brought about, it is believed, by an undue elevation of the domain of the universal. For these thinkers, this fate is to be avoided only by a proper emphasis on the particular and/or the singular.

In this chapter, I want to question the dissolution or at least subordination of the domain of the universal in political thought, and I shall do so by examining the thought of Simon Critchley (who subordinates the universal to a politics of particularity) and Michael Hardt and Antonio Negeri (who subordinate the universal to a politics of singularity). I shall argue that a neglect of the universal effectively gives rise, yet again, to the end of politics. When stubborn particularity is valorized above universal imperatives, the neutral contingencies of life themselves become a moral good. As Alain Badiou has provocatively put it, "multiculturalism" is not an ideology or an ethical principle but empirical description.[16] But in the absence of genuinely universal political imperatives, empirical description *becomes* morally weighted. What is comes to be reconceived as what ought to be. This is, in effect, the condition of liberal pluralism, which is, as Badiou again points out, such a perfect accomplice of global capitalism. Critchley, of course, is by no means a purveyor of the latter, but I shall suggest that his thought lacks adequate resources for genuine change, with the result that his prescriptions look all too much like a version of the liberal plural world we currently inhabit, a less blighted version of the status quo. Hardt and Negri are certainly more radical in their ambitions, and their passion for revolutionary change is all too evident. But their passion looks destined to remain an unfulfilled desire, as once again, they appear to lack the theo-

---

16. See Badiou, *Ethics*, 26–27.

retical resources that would give that desire any hope of consummation. In what follows, I want to suggest that these deficiencies arise through a neglect of the domain of the universal. To this end, let us turn first to the work of Simon Critchley.

Politics of the Particular: Simon Critchley

In *The Ethics of Deconstruction: Derrida and Levinas* (1992), Critchley argued that attempts to develop an ethics and politics on the basis of Derridean deconstruction had reached something of an impasse. While arguing that deconstruction was not ethically neutral, and that there was a positive ethical promise or dimension at the heart of the deconstructive operation, he nonetheless perceived that Derridean deconstruction alone was inadequate as a resource for the development of a substantive and effective ethics and politics in the contemporary world. He accepts that "deconstruction can certainly be employed as a powerful means of political analysis." By showing, for instance, how an oppressive regime "is based on a set of undecidable propositions," deconstruction can play an important role in the act of subversion.[17] But, he goes on to ask,

> how is one to account for the move from undecidability to the political *decision* to combat that domination? If deconstruction is the strictest possible determination of undecidability in the limitless context of, for want of a better word, experience, then this entails a suspension of the moment of decision. Yet, decisions have to be taken. But how? And in virtue of what? How does one make a decision in an undecidable terrain? I would claim, with Laclau, that an adequate account of the decision is essential to the possibility of politics, and it is precisely this that deconstruction does not provide.[18]

Critchley's solution to this problem is to provide a Levinasian supplement to Derridean deconstruction. He argues that Levinas supplies what Derrida lacks, namely, a substantive account of the political that can move one beyond the stalemate of undecidability. His claim is that "politics provides the continual horizon of Levinasian ethics, and that the problem of politics is that of delineating a form of political life that will repeatedly interrupt all attempts at totalization."[19] He says that Levinas's approach to the po-

---

17. Critchley, *Ethics of Deconstruction*, 199.
18. Ibid., 199–200.
19. Ibid., 223.

litical emerges directly out of his phenomenological account of the ethical. In particular, the preeminent danger of the political is that of totalization. Just as, in the ethical sphere, there is an intrinsic link between ontology and violence, so also, for Levinas, totalitarianism in politics arises from an ontological conception of the task of the philosopher or political theorist, which itself subordinates the ethical to the political. As Critchley says, "The primacy of politics is the primacy of the synoptic, panoramic vision of society, wherein a disinterested political agent views society as a whole. For Levinas, such a panoramic vision, not only that of the philosopher but also that of the political theorist, is the greatest danger, because it loses sight of ethical difference—that is, of my particular relation to and obligations towards the Other."[20]

Furthermore, Levinas's critique of totalizing political regimes is not only directed at those that are explicity totalitarian. As Critchley points out, Claude Lefort, Jean-Luc Nancy, and Philippe Lacoue-Labarthe have all shown that the problem of totalitarianism is not a problem unique to explicitly totalitarian regimes. A "soft"—more subtle but nonetheless very real—form of totalitarianism may be seen in operation in other political dispensations, including those of liberalism. He says that Levinas's strictures are directed also at "liberal politics, in so far as it has been dominated by the concepts of spontaneity, freedom and autonomy. In the 1990 Preface to a republished essay, [Levinas] wryly notes, 'We must ask ourselves if liberalism is all we need to achieve an authentic dignity for the human subject.' The Levinasian critique of politics is a critique of the belief that only political rationality can answer political questions."[21] These are certainly important insights, and they will no doubt have an important part to play in any contemporary political reflection. But if the task at hand is to develop a political disposition on the basis of Levinas's phenomenology of ethics—as Critchley is explicitly attempting to do—then what particular political vision begins to emerge?

The political life envisaged is one constituted by an "open community" interrupted by the "moment of transcendence" (in the Levinasian sense) which would guard against immanentism, totalization, and totalitarianism. "Political space is an open, plural, opaque network of ethical relations which are non-totalizable and where 'the contemporaneity of the multiple is tied around the dia-chrony of the two'. Levinasian politics is the enactment of plurality, of mutliplicity."[22] But what does it mean in practice to enact a

20. Ibid., 222.
21. Ibid.
22. Ibid., 225.

politics of plurality, of multiplicity? Certainly, Critchley expands upon his conception of Levinasian politics at some length, but, informative though this discussion is, it has to be said that the positive political vision does not move much beyond this. Admittedly, given the Levinasian starting point, it would be inappropriate to look for a detailed, positive, systematic political proposal, because this would be to fall back into the metaphysical, panoptical, and therefore totalitarian vision that Levinas guards against. But while heeding this salutary warning, one may well ask whether we should not expect more of an effective political vision than that with which Critchley supplies us. For it has to be said that what is offered here is a peculiarly negative vision, which guards against violence, totalitarianism, closure, and the reduction of difference. In its positive prescriptions, however, it is much less rich. And this raises the whole question of the complicity of a Levinasian political perspective with that of liberal pluralism. Now we have already observed that liberalism as a political project also falls prey to Levinas's antitotalitarian strictures. It would be misleading to view Levinas as providing a postmodern justification for the modern liberal political agenda. Furthermore, Critchley himself makes clear that he does not view his own Levinasian defense of democracy as a defense of currently existing liberal democracy. His own vision of democracy he defines as "the politics of ethical difference, political difference at the service of ethical love."[23] As such, democracy for Critchley does not exist; it is an "infinite task," something that comes without finally arriving. Nonetheless, for all that Levinas and Critchley wish to see themselves as critics of (post)modern liberal pluralism, it has to be asked whether their ethical and political philosophies are positive enough, substantial enough, specific enough, and different enough to serve as an effective bulwark against the liberal pluralism that is so much an accomplice of contemporary capitalism.

I would suggest that they are not, but that this conclusion really ought not to surprise us. We have observed the ways in which Critchley believes that Derrida's deconstruction *alone* provides insufficient resources for an effective political project. One way of understanding Critchley's reservations in this respect (although he himself does not express them in these terms) is to say that the move from undecidability to decision is ultimately problematic because Derrida's deconstructive disposition is ultimately predicated on the elevation of the domain of the *particular*. As Derrida repeatedly insisted, deconstruction is not, and does not claim to be, yet another "philosophy" in a long line of philosophies, and one might say that one way in which it is not yet another such philosophy is that it does not prescribe any normative

23. Ibid., 240.

universal. Rather, it is an attempt to articulate the conditions of a quasi-transcendental, the conditions that are effectively necessary for every universal system, every "philosophy." Thus, deconstruction is not a new universal but is, rather, parasitic on all possible universals; it is committed to exposing the stain of particularity that contaminates all universals. It does this not in order to foster the illusion that we can somehow do without universals, but rather to show how every universal is destabilized by the particularities it tries to exclude or contain. These particularities that can never be completely excluded or contained serve to destabilize every universal and thus install an inevitable and unavoidable undecidability.

Such deconstructive interventions may well have an indispensible role to play in political reflection and action, especially in situations where the domain of the universal is threatening to overwhelm and where the domain of particularity is in danger of being forgotten. But the shift from the undecidable to the political *decision* is not one that deconstruction itself can make, for this shift can only be made through the invocation of a universal perspective. This is because it is precisely such a perspective that ensures that the decision is not merely an arbitrary and therefore meaningless leap. In other words, one accepts the reality of the quasi-transcendental condition of undecidability (to which deconstruction draws attention), while simultaneously taking the risk of enacting a meaningful political decision (the universal grounds for which deconstruction does not itself claim to provide). Understood in these terms, one can see why Critchley believes deconstruction cannot provide an adequate account of the political decision. In my terms, this is because this can only be done by looking away from deconstruction's elucidation of the particular toward an adequate political vision of the universal.

But this is precisely what Critchely does *not* do. Instead, he looks to Levinas, who in many ways repeats the structural problematic we have here been elucidating. Just as we have said that Derrida does not seek to construct a new universal, a new "philosophy," so it must also be said that what Levinas does not do—indeed he explicitly repudiates the task—is to construct an ethics. Rather—and here the structural similarities with Derrida's project ought to be clear—he is concerned with elucidating the quasi-transcendental conditions for all conventional ethical systems. Again, this phenomenology is not without ethical and political effects; in this case, it issues a "call" to which all conventional ethics are answerable. So too, as we have seen in earlier chapters, a politics must always be answerable to the ethical. A politics that is not so answerable is thereby deemed illegitimate; a politics is legitimated insofar as it yields to the demands of the ethical, the singular Face of the Other. Of course, a politics cannot be *consistent* with the ethical, just as the universal cannot be consistent with the singular. But the universal can *yield* to the singular, and that, in effect, is what Levinas's political prescription amounts to. The universal must yield to the singular because, if it does not, its totalitarian (unyielding) logic will do violence to the singular, to the Face of the Other. All this we have seen in earlier chapters. But the important point here is that Levinas does not actually construct a politics. His contribution to political thought has been to emphasize that which all forms of politics should *avoid*: totalitarianism, violence, fascism. What he does not do is provide a positive, substantive vision of that which politics should *promote*. And, of course, he hesitates to do this because it would involve him in invoking an explicit universal and would thus put him at risk of totalization.

In his more recent work, Critchley has developed his account of the relationship between the ethical and the political, but he has done so in a way that extends rather than repudiates his earlier conception. He continues to ground his project in fundamentally Levinasian insights on the nature of both subjectivity and the ethical itself. Critchley does now acknowledge, however, the potentially destructive because hyperbolic nature of the ethical demand in Levinas's work, of the kind we elucidated in chapter 1. He admits that "there is an undoubted ethical extremism in Levinas which, in my presentation of his work, centres around the theme of the subject as trauma. That is, Levinas seems to be describing ethical responsibility as the maintenance of a permanent state of trauma."[24] We have ourselves brought out the damaging implications of this in earlier chapters.

But rather than seeing this as providing grounds for turning *away* from Levinas, Critchley instead wants to remain true to Levinas while simultaneously finding ways of mitigating these extreme effects, rather in the way that we earlier saw Caputo to do. He wants to expose the subject to the trauma of the ethical encounter, but at the same time wishes to prevent it from being crushed. In order to do this, he turns to psychoanalysis and its notion of sublimation. The specific form of sublimation that Critchley commends is that of humor and comedy. This is because, following Freud, he sees many forms of humor as resulting from a split between the ego and the superego. Humor occurs when the superego observes the ego from on high and affirms its finite, limited insignificance. This acknowledgment of finitude and insignificance is liberating, and it is this liberation that lies at the heart of the humorous. As he puts it, "humour recalls us to the modesty and limitedness of the human condition, a limitedness that calls not for tragic affirmation but comic *acknowledgement*, not heroic authenticity

24. Critchley, *Ethics-Politics-Subjectivity*, 205.

but laughable inauthenticity."[25] By means of such a humorous affirmation of finitude, the trauma inflicted on the subject by the demand of absolute responsibility might be mitigated. Critchley delineates these suggestions at some length, but for our purposes it is sufficient to note the way in which he understands the deficiencies of Levinas's outlook to be things that may be overcome while ultimately remaining true to and within the parameters of that Levinasian milieu.

Likewise, when we turn to the recent developments in Critchley's political thought, we find—as we would expect from a follower of Levinas—that he is still promoting a politics "that arises from the infinite demand of an ethical commitment."[26] Thus, while Critchley recognizes the political necessity of the domain of the universal, he continues to subordinate it to that of particularity. Just as the political arises out of and is thus subordinate to the ethical, so too the universal is a secondary supplement to the primary particularist foundation. This is made very clear when he says that "the logic of political nomination, I take it, is that a determinate particularity in society is hegemonically constructed into a universality. That is, the universal is not read off from the script of some pre-given ontology but posited in a specific situation. Universality is constructed in a specific context in relation to what Gramsci calls common sense . . . beginning from a position of emptiness, a particular group posits the fullness of the universal and hegemonically articulates that universality in political action, thereby becoming a political subject."[27]

What motivates this *subordination* of the universal to the particular is, as with Levinas, a fear of totality and its violence: "what has to be continually criticized in political thinking is the aspiration to the full incarnation of the universal in the particular, or the privileging of a specific particularity because it is believed to *incarnate* the universal."[28] It should be conceded that the domain of the universal does potentially harbor totalitarian outcomes, and this is why it must always be exposed to the domains of the particular and the singular, so as to guard against this. But this exposure should always occur in such a way that the question of which has priority is never finally settled and is always in active negotiation. The problem with the *perpetual* subordination of the universal of the kind advocated by Critchley is that this always comes at the price of an attenuation of the legitimate ambitions of the political itself. Thus it is that the *negative* character of Critchley's political

25. Ibid., 224.
26. Critchley, *Infinitely Demanding*, 94.
27. Ibid., 104.
28. Ibid., 119.

Part III: The Political

thinking that we have already identified—namely, that it can articulate what it is trying to *avoid*, while being much more reticent about what it positively stands *for*—has been perpetuated in his recent work. In the kind of political anarchism he defends, he says that "what motivates political struggle is a shared experience of certain wrongs and a determination to right those wrongs. What ties together the highly disparate groups that make up demonstrations of the kind we have seen so often in recent years is not a common set of theoretical doctrines, such as Marxism, but rather a shared sense of grievance and wrong, namely that unrestrained multi-national corporate, military capitalism is wrong, that war is the wrong response to 9/11, etc., etc., etc."[29] So the inspiration for these kinds of political movements is not a universal vision ("a common set of theoretical doctrines") but a contingent coalescing around what particular groups or individuals are *against* ("a shared sense of grievance or wrong").

Furthermore, this lack of positive prescription, this absence of a guiding positive universal vision, feeds into a markedly modest account of what political thought and action may expect to achieve. Of course, there are circumstances in which such political modesty may be appropriate; but again, any curtailment or limiting of the ambitions of the universal imperative should occur in the context of specific situations, through judgments that must repeatedly be made anew. What is much more problematic is when this modesty and limitation is adopted not as a practical strategy in negotiating specific encounters between the universal, the particular, and the singular, but as a positive principle in the political position itself. Again, when this happens, political ambitions become a priori attenuated. This is made clear when Critchley says that "it is the material drive of social being that calls the state into question and calls the established order to account, not in order to do away with the state, desirable though that may be in some utopian sense, but in order to better it or attenuate its malicious effects."[30]

But is this sufficient? Is it enough to develop a form of political thought that is willing to rest content with bettering state capitalism or mitigating its worst aspects? I have already suggested that we should refuse any forced alternative between passive resignation and total transformation. Against Badiou, I argue in favor of a politics that works *within* the constraints of the currently prevailing configuration while *also* working for a complete transformation. So I am not in principle opposed to the kind of gradualism that Critchley seems to be commending. But the point at issue is that such gradualism should always be regarded as incomplete, as a mere staging post

29. Ibid., 126.
30. Ibid., 117.

toward something else. It should not be elevated into a principle of political thought; neither should a complete transformation be a priori dismissed as "utopian." This is perhaps why Žižek asks, "Does not Critchley's position, then, function as a kind of ideal supplement to the Third Way Left: a 'revolt' which poses no effective threat, since it endorses in advance the logic of hysterical provocation, bombarding the Power with 'impossible' demands, demands which are not meant to be met?" It "poses no effective threat" because it makes its demands of the regnant Power rather than striking at the heart of the legitimacy of that Power itself. Žižek continues: "Critchley is therefore logical in his assertion of the primacy of the Ethical over the Political: the ultimate motivating force of the type of political interventions he advocates is the experience of *injustice*, of the ethical unacceptability of the state of things."[31]

While it may be possible for one to attempt to develop a politics in a way that is inspired by, answerable to, and consistent with Levinas's thought, there is a sense in which any such enterprise is in principle compromised from the start. For it is an attempt to develop a politics on the basis of principles that themselves seek to *limit* the political; an attempt to develop a positive political vision on the basis of a way of thinking that emphasizes what politics should *avoid*; an attempt to develop a universal vision on the basis of a commitment to the sovereignty of the *singular* (the Face). Kenneth Reinhard has argued that the

> fundamental disjunction [in Levinas's thought] between the conditions of ethics (and the neighbor) and politics (and the citizen, on the model of "fraternity") should preclude any attempt to draw political consequences from Levinas's theory of the neighbor. What is truly radical in Levinas's thought is precisely this impasse, the fact of the unbridgeable gap between ethics and politics: insofar as ethics involves the encounter of the *two* of the neighbour and the self, it cannot conceive of the *three*, the symbolic representation and mediation on which politics is based; ethics is inherently apolitical, must wilfully ignore what would be fair and for the general good.[32]

If this is so, then, in principle, the endeavor to build a Levinasian politics would seem to be skewed—an attempt to build on a foundation that itself warns against the desire to build. We have seen what the practical outcomes are in Critchley's political thinking; it results in a political vision that is rather clearer about what it is against than what it is for. Faced with

---

31. Žižek, *Parallax View*, 333–34.
32. Reinhard, "Toward a Political Theology of the Neighbor," 48–49.

the political stasis induced by Derrida's undecidability, what was needed was the turn to a universal perspective that would enable one to turn from such undecidability toward a decision. Instead, Critchley turns to another thinker who, like Derrida, seeks structurally to *limit* any such universals. Thus, I would argue that although Critchley was correct to say that Derrida's deconstruction stands in need of an ethical and political supplement, he was mistaken in looking to Levinas to provide it. For in looking to Levinas, he was looking to someone who replicated, in his own register, the very structural characteristics in Derrida that had given rise to the requirements for a supplement in the first place. In other words, in turning to Levinas, he was turning to someone who was as much in need of an ethical and political supplement (a universal, I would argue) as was Derrida. It is not so much that Derrida stands in need of supplementation by Levinas, but rather that Derrida *and* Levinas together stand in need of an ethical and political supplement from elsewhere. Both need the complement of an unequivocal universal.[33]

But at this point, it is important for us to consider another way in which the domain of the universal is downplayed in current political thought. Whereas Critchley insists that universality must give way to the sway of particularity, another line of analysis suggests that the domain of the universal must give way to the sovereignty of the singular. As I have already suggested in chapter 3, the most prominent purveyors of this line of argument are Michael Hardt and Antonio Negri, followed also by Kenneth Surin. It is to their thought that I shall now turn.

Politics of the Singular: Hardt and Negri

It is important to note here the implications of this elevation of singularity rather than particularity. In one respect, it denotes a sharp differentiation from the line of analysis developed by Critchley, while in another, we see the two approaches drawing closer together. The demarcation is most clearly evident in Hardt and Negri's rejection of the elevation of particularities embodied in postmodern thought. This is manifested when they ask, "what if a new paradigm of power, a postmodern sovereignty, has come to replace the modern paradigm and rule through differential hierarchies of the hybrid and fragmentary subjectivities that [postmodern] theorists celebrate? In this case, modern forms of sovereignty would no longer be at issue, and

---

33. The same point might also be made in relation to the work of the Italian philosopher Gianni Vattimo. For a discussion of Vattimo's work along these lines, see Hyman, "Must a Post-metaphysical Political Theology Repudiate Transcendence?"

the postmodernist and postcolonialist strategies that appear to be liberatory would not challenge but in fact coincide with and even unwittingly reinforce the new strategies of rule!"[34] So for Hardt and Negri, the new enemy, which they deem "Empire," is not only resistant to the postmodern political emphases on particularities, differences, and fluidity, but actually thrives on them. Again, they say that

> the affirmation of hybridities and the free play of difference across boundaries... is liberatory only in a context where power poses hierarchy exclusively through essential identities, binary divisions, and stable oppositions. The structures and logics of power in the contemporary world are entirely immune to the "liberatory" weapons of the postmodern politics of difference. In fact, Empire too is bent on doing away with those modern forms of sovereignty and on setting differences to play across boundaries. Despite the best intensions, then, the postmodernist politics of difference not only is ineffective against but can even coincide with and support the functions and practices of imperial rule.[35]

On the other hand, there is another sense in which their analysis draws closer to that of Critchley, namely, in their subordination of the domain of the universal. For Hardt and Negri, their suspicion of universalism appears to derive from their conviction that it is bound up with the notion of transcendence, which they believe brings in its wake hierarchy, tyranny, and oppression. They express this line of argument clearly when they say that transcendence "leads quickly to the imposition of social hierarchy and domination. Antihumanism, then, conceived as a refusal of any transcendence, should in no way be confused with the *vis viva*, the creative life force that animates the revolutionary stream of the modern tradition. On the contrary, the refusal of transcendence is the condition of the possibility of thinking this immanent power, an anarchic basis of philosophy."[36] This analysis is predicated on a particular genealogical account of the development of modernity. On this reading, modernity opened the way for the constitution of this immanent power; indeed, they define the modern as the foundation of a "revolutionary plane of immanence," inaugurated at the end of the thirteenth century by Duns Scotus. But in the wake of the abolition of the ontological dualism of the premodern, it became necessary to replace it with a "functional" dualism that was necessary for disciplinary reasons. The

34. Hardt and Negri, *Empire*, 138.
35. Ibid., 142.
36. Ibid., 91–92.

multitude could not be understood as being in "a direct, immediate relation with divinity and nature, as the ethical producer of life and the world" (as was the case with Spinoza, one of Hardt and Negri's philosophical heroes), as this would have given rise to a "subversive delirium." Instead, a mediation was needed, a "sort of weak transcendence," whereby the multitude would "yield to a preconstituted order."[37] This "weak transcendence" was installed by Descartes and then taken to its apotheosis by Kant.

In this second mode of modernity, the aim was to "eliminate the medieval form of transcendence, which only inhibits production and consumption, while maintaining transcendence's effects of domination in a form adequate to the modes of association and production of the new humanity. The center of the problem of modernity was thus demonstrated in political philosophy, and here was where the new form of mediation found its most adequate response to the revolutionary forms of immanence; a transcendent political apparatus."[38] In particular, Hobbes's conception of absolute sovereign rule plays a major part in the modern construction of this apparatus. So modernity was marked by an incomplete overcoming of transcendence. A weak or quasi-transcendence was retained because of its disciplinary function, a function that was essential to the modern development of profit and capital. For Hardt and Negri, therefore, emancipation from the forces of capital is to be achieved by completing modernity's incomplete revolution vis-a-vis transcendence. Only then will the disciplinary structure be dissipated and the multitude freed to take control of its own destiny. This is something the multitude must do for itself free from any answerability to a transcendent measure: " . . . in contrast to those who have long claimed that value can be affirmed only in the figure of measure and order, we argue that value and justice can live in and be nourished by an immeasurable world. Here we can see once again the importance of the revolution of Renaissance humanism. *Ni Dieu, ni maître, ni l'homme*—no transcendent power or measure will determine the values of our world. Value will be determined only by humanity's own continuous innovation and creation."[39] So Hardt and Negri certainly recognize the need for an exteriority with which the logic of capital, of Empire, may be subverted. But this exteriority must be found *within* this immanent world—not in a transcendent source of meaning, values, and truth, but in an unequivocally human source. The exteriority—the source of revolution—comes from the excessive desire that constitutes the

---

37. Ibid., 78–79.
38. Ibid., 83.
39. Ibid., 356.

potential of the multitude, an excessive desire that, freed from slavery to the transcendent, will create and subvert.

It is this analysis that underpins the turn from universality to singularity. A "transcendent measure" is seen to be inseparably linked with universalism. Universalism derives its authority from the manner in which it *transcends* currently prevailing contingent particularities and singularities. It is precisely this transcendence that underpins the universal authority; and this universal authority serves to *discipline* the particularities and singularities over which it presides. Freed from this transcendent and universal authority, particularities and singularities may be allowed to come into their own. In this context, how might we understand Hardt and Negri's elevation of the singular over the particular? One way of doing so is to see the universal and the particular as being dialectically implicated. We might say that particularities are *effects* of universals. Thus, to use an example of Hardt and Negri's, if "the people" is one and universal, individuals are particular manifestations of this One. The differences intrinsic to particulars are always secondary in relation to the sameness of the one universal. Differences are only apparent manifestations of a more real, if latent, unity. On this understanding, when the universal dies, particulars are cut adrift from their transcendent moorings. The differences of particularities become sheer differences, and the death of the universal rules out, in principle, any overcoming of this sheer difference. The result is impotent contingency, helpless victimhood. This is why, in the wake of the death of transcendent universals, the way forward is not to embrace a rule of orphaned particulars. This would lead to little more than the assertion of sheer differences, without prospect of any commonalities, and with the absence of the latter, tragic resignation would appear to be the only political outcome.

Instead, therefore, one should look to singularities, the differences between which are irreducible and not merely secondary to a universal oneness. If these singularities are to make common cause, they may do so on their own account and are not by definition required to look to a now defunct universalism in order to provide an identity or unity. This is why the notion of "the multitude" (standing in direct contrast to "the people") is so important to Hardt and Negri: "The multitude is composed of a set of *singularities*—and by singularity here we mean a social subject whose difference cannot be reduced to sameness, a difference that remains different. The component parts of the people are indifferent in their unity; they become an identity by negating or setting aside their differences. The plural singularities of the multitude thus stand in contrast to the undifferentiated unity of the people."⁴⁰ But neither is the multitude "fragmentary, anarchical, or incoherent." Such pluralities ultimately collapse into one indifferent whole and are thus not composed of singularities at all. Rather, "The multitude designates an active social subject, which acts on the basis of what the singularities share in common. The multitude is an internally different, multiple social subject whose constitution and action is based not on identity or unity (or, much less, indifference) but on what it has in common."⁴¹ Furthermore, "Whereas the individual dissolves in the unity of the community, singularities are not diminished but express themselves freely in the common."⁴² But the political challenge that confronts this immanent world of singularities is how to develop some notion of "exteriority" on which all hope of radical or revolutionary change would seem to be predicated. Is not the current political impasse defined by precisely this lack of "exteriority"? And does not a world of immanent singularities not serve only to reinforce it? Without any transcendent universal, where is any such "exteriority" to be found? The challenge, in other words, is to find a way of combining a political commitment to "exteriority" with an ontological commitment to immanence.

A priori, this would seem to be an inauspicious undertaking. At the heart of any ontology of immanence, is not any kind of genuine exteriority implicitly if not explicitly precluded? This question was, of course, famously asked by Heidegger. He suggested that the project of Western metaphysics was always likely to culminate in immanence because of the way in which the whole endeavor was founded upon the immanent subject. As he comments, "Objectifying, in representing, in setting before, delivers up the object to the *ego cogito*. In that delivering up, the *ego* proves to be that which underlies its own activity (the delivering up that sets before), i.e., proves to be the *subiectum*. The subject is subject for itself. The essence of consciousness is self-consciousness."⁴³ When the essence of consciousness is self-consciousness, any kind of exteriority would seem to be precluded: "If man meets only himself, he never encounters otherness or difference."⁴⁴ In this situation, as Heidegger again puts it, "man has risen up into the I-ness of the *ego cogito*. Through this uprising, all that is, is transformed into object. That which is, as the objective, is swallowed up into the immanence of subjectivity."⁴⁵ The

40. Hardt and Negri, *Multitude*, 99.
41. Ibid., 100.
42. Ibid., 204.
43. Heidegger, *Question Concerning Technology*, 100. Quoted in Taylor, *Altarity*, 39.
44. Taylor, *Altarity*, 40.
45. Heidegger, *Question Concerning Technology*, 107. Quoted in Taylor, *Altarity*, 40.

instrumentalism intrinsic to such an ontology is clear, as Heidegger again specified. All that is in the world becomes "things," which are instrumentalist tools to be utilized by the centered metaphysical subject. All that is not-I is secondary and is subordinated to the whims and desires of the primary and centered I. For Heidegger, all the horrors of technological capitalism may be traced back to the dominance of this metaphysical way of thinking.

Kenneth Surin, while endorsing the ontological vision being propounded by Hardt and Negri, is nonetheless acutely aware of this challenge. In particular, he is aware that the problem of politics today lies in the absence of any kind of otherness or exteriority. This absence promotes the conviction that what is, is what ought to be, and thus also the conviction that there is no alternative to the current liberal-capitalist configuration. He says that "politics today is postpolitical precisely to the extent that there is no . . . exteriority to the political as it actually exists, no enabling point in the so-called liberal democracies from which to pose a genuine social democracy against the regnant liberalism, let alone one that will overturn the system in its entirety. The project of liberalism can be viable only if it is predicated on the need to find this exteriority once more. Only then will there be an alternative to the mutually reinforcing relationship that exists between this neoliberal conjuncture and world-integrated capitalism."[46] Indeed, in this context, he acknowledges that any ontology that posits a genuine transcendence, a beyond or some kind of otherness does immediately thereby possess a political advantage. More specifically, he says that the fact that Christianity affirms a rationality of a desire grounded in something *beyond* is its "remarkable ontological asset." This is because it "enables Christianity ceaselessly to move beyond the limits necessarily constituted by the given."[47]

In other words, Surin acknowledges that the great advantage of a transcendent ontology is precisely that it provides that exteriority which is necessary for any emancipatory political project. An immanent ontology does not immediately have that advantage, but nonetheless Surin believes that it is possible to unleash a liberatory exteriority *within* an ontology of absolute immanence. Tracing the genealogy of such a vision back through Deleuze, Spinoza, and Duns Scotus, Surin says that "the Scotist axioms that reality is to be approached by the will guided by love, and that reality is constituted by worlds of singularities, events, and virtualities, and not of subjects and objects, allows all these items to be 'expressively' distributed: all kinds of possible worlds, extending to a potential infinity, can express the same singularity, event, or virtuality, so there is from the beginning a complete

---

46. Surin, "Rewriting the Ontological Script of Liberation," 253.
47. Ibid., 259.

preemption of any bureaucratic administration of these 'expressive' distributions and the worlds in which they are located."[48] He says that on this view, the constitution of reality is politicized; the distribution of expressivities is governed by a logic of ceaseless proliferation. Surin then goes on to clarify the way in which this Scotist-Spinozist-Deleuzean vision, as articulated by Hardt and Negri, fulfils the recognized political need for a genuine exteriority, while at the same time remaining unequivocally immanent.

> With this uncontainable production of expressivity, there is an absolute "beyond" for all that is given. As the horizon for the critique of anything that is given, this "beyond" is precisely the exteriority needed for any viable project of liberation. This infinity of expressivities and their associated possible worlds is rigorously immanent and materialist. Without being transcendent (there being no universal subject and universal object for it to transcend), it serves as a transcendental field for the becoming of new multiplicities, each new multiplicity being potentially another name for a new kind of political agent living for a liberation that the old sovereignties are unable to forestall.[49]

So there is no recapitulation here of liberalism's modest desire to mitigate the severity of violence and tyranny. There is a quest for genuine change, for a different regime of truth and power, the precise nature of which cannot be specified in advance (it is precisely the "excessive" nature of the desire fueling this revolutionary impulse that precludes such prediction). It is this unknown future, this unpredictability that bestows the exteriority that is deemed to be necessary for any project of liberation. But it is also necessary to ask whether the immanent ontology that is intrinsic to this vision actually advances the cause for change and liberation. Or does it, on the contrary, serve as a stumbling block? The repudiation of transcendence brings with it also a turn away from the domain of the universal, and for Surin (and Hardt and Negri) it entails an affirmation of singularities, expressively distributed, extending out to a potential infinity, which ceaselessly proliferate. This potential infinity frees one from bondage to the given. But without a universal to guide this ceaseless proliferation, how much confidence might we have in the political potential of such an ontology? Does this kind of ceaseless proliferation necessarily lead in an emancipatory direction?

In this respect, it is important to observe that the ontology that is being commended *coincides* with the ontology that is being resisted. This is because one of the defining features of capitalism is its immanence; that

48. Ibid., 262.
49. Ibid.

is to say, capitalism recognizes no transcendent norm or standard of judgment to which it is subject: it is powered by the purely immanent forces of supply and demand, which are themselves effects of the desires of the centered subject, specifically the immanent desire for maximum profit. As Terry Eagleton has observed, "The advanced capitalist system is inherently atheistic. It is godless in its actual material practices, and in the values and beliefs implicit in them, whatever some of its apologists may piously aver."[50] Indeed, it is difficult to see how an immanent worldview could give rise to anything other than a capitalist economy, to which it is singularly well suited. Of course, Hardt and Negri are not unaware of this complicity. They point out that capital "operates on the plane of *immanence*, through relays and networks of relationships of domination, without reliance on a transcendent center of power. It tends historically to destroy traditional social boundaries, expanding across territories and enveloping always new populations within its processes."[51] For Hardt and Negri, capitalism's displacement of transcendence with immanence is a positive development. In this (typically Marxist) sense, the advanced form of capitalism they designate as "Empire" is better than what went before. As we have already observed, they argue that in the early modern period, a "weak" transcendence was retained in the form of political sovereignty. This political sovereignty was necessary for capitalism in the short term in order to provide the stable conditions in which it could flourish. But in the long term, it became a stumbling block to the development of the pure immanence that capitalism in its most advanced form requires. Hence, it was necessary that this quasi-transcedence in the form of modern political sovereignty be finally abolished.

If this development was in the long-term interests of capital, then it was also simultaneously in the best interests of the revolutionary potential of the multitude. For now the multitude is liberated from the order and discipline that transcendence necessarily imposes. The excessive desire of the multitude is now freed to be channeled in a revolutionary direction. Apart from the fact that the validity of this whole narrative depends upon the presupposition that transcendence is necessarily tyrannous, which is at the very least questionable, it must also be noted that it further depends on the quintessentially Marxist notion of capitalism (and in this case the advanced form of capitalism designated "Empire") as a "necessary stage" that in at least some ways represents an *advance* toward the anticipated revolution. For Marx himself, this aspect of his analysis was underpinned by a *teleology* which, as John Milbank has suggested, is the "least defensible" aspect of

50. Eagleton, *Reason, Faith, and Revolution*, 39.
51. Hardt and Negri, *Empire*, 326.

Part III: The Political

Marxism.[52] For Hardt and Negri, this necessary teleology is presumably expunged by their thoroughgoing immanence. This is confirmed when Negri specifies his task as being, as we have seen, to provide an ontology of the political subject "outside of all teleology and within the postmodern conditions of absolute immanence."[53] And, as they both say, "Teleology now can only be called ignorance and superstition. . . . Just as humans are born with no eternal faculties written in their flesh, so too there are no final ends or teleological goals written in history. Human faculties and historical teleologies exist only because they are the result of human passions, reason and struggle."[54]

In which case, the only thing that tells against the possibility of advanced immanentist capitalism entrenching itself ever more firmly is a confidence that the excessive desire of the mutitiude will be turned in a revolutionary direction. But on what, precisely, is this confidence based? The realization of the optimistic scenario that Hardt and Negri portray is certainly a contingent possibility; but what makes it any more likely than the realization of an equally contingent and at least as plausible scenario whereby the excessive desires of the multitude are channeled in other ways that reinforce rather than contest the dominant sway of capitalism? As John Milbank has pointed out, "there is simply no truth in the Marxist assumption that, once freed from the shackles of oppression, people will 'by reason' choose equality and justice. To the contrary, in the light of a mere reason that is not also vision, *eros*, and faith, people may well choose the petty triumphs and superiorities of a brutally hierarchic *agon* of power or the sheer excitement of a social spectacle in which they may potentially be exhibited in triumph."[55] Indeed, given the propensity of capitalism to clothe itself in a democratic and participatory garb, given its apparent victory in the war of populist propaganda, does this not appear to be a much more likely scenario?[56]

Hardt and Negri are aware of this challenge, although whether they adequately address it is another question. They refuse, of course, the institutionalization or even organization of collective resistance. They acknowledge that "the multitude does not arise as a political figure spontaneously and that the flesh of the multitude consists of a series of conditions that are ambivalent: they could lead toward liberation or be caught in a new regime

---

52. Milbank, *Being Reconciled*, 163.
53. Negri, "Political Subject and Absolute Immanence," 231.
54. Hardt and Negri, *Multitude*, 195, 221.
55. Milbank, *Future of Love*, 260.
56. For a detailed analysis of this propensity, see Frank, *One Market Under God*.

of exploitation and control. The multitude needs a political project to bring it into existence."[57] But of what precisely does this political project consist? It is at this point that Hardt and Negri become notably vague. They look to a "global cycle of struggles" that "express grievances against the injustices of our current global system," and in light of these, they seek to "rethink the concept of democracy."[58] This democracy would be rooted in the notion of the "common," which is "both presupposition and result" inspired by a political concept of love.[59] All of this is analyzed at length and supplemented by a wealth of illustrations.

But, as we said of Critchley's project, while it is very clear what Hardt and Negri are against, this is not ultimately derived from a positive universal vision. Their only unequivocal "goods" seem to lie in the principles of immanence and singularity. But there is nothing intrinsic to these concepts that would lead them necessarily in the direction of the democracy of the common, rooted in love, toward which Hardt and Negri gesture. The only thing that would seem to sustain this transition is a commitment to some form of vague optimism. Even the figure of "poverty" that looms so large in their analysis would seem to be ambivalent in its potential outcomes. Negri asserts that "poverty does not represent merely the content of the resistance of the multitude but also the site where its power reveals itself."[60] But what if the "biopower that puts power to work so as to exploit it" does its job so well that the exploited do not even perceive their state as being one of "poverty"? Or, even if they do, what if they regard such a state as being, for instance, "inevitable," "natural," and something from which they can escape *only* by attempting to participate wholeheartedly in the very regime that has produced that poverty? Presumably, what is needed in such circumstances is a decisive critical intervention. But is this best effected by means of a mode of thought that reaffirms the very immanence of the system that is to be disturbed, interrupted, and, ultimately, overthrown? What order there is in capitalism (which is not to deny that there is a very real order) emerges spontaneously out of the immanent operation of the differential forces of supply and demand.[61] Is the immanence of capitalism best resisted through the celebration of immanence?

57. Hardt and Negri, *Multitude*, 212.
58. Ibid., 217, 328.
59. Ibid., 350–51.
60. Negri, "Political Subject and Absolute Immanence," 238.
61. For an analysis along these lines, see Taylor, *Moment of Complexity* and *Confidence Games*.

Part III: The Political

This strategy of ever-deeper immersion within the logic of the currently prevailing social conditions would seem only to affirm and reinforce those conditions *unless* one of two things were to occur. The first would be the affirmation of a Hegelian-Marxist type faith in a necessary teleology, whereby to affirm and intensify the present system is also simultaneously to subvert it. And yet, we have seen that such a teleology is ruled out by Hardt and Negri as being a reinstatement of the retrograde principle of transcendence. The second (and this too is not entirely divorced from the Hegelian-Marxist notion of dialectic) would be the existence of an exteriority *within* the present system, which, if unleashed, would lead to the ultimate subversion of that system. It is this latter path that Hardt and Negri take, the exteriority in question being the excessive desire of the multitude. The difficulty for Hardt and Negri here is that this second path—which they affirm—is intimately bound up with the first path—which they reject. It is the first principle—the teleology—that ensures that the second principle—the immanent exteriority—does its work of subversion in a positive and quasi-predictable way.

But it is important to note here that these two paths are linked in such a way that subversion pure and simple is *not* all that Hardt and Negri are left with; on the contrary, there is a profound historical optimism in their work that suggests that the Hegelian-Marxist teleology has not in fact been repudiated in the way that they claim. This tendency in their work has also been detected by Žižek. He says that Hardt and Negri "bring us back to the Marxist confidence that 'history is on our side,' that historical development is already generating the form of the Communist future. If anything, the problem with [Hardt and Negri] is therefore that they are *too* Marxist, taking over the underlying Marxist scheme of historical progress ... they rehabilitate the old Marxist notion of the tension between productive forces and the relations of production: capitalism already generates the 'germs of the future new form of life,' it incessantly produces the new 'common,' so that, in a revolutionary explosion, this New should just be liberated from the old social form."[62] But to what extent is this kind of historical-teleological optimism warranted? There are good grounds for thinking it is not. For one thing, as John Milbank has pointed out, following Jean-François Lyotard, "the extreme formalism of capital, its ability to define all the variety of human needs, labour and products as basically 'the same,' make it inherently 'tautologous,' and the least self-contradictory of social systems, in the sense that it is uniquely able to remain self-identical in the most various situations. As Lyotard suggests, it is a *dispositif de regulation de la conquête*, because

---

62. Žižek, *Parallax View*, 266.

Passivity

its tautologous character means that it can always *precisely* measure what threats it is under, and so automatically make a corrective response."[63] In this sense, capitalism's contradictions can always be overcome or corrected so as to ensure its own perpetual survival. There are no contradictions that will ultimately be irreducible.

Žižek's analysis is different—and in this respect (as in others) he follows Lacan rather than Lyotard—although it too casts doubt on the kind of historical confidence expressed by Marx and perpetuated by Hardt and Negri. In a sense, he argues that the contradictions of capitalism, far from bringing about its eventual destruction, actually serve as its condition of possibility. He says that

> what Marx overlooked is that—to put it in classic Derridean terms—this inherent obstacle/antagonism, as the "condition of impossibility" of the full employment of the productive forces, is simultaneously its "condition of possibility": if we abolish the obstacle, the inherent contradiction of capitalism, we do not get the fully unleashed drive to productivity finally delivered of its impediment, we lose precisely this productivity that seemed to be generated and simultaneously thwarted by capitalism—if we take away the obstacle, the very potential thwarted by this obstacle dissipates. That is Lacan's fundamental reproach to Marx, which focuses on the ambiguous overlapping between surplus-value and surplus-enjoyment.[64]

What both of these analyses suggest (and they are not mutually exclusive) is that the Marxist confidence in historical progress is misplaced. Capitalism may, by its nature, be subject to numerous ruptures, crises, and contradictions, but nothing leads us to suppose that these more or less traumatic experiences will lead to its own self-destruction. On the contrary, experience suggests that capitalism is remarkably resilient, flexible, and self-correcting even when the ruptures are of such a magnitude as to bring it to the brink of an abyss.

What, then, if Hardt and Negri were to take leave of this residual belief in historical progress? What if they were more rigorously self-consistent in their denial of the notion of teleology? One answer might be (and this is perhaps why they might wish to avoid it) that it would bring them close to the structural operations of Derridean deconstruction. As Derrida himself realized, deconstruction is a radical rewriting of Hegelianism, Hegelianism

---

63. Milbank, *Theology and Social Theory*, 194, with reference to Lyotard, *Économie Libidinale*, 187–88.

64. Žižek, *Parallax View*, 266–67.

Part III: The Political

minus that most Hegelian of all concepts—teleology. In which case, Hardt and Negri may be closer to Derridean deconstruction than they are willing to admit. If this is so, then there are several damaging consequences. For one thing, it has never been maintained that an intrinsic aspect of the deconstructive operation is necessarily to overthrow in a revolutionary sense. That a system is liable to deconstruction (and insofar as deconstruction is conceived as a quasi-transcendental, every system is indeed so liable) does not constitute grounds for its rejection or negation. Deconstruction—as an immanent exteriorty—might well subvert and destabilize the system, *while that system as a whole remains in place.*[65] This is why Derrida expressed reservations about the notion of revolution—of an absolute break—as an intrinsically metaphysical concept. The same might be said to apply to Hardt and Negri and their own espousal of an immanent exteriority. It may well be that the excessive desire of the multitude will subvert and destabilize the regime of Empire, while at the same time, that regime as a whole remains in place. Once again, it seems that Derrida himself is more clear-sighted as to the implications of his immanent exteriority than are Hardt and Negri.

Indeed, I would argue that it is the subordination of the domain of the universal that is common to both Derrida on the one hand and Hardt and Negri on the other that gives rise to this political impotence. This is why I argued in the earlier part of the chapter that the resources of both Derrida and Levinas are politically insufficient; there is a need for some form of universal. But we might say that the political prospects for Hardt and Negri are even worse than they are for Derrida. For there is nothing in Derrida's deconstruction that in principle rules out the possibility of it being parasitic upon a universal (indeed the whole notion of supplementation bears witness to the unavoidability of such parasitism); neither is there anything that is in principle opposed to the notion of transcendence (again, deconstruction itself seems to call forth such transcendence). Hardt and Negri, on the other hand, explicitly set themselves against both universalism and transcendence and thereby cut off the only possible resource for the effectualization of radical change.

In this respect, it could be argued that Don Cupitt is more clear-sighted on the implications of this "immanence without reserve" than are Hardt and Negri. Like them, Cupitt has long been concerned to expunge all traces of transcendence from philosophical thought, and instead propounds an ontology of thoroughgoing immanence. Although Cupitt does not approach this issue as a question of political theory, the arguments he develops are nonetheless strikingly similar to those developed by Hardt

---

65. See Taylor, *Moment of Complexity*, 65.

and Negri on this specific issue. It is perhaps not surprising that Deleuzian influences come to the fore in some of Cupitt's writings and that he has described his philosophical outlook as a form of "energetic Spinozism." Although the natures of their respective projects are markedly distinct, it is nonetheless the case that Cupitt shares with Hardt and Negri a commitment to an unequivocally immanent ontology, a common philosophical lineage in Spinoza and Deleuze in particular (less so Duns Scotus in Cupitt's case) and that the justification for this ontology and intellectual trajectory is that it is the one best able to liberate from hierarchy and tyranny.

But whereas, as we have seen, Hardt and Negri continue to propound a Marxist optimism, Cupitt recognizes that without a transcendent or universal intervention, there can be no grounds whatever for anything other than a politically "free" liberalism and an economically "free" capitalism. Cupitt has the merit of being quite explicit about this. He says that "the late capitalist economy promises the most perfect synthesis of total social organization and total personal fulfilment yet achieved on earth. . . . It is not easy to get any critical leverage against late capitalism. Those who call it materialistic—confident, somehow, that that is a serious charge—forget that by its elegant synthesis of order and freedom, duty and desire, it has largely fulfilled the dream of Western Christian thought at least from Augustine to Hegel."[66] Cupitt is aware, too, of what would be needed to effect some kind of critical leverage against capitalism, namely, some form of transcendent universal intervention of the kind that he believes now to be impossible. As he continues, "Nobody has access to an extra-cultural and purely independent standard by which to determine what is 'really' to be desired by human beings, and what 'really' should satisfy their desires. There is no superior or 'natural' reality by contrast with which the world of late capitalism is mere appearance. I cannot usefully condemn it as frothy if there is nothing but froth."[67] Gillian Rose has observed that Cupitt presents himself as "a holy celebrant of the market-place" and does so in the interests of a "dynamic pluralism." But she sees the apparent "freedom" being inverted into a new "tyranny." As she puts it, "Cupitt glorifies markets—for commodities, languages, political interests and religions—as plural and labile. But the market thus enthroned in the middle becomes a remorseless and authoritarian universal."[68] In other words, by renouncing the domain of the universal, he has ended up by reinstating it. But it is a universal that embodies—rather than confronts—the capitalism from which our other thinkers seek liberation.

66. Cupitt, *Time Being*, 78, 79.
67. Ibid., 79.
68. Rose, *Judaism and Modernity*, 47.

Part III: The Political

It seems that any explicit attempt to do without a universal will always end up by unwittingly reinstating one after all. The thinking here seems reminiscent of that of Badiou, as discussed earlier in the chapter, when he said that the contemporary valorization of particulars ends up by unwittingly promoting a universality of particulars, such that universalism has not in fact been escaped. Again, we see the same kind of point being made by Milbank when, against Lyotard, he insists that it is illusory to suppose that we can dispense with metanarratives. Even Lyotard's attempt to dispose of them entails the performative instalment of yet another. In which case, the question before us is not whether to adopt a universal, but which one. If we refuse to answer this question, we will discover that it will be answered for us, as we find ourselves subject to the "remorseless and authoritarian universal" of the market.

So it would seem that without explicit recourse to a universal perspective, the resources for any effective resistance to contemporary capitalism will always prove elusive. Indeed, our discussion of the respective projects of Critchley and Hardt and Negri in this chapter indirectly confirms this line of analysis. Certainly, none of these thinkers repudiates the domain of the universal in as unequivocal a way as does Cupitt, and none of these thinkers is happy to embrace contemporary capitalism in quite the way that he does. Nonetheless, what we have observed is that all of them do at the very least subordinate the domain of the universal, and locate the activity of political resistance on the planes of the particular and/or the singular. And we have seen that the result of their so doing is to blunt the edges of their swords of resistance. Without it, a certain passivity seems inevitably to result, and the political itself becomes endangered. If political thought is to be adequate to the task of effective resistance, it seems, the domain of the universal is unavoidable.

5

VIOLENCE

We have seen some of the difficulties that ensue when the political is approached, thought, and enacted by means of an ultimate prioritizing of the domains of the particular or the singular over that of the universal. We identified some of the most prominent voices in recent political thought who have been espousing precisely such an elevation of particularity or singularity. But theirs are by no means the only voices in current political theory. On the contrary, there have been others who have been advocating precisely the opposite approach, namely, a political prioritizing of the domain of the universal. Most prominent among them have been the voices of Alain Badiou, Slavoj Žižek, and John Milbank. For all the substantial differences between their respective projects, it would not be misleading to understand all three as advocating the primacy of the domain of the universal in political thought and practice, and as protesting against what they perceive to be the contrary and fatal elevation of particularity in contemporary postmodern philosophy and culture. Indeed, they see a deadly complicity between this philosophy and culture and contemporary global capitalism, a complicity first discerned by Fredric Jameson and David Harvey some decades ago. In the contemporary context, therefore, to propose an understanding of the political that locates it precisely in the *tension* between the universal, the particular, and the singular is to set oneself against a voluble tendency that seeks to assert the unequivocal *primacy* of the domain of the universal. The urgent task for any such proposal, therefore, is to address this assertion. In what follows I shall interrogate what it means in political terms to prioritize the universal in this way. I shall question whether the political is best understood in terms of the dominance of the universal and question the desirability of the understanding of the political that emerges.

Part III: The Political

The Universal and Violence

In order to understand the current resurgence of universalism in political theory, it is necessary to see the way in which the phenomenon is fundamentally reactive. Most obviously, of course, it is reacting against the global sovereignty of capitalism and the ways in which this sovereignty has infiltrated so many spheres of life—cultural, ethical, philosophical, and so forth. In the introduction to the English translation of *Being and Event*, Badiou specifies the context within which and against which he was writing. On the one hand, there was the universal sway of what he terms "capitalo-parliamentarianism"—the alliance between the unquestioned sovereignty of the market and parliamentary "democracy," with the latter increasingly coming to work within and as a handmaid of this global market system. On the other hand,

> one had the widespread presence of relativism. Declarations were made to the effect that all cultures were of the same value, that all communities generated values, that every production of the imaginary was art, that all sexual practices were forms of love, etc. In short, the context combined the violent dogmatism of mercantile "democracy" with a thoroughgoing scepticism which reduced the effects of truth to particular anthropological operations. Consequently, philosophy was reduced to being either a laborious justification of the universal character of democratic values, or a linguistic sophistry legitimating the right to cultural difference against any universalist pretension on the part of truths.[1]

It is this latter rendering of philosophy against which Badiou, Žižek, and Milbank are reacting. This is what might broadly be described as "postmodern" philosophy, which, for our current thinkers, induced political paralysis, the kind of paralysis we exposed in the last chapter. This was not only because philosophy and politics were being deprived of the means of effective intervention, but also because the logic of the valorizing of particularity fed into and supported the very thing that was thought most needed to be resisted, namely, the "universal" logic of global capitalism. This is brought out clearly when Badiou says that the unifying factor behind the extolling of communitarian partciularisms is "monetary abstraction, whose false universality has absolutely no difficulty accommodating the kaleidoscope of communitarianisms. . . . The senescent collapse of the USSR . . . unleashed empty abstraction, debased thought in general. And it is certainly not by

---

1. Badiou, *Being and Event*, xii.

renouncing the concrete universality of truths in order to affirm the rights of 'minorities,' be they racial, religious, national, or sexual, that the devastation will be slowed down."[2] Indeed, this well articulates the motives lying behind the recently prominent return of universalism in philosophy, critical theory, and theology.

But perhaps the crux point at issue between the postmodern sensibility in ethics and politics and that represented by Badiou and Žižek in particular is located in the question of *violence*. It is in the name of "overcoming" violence that postmodernism undertakes its deconstruction of universals, while Badiou and Žižek frankly accept the necessary connection between universalism and violence. Both have made a plea for the inauguration and enactment of violence as being of the essence of the political. (The theologian Milbank, of course, dissents from his atheist colleagues Badiou and Žižek at this point, while avoiding the illusion that one can renounce violence *tout court*.) But there is a great deal at stake here, and the question of violence is one that is worthy of extended discussion. Furthermore, there is often a great deal of obfuscation in evidence in discussions around this point. What sort of violence is being invoked here? What violence might be thought necessary and what might be thought evil? Is violence the route to (political) salvation or can it only be a road leading to perdition?

In his book *Violence* (2008), Žižek argued that the mantra of contemporary society is to "oppose violence," underscored by the conviction that there is no such thing as "good" or "necessary" or "unavoidable" violence.[3] Žižek cites a text written by Jean-Marie Muller for UNESCO as exemplifing this outlook. Muller says that "it is essential to define violence in such a way that it cannot be qualified as 'good.' The moment we claim to be able to distinguish 'good' violence from 'bad,' we lose the proper use of the word and get into a muddle. Above all, as soon as we claim to be developing criteria by which to define a supposedly 'good' violence, each of us will find it easy to make use of these in order to justify our own acts of violence."[4] But for Žižek, this is too easy. For one thing, it fails to distinguish empirically between different types of violence, some of which are inescapable features of life itself. To repudiate violence *as such* is simply not possible.

For one thing, it might be said that violence is intrinsic to language as such: "What if . . . humans exceed animals in their capacity for violence precisely because they *speak*. As Hegel was already well aware, there is something violent in the very symbolisation of a thing, which equals its

---

2. Badiou, *Saint Paul*, 6–7.

3. Žižek, *Violence*, 9.

4. Quoted in ibid., 53.

mortification. This violence operates at multiple levels. Language simplifies the designated thing, reducing it to a single feature. It dismembers the thing, destroying its organic unity, treating its parts and properties as autonomous. It inserts the thing into a field of meaning which is ultimately external to it."[5] Gillian Rose has further drawn our attention to the way in which to be human is always to be caught up in violence in some sense. Even acts of peace and love are complicit with violent outcomes in ways that we often cannot immediately perceive or foresee. As she says, "'violence' cannot be isolated without being posited as the lowest common denominator of action, whether good or bad; while if, on the contrary, it is presupposed, there is no need to theorize it as such. All isolating of 'violence' is therefore suspicious unless the ethical is suspended and its historical and legal precondition recognized."[6] Her criticisms of thinkers often revolve around the various ways in which their thought attempts to cover over or ignore this fact—what she describes as attempts to "mend" the broken middle. These are false idealizations that fail to deal with life in its concrete reality. Thought that remains true to this reality must frankly accept and tarry with this necessarily inescapable violence.

At another level, Žižek says that the "blanket" repudiation of violence obscures the critical fact that there are different *types* of violence, and ignoring this fact can only exacerbate the most malignant violence. In particular, he makes a distinction between *subjective violence* (visible acts of violence perpetrated by subjects) and *systemic violence* (less immediately visible, intrinsic to a system, economic, political and/or cultural). Of the latter, he says, "We're talking here of the violence inherent in a system: not only direct physical violence, but also the more subtle forms of coercion that sustain relations of domination and exploitation, including the threat of violence. . . . Is there not something suspicious, indeed symptomatic, about this focus of subjective violence—that violence which is enacted by social agents, evil individuals, disciplined repressive apparatuses, fanatical crowds? Doesn't it desperately try to distract our attention from the true locus of trouble, by obliterating from view other forms of violence and thus actively participating in them?"[7] This is the problem with the contemporary outlook. The forgetting of the difference between types of violence means that all efforts are devoted to the combating of subjective violence (which is understood simply as "violence") while systemic violence is rendered almost invisible, with the result that the violence perpetrated is all the greater. Milbank seems to

---

5. Žižek, *Violence*, 52.
6. Rose, *Broken Middle*, 152.
7. Žižek, *Violence*, 8–9.

agree in this respect when he says that "looking at violence is actually *more violent* than participating in violence—that to be violent *is* actually to survey in a detached, uninvolved fashion a scene of suffering; the *most* violence lies in an occulted violence."[8] This is why, for both Žižek and Milbank, violence may be *required*. For simply to renounce violence, thus passively accepting what is, may involve colluding with the perpetuation of a systemic violence, which could be seen as the most malignant form of violence possible.

If this is so, then there are clearly all sorts of violence—benign, malign, unavoidable, necessary, and perhaps even transcendental. But if a "blanket" rejection of all violence is both impossible and dangerous, so too would be a "blanket" acceptance of it. Sensitivity to the fact that violence manifests itself in heterogeneous forms heightens the question of what may be a necessary violence that must be taken up, as opposed to a malignant violence that must be combated. How, ultimately, is one to discriminate? This is related to a question that is particularly pertinent for our purposes, namely, the question of the extent to which unacceptable or malign violence is a necessary symptom of the imposition of universals. Are universals, precisely by virtue of the fact that they are universals, intrinsically and malignantly violent? Is it the case that only certain kinds of universals carry violence in their wake, or is *every* universal, by virtue of the fact that it is universal, intrinsically violent? In other words, does universalism have malignant violence inscribed into the very heart of its structure?

To raise this question is, of course, to confront Badiou and Žižek's real target—postmodern philosophy. In its assertions that every universal is violent, that every doctrine is dogmatic, postmodernism expresses the conviction that universalism is *structurally* violent, regardless of its particular content. Thus, every universal must be undercut by the particular, whether this means that it must be deconstructed (Derrida) or exposed to the vulnerability of the Face (Levinas). This sensibility has been well expressed in a distinctively Levinasian manner—and in relation to Badiou's work in particular—by Regina Schwarz. It is clear that her primary objection to Badiou's unequivocal prioritizing of the universal is the inevitable violence and totalitarianism that this entails. As she says, "Badiou, seeing Paul as exemplary in his community building by conversion, is willing to run the attendant risks of totalitarianism and fundamentalism. Levinas, fearing totality with its connotations of intolerance and fascism, would be faithful to Revelation without any attempt to convert others."[9] Schwarz says that this does not mean that Levinas displays an indifference to truth; neither does

8. Milbank, *Being Reconciled*, 28.
9. Schwarz, "Revelation and Revolution," 106.

Part III: The Political

he embrace any notion of private truth. Rather, he espouses "a universal in which each person acts in accord with their apprehension of a revelation, a revelation of responsibility—not of resurrection. In Badiou, being faithful to the Truth-Event requires speaking that truth, persuading others of that truth, organizing it politically—only then is it universal. For Levinas, the universal truth of revelation issues in a completely different regard for the other: he is not the object of persuasion, he is the one for whom I am responsible."[10]

Badiou would not dispute that this is indeed the logical outcome of his position; indeed, he explicitly endorses it. The politics of the "event" presupposes a universalism that cuts across and overturns all particularities and, as such, is intrinsically violent. This must frankly be accepted. Furthermore, its status as a universal means that it is not simply true *for me*, but universally, *for all*. One thus has a duty to implement it, to carry it out, put it into effect, and so forth. This is the procedure that constitutes the militant political subject. This is the work of conversion, of bearing witness to this truth. Badiou expresses this as follows:

> every universal singularity is presented as the network of consequences entailed by an evental decision. What is universal always takes the form $\varepsilon \to \pi$, where ε is the evental statement and π is a consequence or a fidelity. It goes without saying that if someone refuses the decision about ε, or insists, in reactive fashion, in reducing ε to its undecidable status, or maintains that what has taken on a valence should remain without valence, then the implicative form in no way enjoins them to accept the validity of the consequence, π. Nevertheless, even they will have to admit the universality of the form of implication as such.[11]

To this extent, Badiou is surely correct. If the domain of the universal is to be intelligible *as* universal, this must surely mean fidelity to its truth and a commitment to its dissemination, and thus must entail speaking, persuading, organizing, and converting.

Are such commitments and such activities *violent*? Surely they are not intrinsically so, or at least, they are not unacceptably so. For is not such speaking, persuading, organizing, and converting going on every day on the part of politicians, journalists, academics, and, indeed, in the conversations of everyday life? Paradoxically, in our current world, perhaps the only groups who are not permitted to undertake such conversion activities are religious communities themselves. Meanwhile, the evangelists for free

---

10. Ibid.
11. Badiou in Badiou and Žižek, *Philosophy in the Present*, 39–40.

Violence

market capitalism have engaged in missionary activity with zeal and with conspicuous success. People seek to persuade and convert because they are convinced that the values they hold and the truths to which they are committed have a validity beyond themselves, because they believe them to be, in precisely this sense, universal. Indeed, it is difficult to see how politics would proceed without such a conception of a universal and its accompanying activities of persuasion and conversion—whether at the mundane level operating within current norms and practices or whether operating toward a revolutionary horizon that seeks quite other norms and practices. But there is surely nothing intrinsically—or unacceptably—violent about such acts. Of course, they have the potential to become coercive, and it is at this point that they might be thought to become *unacceptably* violent. To speak of coercion here, however, is perhaps to approach the nub of the issue because it is the potentially *coercive* character of such persuasion and conversion toward which reservations are often being expressed. Schwarz does not sufficiently distinguish here between what we might think of as legitimate acts of persuasion and conversion on the one hand and unacceptably coercive ones on the other. Indeed, the fact that she does not do so reveals the extent to which she—along with the mainstream of postmodern philosophy—believes such activity to be *intrinsically* coercive and unacceptably violent.

Clearly, such persuasion and conversion activities have within them the potential to become coercive. The much discussed policy of Augustine toward heretics encapsulated in his exhortation to "constrain them to come in" bears witness to this. But this latent coercion will only become manifest, I suggest, if the domain of the universal is given unequivocal priority over the domains of the particular and the singular. It is the mutual interplay of the universal, the particular, and the singular that allows for a politically fruitful commitment to a universal while at the same time preventing this universal commitment from becoming coercive. This interplay or mutual qualification can be seen to be manifested at a theoretical and at a phenomenological level.

First, at the theoretical level, it is important to acknowledge that we never have access to a universal without its mediation through a particular. In this sense, every universal is contaminated by a particular. Indeed, Žižek has well brought out this point. In doing so, he claims that it is important to note that this acknowledgment does *not* entail the relativist notion that every universal is *really* just a mask for a particularity—that every universal is, at base, reducible to a particularity. This would be to acknowledge the unequivocal sovereignty of the particular. But, he says, it is important to

Part III: The Political

recognize that the All of universality is always sustained by a One, and he says that an exemplary case of this

> is provided by a quick glance at any manual of philosophy. Every universal, all-encompassing notion of philosophy is rooted in a particular philosophy. There is no neutral notion of philosophy to be divided into analytical philosophy, hermeneutic philosophy, etc.; every particular philosophy encompasses itself and (its view on) all other philosophies. Or, as Hegel put it in his *Lessons on the History of Philosophy*, every epochal philosophy is in a way the whole of philosophy, it is not a subdivision of the whole but this whole itself apprehended in a specific modality. What we have here is thus not a simple reduction of the universal to the particular, but rather a kind of *surplus* of the Universal. No single universal encompasses all particular content, since each particular has *its own* universal, that is, it contains a specific perspective on the entire field.[12]

Žižek goes on to point out, as we did at the end of the last chapter, that every attempt to dispense with universality is illusory, since some reference to universality is inherent to speech as such. Indeed, we might say that this insight is displayed in the often discussed and alleged incoherence of any strictly relativistic philosophy. In making the claim that "all is relative" one is thereby making a (universal) claim that is itself exempt from the relativism that is being ascribed to everything else. In this sense, the dimension of the universal is unavoidable no matter how much one may seek to avoid it. But if unavoidable, it is also impossible, at least in a purely unequivocal sense, that is to say, in a way that is uncontaminated by the stain of particularity. Thus, Žižek goes on to say that "the thing to do is not to claim or openly admit that we only speak from our particular position (this association already involves a view of totality within which our particular position is located), but to admit the irreducible plurality of the universals themselves. The discord is already at the level of the universal, so that the only true self-restraint is to admit the particularity of one's own universal."[13] What this recognition does, I suggest, is to inject a certain degree of *restraint* or equivocation into what Schwarz characterizes as the missionary imperative intrinsic to every universal perspective. In other words, the domain of particularity emerges to guard against a violent impulse that might otherwise overtake a universalism without reserve. This is not to suggest, of course, that particularity will *always* take precedence over the universal. As we have said before, this

12. Žižek, "Selfhood as Such Is Spirit," 28–29 n. 27.
13. Ibid.

relationship is a dynamic and always changing one. The important point at issue here is that such judgments must be made interminably and cannot be settled once and for all.

Second, this theoretical observation may also be made phenomenologically. While the universal missionary imperative may seek to impose itself, may seek to use violence to do so and may ultimately resort to the destruction and thus killing of the other, it is the domain of the particular—along the lines of the appearance of the Face in a Levinasian sense—that may call such violent destruction into question. Such persuasion and conversion must be tempered by the stubborn particularity embodied by the neighbor before me. Indeed, without this, we could not meaningfully speak of persuasion or conversion at all. What Schwarz does not perhaps sufficiently credit is that the persuasion and conversion that she fears is in fact only intelligible in terms of an "other" that initially resists these attempts, but that gradually (noncoercively) comes to see (or not see) the persuasiveness of the universal vision that is being commended. For the notions of persuasion and conversion to be intelligible, they require the consent of the one who is being persuaded and converted. Without such consent, we would no longer be talking of persuasion and conversion at all. Milbank seems to agree when he says that Christianity, for example, "certainly requires in the end *free consent* to the truth." But, he continues, "it does not fetishize this freedom merely as a correct mode of approach: truth is what most matters, and moreover a *collective* commitment to the truth, since truth itself is the shareable and the harmonious. Thus in certain circumstances, the young, the deluded, those relatively lacking in vision require to be coerced as gently as possible."[14]

Milbank is right to draw attention here to a certain tension or equivocation between conversion and consent. The domain of the universal demands conversion, while that of the particular demands consent. If Milbank is indeed bearing witness to this equivocation, that is well and good. But there are hints that he wishes, a priori, to elevate the domain of the universal ("truth is what most matters," with the result that "gentle coercion" is legitimized), while modern liberalism, in contrast, a priori elevates the domain of the particular—consent, freedom itself. But both are problematic attempts to overcome thoroughgoing equivocation. The tension between the demands of the universal (conversion) and the particular (consent) must be resolved only in singular situations. One can argue thus while also acknowledging that "truth is what most matters." But given that truth is never simply "present" and emerges precisely in the interplay between the universal and the particular, given that every universal truth is "contaminated" by

---

14. Milbank, *Being Reconciled*, 38.

Part III: The Political

particularity, given the unavoidable possibility of error, this equivocation between conversion and consent must repeatedly be negotiated anew. Our fidelity to the universal may well call us to persuade and convert, but our acknowledgment of the necessity of the particular likewise commits us to persuasion and conversion rather than coercion and obliteration of the particular other who is the object of that conversion. What the coherence of the political would seem to depend on is precisely this interplay between the universal and the particular in such a way that neither is a priori privileged over the other.

To what extent, however, is this interplay perpetuated in the thought of Badiou and Žižek, the thinkers to whom Schwarz made her Levinasian plea in favor of particularity? Clearly, they bear witness to a necessary equivocation of the kind I am here commending. But, as we saw in chapter 1, Levinas likewise bears witness to the equivocation of the ethical, but in a way that is penultimate rather than irreducible, and the same may be said of Badiou and Žižek. How close Žižek comes to the kind of equivocation that I am commending may be seen in the passage already quoted in which he emphasizes the stain of particularity that is constitutive of every universal. But for both Badiou and Žižek, it does seem that such equivocation must finally be overcome.

Politics of the Event: Badiou

We have already seen the way in which Žižek bears witness to the "irreducible plurality of the universals themselves." Badiou develops his own way of articulating this insight, as has been pointed out by John Milbank. Badiou's criteria for the emergence of a Truth-Event are entirely procedural, as many have acknowledged. A true event is made true not by its specific content but by the manner of its appearing. As Milbank therefore comments,

> The consequence here would be, as he sometimes seems to imply, that the *only* mark of the true is its break with old systems and invention/discovery of a new mode of operation in art, politics, science, and love (the four categories that he sees as both defining our humanity and as composing in their interrelation the true subject matter of philosophy, as Socrates first realised). In this way, the "universality" of truth-processes would collapse back into anarchic manyness expressing only a nullity, and there would be no way to discriminate between one new eventful

possibility and another (nor indeed did Badiou suggest any such way).[15]

So what seems to be envisaged by Badiou, according to Milbank, is the coexistence of multiple Truth-Events. While they may be incompatible at the level of their content, it is not their content that constitutes them as Truth-Events; it is, rather, the procedure that brings them into being. It is admitted therefore that universals are plural, as was admitted by Žižek, although their respective routes of reaching these conclusions are somewhat different. Milbank goes on to say that "if for Badiou the many different truth-processes are compatible with one another, then it does not seem satisfactory to say, as he does, that the public measure of their legitimacy is merely the noninterference of one process with another. For this lapse into liberalism . . . implies a permanent static appearing of a formal logic of noninterference and clearly demarcated distribution of boundaries of discourse to prevail over the unpredictability of a newly emerging Event, which must surely include the capacity to revise any such boundaries."[16]

How are we to make sense of what is going on here? For one thing, it is important to distinguish between the different "levels" on which Badiou is operating. On the one hand, he is operating at the level of the universal Truth-Event itself. Here we see the universal imperative to convert, to implement the truth in such a way that it is not hindered by the contaminating and disabling trace of particularity. But in his description of the generic procedure of the Truth-Event, Badiou is ascending to a "meta-" level of description that would have been inconceivable to St. Paul and other proselytes for universal truths. For them, there can be no question of any "meta-" level above and beyond their universal truth. But this is, of course, precisely what distinguishes Badiou from other such proselytes. Milbank is perhaps being unduly pejorative in describing this move as an instance of "liberalism," but it has also to be admitted that there is an element of truth in the characterization. This is because by ascending to this "meta-" level and developing his account of the generic procedure of the Truth-Event, Badiou has effectively undercut the *absolute* pretensions of each universal. He must acknowledge (as we have seen Žižek to do) an irreducible plurality of universals and must concede their coexistence. In this sense, the commitment to universals is diluted by a recognition of plurality.

But at the same time, Milbank's characterization might be thought unduly pejorative because we might say that Badiou is here bearing witness to the necessity of equivocation. In other words, we might see his

15. Milbank, "Return of Mediation," 214.
16. Ibid., 215.

Part III: The Political

procedure as being akin to that of Žižek as just discussed. In viewing each universal Truth-Event as a *particular* manifestation of a *universal* generic truth-procedure, Badiou has admitted to the inevitability of the domain of the particular—that every universal is articulated from a *particular* standpoint. As we saw in our discussion of Žižek, this need not lapse back into a postmodern-liberal-relativist assertion that every universal is *merely* a mask for sheer particularity. This is why Milbank's "liberal" characterization is unduly pejorative. For liberalism would want to prioritize unequivocally the domain of particularity; all universals would be *reduced* to particulars. Badiou, on the other hand, might be viewed in this mode as bearing witness to equivocation; that every universal, if not merely a particular, is nonetheless contaminated by particularity. Viewed thus, Badiou might be thought to be articulating a form of the equivocation between the universal, the particular, and the singular that I am arguing is constitutive of the political as such.

But the problem here is that Badiou does not consistently develop this equivocal disposition. On the contrary, he quickly lapses back into the unequivocal assertion of the priority of the universal that does not quite fit with the equivocation that he otherwise exposes. Indeed, in many places in his work he appears to proceed with a forgetfulness of the equivocation he has exposed in his acknowledgment of the existence of multiple universals. This is where Badiou's commitment to coercive violence comes most clearly to the fore, and can be seen particularly in his positive, if also ambivalent, appraisal of Rousseau. The ambivalence may be seen when Badiou says that "what I will argue here is that Rousseau clearly designates the necessity, for any true politics, to articulate itself around a generic (indiscernible) subset of the collective body; but on the other hand, he does not resolve the question of the political procedure itself, because he insists on submitting it to the law of number (to the majority)."[17] As for that aspect of Rousseau's thought that Badiou positively embraces, he expands on this in the passage that follows:

> Rousseau's hostility to parties and factions—and thus to any form of parliamentary representativity—is deduced from the generic character of politics. The major axiom is that "in order to definitely have the expression of the general will, [there must] be no partial society in the State." A "partial society" is characterized by being discernible or separable; as such, it is not faithful to the event-pact. As Rousseau remarks, the original pact is the result of a "unanimous consentment." If there are opponents, they are purely and simply external to the body politic, they are

---

17. Badiou, *Being and Event*, 346.

> "foreigners amongst the Citizens." For the eventual ultra-one evidently cannot take the form of a "majority." Fidelity to the event requires any genuinely political decision to conform to this one-effect; that is, to not be subordinated to the separable and discernible will of a subset of the people. Any subset, even that cemented by the most real of interests, is a-political, given that it can be named in an encyclopaedia. It is a matter of knowledge, and not of truth.[18]

One does not need to be a defender of currently existing parliamentary democracy or what Badiou calls "capitalist-parliamentarianism" to be disturbed by this line of thinking. The logic at work here is clearly totalitarian: particular interests must be wiped away, and those who hold them are "foreigners amongst the citizens"; the general universal will must not be impeded by particularities; dissenting individuals must be incorporated or eliminated. Indeed, it therefore comes as no surprise to find him defending totalitarian political moments, as John Milbank has again pointed out: "According to this [Rousseauian] endorsement, Badiou also defends the French revolutionary terror and the Maoist cultural revolution on behalf of such objective essences (ignoring the questionably 'radical' character of even the aims pursued in both cases)." Milbank refers to this as the "dark side" of Badiou's thought.[19] But this "dark side" emerges as a direct result of Badiou's unequivocal elevation of the domain of the universal and his subordination of the domain of the particular.

If Badiou were to proceed in a way that is consistent with the equivocation that he elsewhere indirectly seems to acknowledge, he would see that the universal toward which he proclaims fidelity is nonetheless proclaimed from a particular standpoint (without this actually destroying its universal status); he would see that the particular neighbor in front of me is not simply an expendable tool to be subordinated to the instantiation of my (particular) universal; he would see this neighbor as potentially resistant to my universal fidelity but also potentially as a subject who may be open to persuasion, to conversion, and also, therefore, potentially a partner in my fidelity to truth. In seeing all of this, he would also see that political change may lie as much in the slow, patient work of persuasion, in the building of consensus, in the conversion of others to my universal cause, and not simply in the imposition of it. Only thus, it might be thought, is genuine political change possible. As Eagleton has commented, "Badiou does not grant the commonplace world enough credence to trust that there may

18. Ibid., 348.
19. Milbank, "Return of Mediation," 236.

be forces immanent within it which are capable of transforming it."[20] To proceed in the way I am suggesting is in no way to capitulate to the unequivocal elevating of particularism that is characteristic of liberal relativist capitalism, and that Badiou rightly condemns. Rather, it is to proceed in the recognition of equivocation, in the negotiation between the necessary and interminable tension between the universal, the particular, and the singular. It is in such negotiation, it might be argued, that the genuinely political is located, whether of the mundane kind operating within current norms and practices, which Badiou despises, or of the kind that works toward the instantiation of new norms and practices. Indeed, it might be said that both kinds of politics stand in need of each other.

It is worth noting at this stage a difference in the respective "solutions" to Badiou's dilemma that Milbank and I are advocating. As has been noted, I agree with Milbank that there is a tension in Badiou's thought between his commitment to the universal logic of a truth procedure and all that that entails on the one hand and his acknowledgment of what I call equivocation and what Milbank calls "liberalism" on the other. But we differ in how we believe this tension is to be overcome. I have been arguing that Badiou should frankly embrace equivocation, whereas Milbank, on the contrary, argues that he should explicitly escape it. As Milbank puts it, "Truly to escape such liberalism, it would seem that Badiou must consider the possibility of a 'meta-truth-process' arising from an Event that is the 'universal of all universals.' He realizes, of course, that Christianity provides just such a possibility but seeks, perhaps incoherently, to confine its Truth-Event to the full emergence of the very idea of a Truth-Event as such, rather than as providing a needed overarching substantive horizon."[21] So for Milbank, when Badiou ascends to the "meta-" level, he should do so in such a way that does not undercut universalism, giving rise to equivocation or, as Milbank sees it, "liberalism," but should, rather, articulate a "universal of all universals," which is, for him, to be found in Christian theology.

But to what extent is this really possible? I have argued elsewhere that when Milbank himself ascends to a "meta-" level beyond the universal level of the Christian metanarrative, he too does so in such a way that seems to put into question the totalizing and universal status of the Christian metanarrative itself. I argued that when Milbank ascends to the level of a "metametanarrative," he actually begins to invoke another kind of narrative that is remarkably complicit with the nihilism that he is otherwise so concerned

---

20. Eagleton, *Trouble with Strangers*, 268.
21. Milbank, "Return of Mediation," 215.

to out-narrate.²² At this "meta-" level, Milbank speaks of many possible versions of truth, each of which is a *mythos*, there being no independent way of adjudicating between them. The only resolution of the differences between them comes when there is a rhetorical victory, when one "persuades" from within one of them that it is "better" or "truer"—that is to say, when one metanarrative "out-narrates" another.²³ In other words, at this "meta-" level, Milbank would seem to perpetuate a version of the very thing for which he criticises Badiou. Whether Christianity (or indeed any other universal metanarrative) could indeed serve the role of a "universal of all universals" in such a way as to halt the proliferation of "meta-meta-" levels and foreclose equivocation is by no means clear. As I have argued before, the process of metanarrative supplementation, by which one "meta-" level is supplemented by another "meta-meta-" level, is interminable. This does not mean that one can do without a metanarrative; on the contrary, Milbank is right to say that it would seem to be unavoidable. But at the same time, the process of supplementation would seem to render a complete, total, and enclosed metanarrative (a "universal of universals") impossible. Hence I suggested that a metanarrative is as impossible as it is unavoidable.²⁴ In the context of this current work, we may view this as bearing witness to the inevitability of equivocation, of the necessary co-presence of the universal with the particular and the singular.

Furthermore, one might also want to question, at the level of *content*, whether Christianity does indeed perceive itself as a "universal of all universals" in the manner that Milbank suggests. Could it not be said that Christianity rules out the possibility of a "universal of universals" precisely because such a standpoint, by definition, belongs to God alone? If Christianity indeed articulates a universal vision, it has to be accepted (as Milbank does in places accept) that this universal is one that is "projected" or articulated from a particular, finite standpoint. The universalism of Christianity is itself contaminated by the particular in this unavoidable way. It is itself caught up in equivocation. But it might be thought that the great virtue of Christianity at its best lies in its recognition of this, in its teaching that the articulation of a "universal of universals" is forever impossible for us as finite beings, because it is a perspective that is the prerogative of God alone. We might also say that Hegel, in his own way, perpetuates this insight in his insistence that the Absolute as such can never be grasped from any finite perspective. He

---

22. See Hyman, *Predicament of Postmodern Theology*, especially ch. 4. See also Milbank's reply in *Theology and Social Theory*, xi–xxxii.

23. See Hyman, *Predicament of Postmodern Theology*, 92.

24. See ibid., 94.

says that each determinate position is "a necessary standpoint assumed by the absolute . . . speculative thinking in the course of its progress finds itself necessarily occupying that standpoint and to that extent the system is perfectly true; but *it is not the highest standpoint.* Yet this does not mean that the system can be regarded as *false*, as requiring and being capable of refutation; on the contrary, the only thing about it to be considered false is its claim to be the highest standpoint."[25] All of which, in turn, is to suggest that the *content* (as opposed to the procedure) of a universal is of more significance than Badiou is willing to credit. These are questions that I shall explore in more depth in the final chapter when I turn more explicitly to theological questions. Finally, however, we must ask about the extent to which Žižek repeats the kind of universalist gesture with its concomitant violence that we have just been discussing in the work of Badiou.

"Bartleby Politics": Žižek

We have already noted that at times Žižek does appear to acknowledge equivocation. We noted this particularly in his acknowledgment of the irreducible plurality of universals and his recognition that every universal cannot avoid being announced from the standpoint of particularity. As any reader of his work will testify, however, such themes appear to be rather subtle and somewhat hidden in relation to the dominant note struck by his work as a whole. Far more predominant and striking are the explicit invocations of the political necessity of violence. He speaks, for instance, of the political need to "smash the Face of the neighbor" and issues pleas for instantiations of ethical violence. As with much else in Žižek's work, one cannot help wondering about the rhetorical character of some of this valorizing of violence. It is by no means always entirely clear what Žižek concretely has in mind when such rhetorical clarion calls are issued. Indeed, one may sympathize with the exasperation expressed by John D. Caputo in this respect when he says, "Žižek has not the slightest impunction about invoking violence and he owes it to his readers to be clear about what he means, how far he would go and under what circumstances."[26] Indeed, such questions often remain elusively unanswered in many of Žižek's texts.

We come close to an answer, however, in his book *The Parallax View* (2006). Here we once again find the explicit invocation of violence, but it is a violence not of terror, killing, and murder, but a violence of passivity, a pure refusal, which, it is argued, is the most effective form of violence in

---

25. Hegel, *Science of Logic*, 580.
26. Caputo, review of *The Monstrosity of Christ*, par. 17.

relation to that which is to be confronted. This, indeed, is what Žižek says he is tempted to call "Bartleby politics":

> perhaps we should assert this attitude of passive aggression as a proper radical political gesture, in contrast to aggressive passivity, the standard "interpassive" mode of our participation in socio-ideological life in which we are all active all the time in order to make sure that nothing will happen, that nothing will really change. In such a constellation, the first truly critical ("aggressive," violent) step is to withdraw into passivity, to refuse to participate—Bartleby's "I would prefer not to" is the necessary first step which, as it were, clears the ground, opens up the place, for true activity, for an act that will actually change the coordinates of the constellation.[27]

In order to clarify what this actually means, Žižek contrasts this approach with the "refusal" of Hardt and Negri, for whom it is a preparatory stage leading to the positive work of constructing a new community, wherein the negative distancing is "overcome" in the subsequent positive building. In contrast, for Žižek, Bartleby's "I would prefer not to" is "a kind of *arche*, the underlying principle that sustains the entire movement: far from 'overcoming' it, the subsequent work of construction, rather, gives body to it."[28] But the second difference from Hardt and Negri's approach is that the Bartleby gesture is not to be reduced, for Žižek, to the attitude of saying "no" to the Empire, but

> first and foremost, to all the wealth of what I have called the *rumspringa* of resistance, all the forms of resistance which help the system to reproduce itself by ensuring our participation in it—today "I would prefer not to" is not primarily "I would prefer not to participate in the market economy, in capitalist competition and profiteering," but—much more problematically for some—"I would prefer not to give to charity to support a Black orphan in Africa, engage in the struggle to prevent oil-drilling in a wildlife swamp, send books to educate our liberal-feminist-spirited women in Afghanistan..."[29]

Thus, as he goes on to say, Bartleby's refusal is not the refusal of a determinate content, but is rather the formal gesture of refusal as such. It is "a signifier reduced to an inert stain that stands for the collapse of the symbolic

---

27. Žižek, *Parallax View*, 342.
28. Ibid., 382.
29. Ibid., 383.

order. . . . There is no violent *quality* in it; the violence pertains to its very immobile, inert, insistent, impassive *being*. Bartleby wouldn't even hurt a fly—that's what makes his presence so unbearable."[30]

So this is a peculiar kind of violence, a violence that "wouldn't hurt a fly," quite different from the violence of revolution, killing, and terror. Or at least, it would *appear* to be quite different. Certainly, for Žižek himself, the merit of this kind of Bartleby violence is certainly not that it is somehow more benign, more constrained, or more delicate. On the contrary, its merit is that this is violence at its purest, the sort of unflinching violence that is needed. Indeed, Žižek agrees with Milbank in one specific respect, namely, that Badiou is prone to fall too far into a "liberal" stance. He points to elements in Badiou's thought that come close to the "antitotalitarian" logic of an endless "to come," which may be seen particularly in his notion that Truth never appears *as such*, that the unnameable Real can never be forced, lest we have an evil terrorist imposition. For Žižek, such a stance does bring Badiou rather close to Levinas.[31] In contrast to this, Žižek would see his own position as more unflinchingly violent, more resolutely universalist and revolutionary. And in this specific respect, we might say that Žižek is right. For the pure refusal of Bartleby politics does seem to embody the logic of revolutionary terror, exemplified in the revolutionary who takes harsh violent measures sustained by love[32] or the Russian revolutionary who has to exercise total discipline over bodily excess, or even the Kantian moralist who must steel himself against the lure presented by human sympathy. What all these stances have in common is, of course, the resolute elevation of the universal over the particular, the deliberate attempt not to be dissuaded from the implementation of the universal by the distracting claim made upon us by the particular. Thus, the claims made upon us of the starving orphan in Africa, the beggar on the street, the victims of the injustice of the economic system are particularist lures to be resisted. Assisting them will detract us from the universal goal of justice; engaging in this *rumspringa* will only perpetuate the given and will thus preclude radical change. As Žižek puts it, "Justice is emphatically *not* justice for—with regard to—the neighbor."[33]

But in this case, what *is* justice for? This whole mode of discourse is, of course, predicated on a fundamental disjunction between the ethical and the political, a disjunction I have already called into question in chapter 3.

30. Ibid., 385.
31. See ibid., 325.
32. See Žižek, "Neighbors and Other Monsters," 186.
33. Ibid., 184.

There, I argued that what was at issue in the debate between Levinas and Žižek was not the disjunction between the ethical and the political, but the disjunction between the particular and the universal. There *is* a disjunction between these last two, but the mistake lies in attempting to deal with this by prioritizing one of them over the other. And here, in Žižek's Bartleby violence and his explicit setting himself against the claims of particular neighbors upon him and us, we see clearly what is at stake in such a priori prioritizing of the universal. Justice, I should argue, is precisely *for*—with regard to—the neighbor. There *is* a continuity here. Is it not the starving orphan in Africa or the beggar on the street who awakens in us the desire for a universal justice, a justice that, if fully achieved, would mean that my neighbor would not need to suffer in this way? This is to return us to the phenomenology of the primordial "origin" of the ethical-political that I sketched out in chapter 3. The particular Face of the neighbor makes its claim upon us *because* of the background multitude out of which it emerges. Our concern for justice for this multitude makes its claim upon us *because* of the responsibility that we feel toward the Face of the neighbor before us. And if this is so, might one not help a neighbor in need *and* at the same time engage in wider political acts (or non-acts) that would be aimed at a justice that would alleviate my neighbor's need in future?

Of course, there is no *easy* continuity here. The universal and the particular are in tension; that, I have been arguing, is of the essence of both the ethical and the political. But if they are in tension, they are not opposed and incommensurable; they are, on the contrary, mutually implicated. Insofar as Žižek bears witness to this tension, he is bearing witness to certain political truths. For instance, he is right to warn that a constant attention to the *particular* demands of the neighbor at the expense of the forgetting of the universal demands of justice will ultimately be dangerous and politically self-destructive. There is something amiss in all our efforts devoted to fending off subjective violence while rendering systemic violence invisible, to feeding the hungry and clothing the naked while forgetting to challenge those very conditions that actually cause people to be hungry and naked in the first place. Indeed, there is a sense in which exclusive attention to feeding the hungry and clothing the naked will perpetuate that hunger and nakedness unless due attention is given to the domain of universal justice. Insofar as he draws attention to this danger, Žižek is bearing witness to a true insight. He sees this danger being perpetuated in much postmodern philosophy and in Levinas in particular, and no doubt he is right to make these charges. But the response to this danger certainly should not be to turn from one imbalance to another, to turn from exclusive preoccupation with the particular to an exclusive preoccupation with the universal.

Part III: The Political

There is a second way in which Žižek may be seen as bearing witness to certain political truths. Although I have suggested that there is a *continuity* between the universal and the particular and an accompanying imperative to pursue *both* the universal and the particular, this suggestion must be set in the context of a wider tension between them, which I have also been attempting to illuminate. For the fact is that in singular situations and circumstances, there will inevitably be a *conflict* between responding to the call of the universal and the particular that can only be solved by a judgment for one or the other. In this sense, Žižek is right to draw attention to a certain conflict between them—that a judgment for one will entail the sacrifice of the other. Such examples may most obviously be thought *in extremis*. Thus, a soldier or a revolutionary fighting for a just cause or against a manifest evil may well find himself in the position of having to kill his neighbor, thereby making a singular judgment in favor of the universal call of justice and against the call of this particular neighbor's Face. A mother, in war or in the midst of some other catastrophe, may find herself making a judgment to save her child even though this may mean contravening the laws of universal justice, perhaps meaning the sacrifice of other children. She would thus be making a singular judgment in favor of the particular call of her child and against the universal call of justice. In these cases, a sacrifice is involved, whereby a judgment in favor of the universal entails sacrificing the particular and vice versa. But these judgments are made in singular instances, without thereby extrapolating from them that such a judgment would always and everywhere be made regardless of the circumstances.

Furthermore, each judgment entails the recognition of tragedy, of the neglect of that domain that is being sacrificed. Thus, the solider or revolutionary who kills an enemy combatant does not do so lightly but in full acknowledgment of the tragedy involved in killing his neighbor and of the necessary sacrifice that is here entailed. So too the mother who saves her child may be tormented by the tragedy involved in the sacrifice of others who may have been neglected. Such judgments may be made in faith and hope that they were right, but also with an awareness that such judgments always involve risk because of the tragic overriding of the neglected domain. To make a judgment *for* one domain while being aware that this tragically entails the *neglect* of the other domain is to acknowledge *both* that such a judgment must be made, is unavoidable, *and* that both the prioritized domain *and* the suspended one simultaneously make an ethical and political call upon us. Such decisions and actions are always perilous and uncertain and are made with no guarantees. This is what it means to be constantly negotiating the tension between the universal, the particular, and the singular. But what must not be done is to attempt to deal with this tension by

Violence

elevating as a matter of principle and in advance of all circumstances one domain over the others. This is what Žižek clearly attempts to do, and we have seen the kind of inhuman denial of finitude that it entails.

That the kind of elevating of universal violence advocated by Žižek entails a denial of human finitude cannot be doubted. We have already observed in an earlier chapter John Milbank's riposte to those Kantians who would argue against the "arbitrary" privileging of our nearest and dearest in the case of a natural catastrophe. Suppose that the nearest and dearest survive in spite of our "piously neutral" refusal to privilege them. Milbank's rhetorical question is, how would they regard us as human beings, as fellow members of a finite and fragile human community? Žižek's political stance seems to abstract us from our position as finite human beings who are both called to love and assist our neighbors and, simultaneously, who stand in need of the love and assistance of our neighbors. Insofar as we are called to be political agents, political change should be sought in such a way that is true to this situatedness and not in a way that repudiates it. In this sense, there is perhaps more truth than Žižek would credit in his comment that "in their love/hatred, revolutionaries are pushed beyond the limitations of empirical 'human nature,' so that their violence is literally *angelic*. Therein resides the core of *revolutionary justice*, this much misused term: harshness of the measures taken, sustained by love."[34] Indeed, Žižek's stance appears to demand that human beings vacate their finite situated status and become instead angelic beings, exiled from the world of particularity, seeking to inaugurate change from a position of transcendent universal purity, a position that is ultimately impossible and unsustainable for human beings in a finite and broken world.

This leads us to probe further the extent to which Žižek's political stance is even logically conceivable. Let us recall again the radical refusals of Bartleby, the refusals of all aspects of what Žižek calls the *rumspringa*, the local political interventions that serve only to sustain the global system. Do something for the environmental cause for ecology? I prefer not to. Do something to overturn racial and sexual injustices? I prefer nor to. Do something to help a starving orphan in Africa? I prefer not to. The problem with this is that it is difficult, if not impossible, to know where to draw the line. The sphere of *rumspringa* is not a clearly defined and identifiable area of activity. Almost every sphere of life is implicated and bound up with the global status quo, the revolutionary overturning of which is being sought. That being so, it is difficult to imagine where the Bartleby revolutionary would stand other than in some imaginary angelic no-man's-land. If *every*

---

34. Ibid., 186.

aspect of our contemporary situation—which is ultimately to say every aspect of life—is met with the radical refusal of Bartleby, with the relentless repetition of "I prefer not to," what space is left to inhabit? It leads us to be not only "suicidally marginal" (to use Žižek's own phrase against him), but seems also to push us out of and beyond the marginal into the suicidal abyss. And when this happens, is one then not abandoned to pure impotence? Are we then not in a position of reinforcing that which Žižek most fears, namely, a state where nothing changes and everything remains the same?

Undoubtedly, a political concern with particularity alone may well lead to that, as we have already conceded that Žižek is right to warn against. But if the logical outcome of Žižek's stance is this kind of suicidally marginal state, will we not likewise have changed nothing and—what is worse—in the meantime, cut ourselves off from the practical call of our neighbors, cut ourselves off from one of the determining features of human solidarity? Furthermore, in unwittingly promoting this suicidal abyss, does not Žižek provide a mirror image of the suicidal negation we observed in Kantian-Levinasian ethics? Whereas we saw Levinas's emphasis on singularity to entail the individual's responsibility for all to the point of a suicidal self-negation, Žižek insists that our responsibility to the universal lies in a commitment to the Nothing (the violent politics of absolute refusal), but again to the point of a suicidal nothingness. Both, I suggest, are led to this juncture from opposite ends, but from their common refusal to dwell within the brokenness of the middle.

To dwell within the brokenness of the middle is to acknowledge the interminable interplay—and tension—between the universal, the particular, and the singular. In explicitly political terms, and to return to the structures with which we began our discussion in the last chapter, it means operating politically within the tension between norms and practices, seeking neither to impose norms upon practices nor to abolish norms in favor of practices. Furthermore, and what is more germane to the discussions we have been discussing in this chapter, it will mean operating politically within a tension between *current* norms and practices and *revolutionary other* norms and practices. The true perpetuation of the political will lie within the refusal of the temptation to restrict political activity solely to current norms and practices or to the inauguration of other norms and practices. Political thought and action that is true to human life as it is lived in the broken middle will need to do both these things simultaneously. It will operate within *current* norms and practices in such a way as to constantly bear witness to a universal ethical and political vision, to seek *local* reforms, correct *particular* injustices, in the mundane and corrupt world of the "capitalist representative democracies" of which Badiou and Žižek are so dismissive. As Eagleton has commented, "one needs an ethics appropriate to the orthopaedic hospital and pre-school playgroup, not just to the death camps and barricades."[35] Of course, to seek local reforms and correct particular injustices would be insufficient, would be to risk doing little more than feeding into and furthering the very injustices one is trying to correct. In this sense, political thought and activity must never be *limited* to current norms and practices. The true end of all politics is indeed the overthrow of current norms and practices in favor of new and transformed ones. In this sense, the universal dimension of politics is indeed indispensable. Furthermore, the revolutionary, universal dimension of politics will not necessarily be as *active* as the local, particularist dimension. Žižek is right to point out that sometimes we should *do* less—that we should withdraw, think, read, bear witness. We have seen that the universal dimension of politics does entail commitment to persuasion and conversion. These are as much parts of political activity as attempting to bring about local and material reform. Consequently, politics may be seen as taking place in all sorts of mundane and ostensibly nonpolitical contexts—one engages in such political persuasion and conversion in the mundane practices, interactions, and conversations of everyday life as well as in the more conventional political arenas.

What I am suggesting, therefore, is that if we are to pay true obeisance to the equivocation between the universal, the particular, and the singular, we must refuse every false choice between local, particular political action within the domain of the given and universal projective political thought and action within the domain of the infinite. We must both help the starving orphan in Africa and seek a fairer taxation and welfare system and *at the same time* work toward and hope for the overthrow of global capitalism as such. To do only one or the other will ultimately usher in the end of politics, which it may well be argued is what we are indeed seeing today. In the former case, it will lead to the apolitical conclusion that nothing will ever change (the situation definitive of most Western democracies), while in the latter case, it will lead to an apolitical disengagement in favor of pure totalitarian violence or suicidal marginalization (the kind of reactive positions embodied in Badiou and Žižek). In the image of David Wood, the political thinker and activist must conceive of himself as operating with binocular vision, thinking and acting in both registers at once.[36] Of course, we have also noted that there *is* a conflict between these two registers. In singular situations and circumstances, one must constantly be making judgments and decisions *between* these two realms. These involve difficult decisions

35. Eagleton, *Trouble with Strangers*, 298.
36. Wood, *Step Back*, 193.

that involve outcomes that can never be guaranteed. When might my intervention within the conventional political realm be serving as an obstacle to wider political change? When might my activities (or nonactivity) on behalf of transformed political norms and practices be exacerbating suffering and injustices in the here and now? Such decisions make the political process of discernment interminable. But whatever the difficulties and risks in these judgments, what must at all costs be avoided is the ending of them by the unequivocal and *a priori* elevation of the universal or the political. Therein lies the end of politics.

One way of summarizing all this is to say that the political lies in the pursuit of both justice and mercy. Neither must be lost from view, even if, in singular situations, we make a necessary judgment to prioritize one or the other. For all their acknowledgment of equivocation which I have done my best to acknowledge in turn, we have nonetheless seen the ways in which Levinas ultimately wishes to prioritize mercy over justice, while Badiou and Žižek ultimately wish to prize justice over mercy. But both, I have been arguing, are politically (and ethically) destructive. Beyond these contemporary voices, we should heed a more antique wisdom. In the British coronation service, the archbishop of Canterbury exhorts the newly anointed sovereign thus: "Be so merciful that you be not too remiss; so execute justice that you forget not mercy."

Part IV
THE RELIGIOUS

6

FAITH

The Ethical and Political and the Return of Religion

At last we arrive at an explicit discussion of what has been present, albeit only implicitly, throughout this study, namely, the religious or the theological. In the preceding chapters, we have been interrogating the ethical and political not on the basis of any specified theological foundation, but simply in terms of some of the most important recent debates on the nature of the ethical and political as such. In the process of so doing, I have argued that the ethical and political, far from being logically incommensurable, as we have seen some prominent voices to have argued, are in fact continuous; they are the same thing looked at from different angles. More specifically, both are constituted by an interplay between the domains of the universal, the particular, and the singular, wherein the omnipresent temptation is to resolve the tensions between these domains by elevating one of them over the other two. The practical outcome of succumbing to this temptation, I have argued, is the ultimate dissolution of the ethical and political themselves. In order to preserve the ethical and political as such, this tension and negotiation between the universal, the particular, and the singular must be perpetuated, and the labor involved in this negotiation must be constantly enacted and reenacted as an ever-present task.

In many ways, however, such an account remains incomplete and, in particular, it remains unduly abstract, formulaic, and structural. As we observed at the end of chapter 2, there is a certain sense in which this is inevitable, given the nature of the analysis being propounded. But one aspect that does require more discussion is the question of the nature or *content* of the universal that we have seen to be both ethically and politically

Part IV: The Religious

indispensable. What sort of universal is here being invoked? Does our discussion of the nature of the ethical and political demand the invocation of a specific kind of universal? Does the character of the ethical and political demand not only the particular structural form I have been outlining, but also that this form be filled by a certain specifiable kind of content? Clearly, what is being sought here is not *any* universal, for our preceding discussions have indicated not only the ethical and political necessity of a universal but also what kinds of universals are to be avoided. In particular, we have seen that those universals that seem internally to demand an a priori subordination of the domains of the particular and the singular ultimately become ethically and politically self-destructive. Indeed, we have observed two specific ways in which universalism in ethics and politics can become problematic.

The first was a Kantian universalism, and we might venture to suggest that the problems intrinsic to this might also be intrinsic to "rational" moral theories more generally. We saw the way in which Kant relentlessly subordinated the domains of the particular and the singular to the sovereign demand of the universal, and we explicated all the difficulties that this entailed. But what was it that impelled this assertion of the sovereignty of the universal? One answer might be that Kantian ethics (and indeed other kinds of "rational" moral theories) are substantively *empty* at the level of their content. It is important to recall in this respect that, for Kant, the moral law cannot be articulated or specified as such; rather, it is something that has to be deduced procedurally. What is precluded is a positive and substantive articulation of the Good in itself. For Kant, the good is that which is produced as the outcome of a rational procedure. As he puts it, "the concept of good and evil is not defined prior to the moral law, to which, it would seem, the former would have to serve as foundation; rather the concept of good and evil must be defined after and by means of the law."[1] Furthermore, he explicitly contrasts this with what he considers the "error of the ancients" in "devoting their ethical investigation entirely to the definition of the concept of the highest good" and thus positing "an object which they intended subsequently to make the determining ground of the will in the moral law. But only much later, when the moral law has been established by itself and justified as the direct determining ground of the will, can this object be presented to the will whose form now is determined a priori."[2] Thus, the good can only be given content procedurally (rationally), not substantively. In which case, rather than a substantive *content* (e.g., love) taking a universal *form*, the universal *form* must itself become the *content*. This is most clearly

---

1. Kant, *Critique of Practical Reason*, 65.
2. Ibid., 67.

seen when Kant insists that a moral action is not that which is in accord with a prior concept of the Good, but rather that which, as an imperative, could be universalized. That is to say, the content of the good is constituted precisely by the formal structure of the universal itself; universal form and substantive content are collapsed into each other.

There is a great deal at stake in this reversal. For where the form and content of the universal are distinct (that is to say, where the universal is deemed to be such by its content rather than by the mere fact of its universalism), it is possible for the universal form to be "suspended" (by means of a dialectical interplay with the particular and the singular) without in any way compromising the sovereignty of the Good at the level of its substantive content. On the other hand, where the form and content of the universal are essentially one (that is to say, where the universal is tautologously deemed to be such by the mere fact of its universal form), the universal can in no way be "suspended" without thereby also compromising the content of the universal itself. It is this, I suggest, that explains why Kant cannot countenance any "suspension" of the universal and therefore why he cannot countenance any compromise, negotiation, or dialectical interplay with the domains of the particular and the singular. This is why, in ethical terms, Kant must rigorously cleanse the universal of the stain of particularity. But it is precisely this imperative, we saw, that lies at the heart of all the problems we identified in chapter 1. When the universal imposes itself without reserve over particularity and singularity, we saw the various ways in which this leads ultimately to the self-destruction of the ethical itself. What is clearly needed, therefore, is a substantive content *by virtue of which* it might be regarded as universal rather than the tautologous version we find exemplified in Kant. In the latter, any kind of negotiation or interplay with the particular or singular becomes impossible without undermining itself as a universal.

The second problematic conception of universalism in ethical and political terms was that identified in the work of Badiou and Žižek. In their work, we saw the assertion of a (non-tautologous) universal content that cuts across the domain of particularity, an unequivocal assertion of sovereignty that we again saw to be ultimately destructive of both the ethical and political. The nature of the relationship of this universal gesture to the Kantian one is ambivalent. On the one hand, it would seem to be markedly different; there is a substantive content to the universal that is something more than the mere fact of its universalism. But on the other hand, there are ways in which these two universalist gestures are indeed more complicit than might initially appear. In some ways, this is most explicit in the case of Badiou. We saw in chapter 5 that what constitutes a Truth-Event for Badiou is the manner of its appearing; the criteria for what counts as a Truth-Event are entirely procedural. We saw that in this particular respect Badiou is indifferent to the specific content of such an event.

Although Žižek's approach is different, it enacts a somewhat analogous move. Although what counts as a universal for Žižek is not a matter of proceduralism in the way that it is for Badiou, it nevertheless seems that the specific content of the universal is less important than the fact that it valorizes the universal as such. In other words, what seems to be most attractive about the Christian legacy for Žižek is precisely its trenchant commitment to universalism. This would seem to bring us perilously close to what I have called the Kantian tautology. In contrast to Kant, there *is* a specifiable content to the universal that is something other than the mere requirement of universalizability. But on the other hand, this specifiable content is embraced *precisely because of* its universal imperative, and it is in this respect that Badiou and Žižek move closer to Kant. It is important to emphasize here the contrast that we saw Kant himself to have drawn between his approach and that of the ancients. Whereas for the ancients there was something intrinsic to the content of the conception or narrative of the Good that led them to reach conclusions about its universal status, for Žižek it is more the fact that the content makes universal claims for itself that makes it authoritative. Thus, in answer to the question of why a particular narrative or content should be regarded as universal, the reply would seem to be "because it claims to embody a universal." When seen in these terms, we begin to see how close Žižek comes to Kant, a proximity we have already noted in somewhat other terms in chapter 3.

In which case, it should not surprise us that Badiou and Žižek lead us to the same practical outcome as did Kant. If it is the very fact of its universalism that commends a particular content to us in ethical and political terms, then it follows that it is precisely that universalism as such that must be perpetuated and enacted. Again, there seems to be no way in which the universal could be "suspended" without compromising the authority of the content itself. In other words, it would again seem to follow that the particular and singular must be subordinated to the universal, which is of course what we observed to occur in the thought of Badiou and Žižek. Likewise, we have also diagnosed why this is so problematic in ethical and political terms. If this is so, then it would seem that the only solution to this specific manifestation of our problem would lie in a return to the methodological procedure of the ancients which Kant was at such pains to deny. If a universal dimension is necessary to the ethical and political in the way we have been suggesting throughout this study, then it would seem that the specific universal invoked must be one that is deemed to be universal on the basis of its intrinsic content, quite apart from any universal claim that it might make for itself. Only when this is so will the "suspension" of the universal be possible, a "suspension" that we have seen to be necessary for the perpetuation of the ethical and political as such. Furthermore, the content would need to be one that would not, in principle, exclude the possibility of such a "suspension." It would be a universal content that would acknowledge the necessity, or at least the possibility, of its own implication and interplay with the particular and the singular. This, in turn, can only come from a substantive content *by virtue of which* the vision is deemed to be universal.

But we have also indirectly identified another way in which the dialectical interplay might be stilled. Albeit in very different ways, we have observed how both Levinas and Žižek precluded the perpetuation of such an interplay through the assumption of a universal or divine task. And both feel impelled to assume such a divine responsibility precisely in the wake of the death of God. In the case of Levinas, we saw that he makes the subject a privileged and centered site that is itself responsible for all others. In spite of all the talk of absolute responsibility and self-denial, there appears to be here an inflation of the subject as that which *alone* bears the burden of ethical responsibility. The subject is constituted by its being called to responsibility for all that which is not itself. The individual ethical subject was seen to bear the weight of the whole world. Eagleton has commented with regard to Levinas here that "universality means being responsible for anyone, not, *per impossible*, for everyone at the same time. To assume that it does, even while insisting on its impossibility, betrays a certain hubris of the infinite, however apologetic and self-castigating in tone."[3] When Eagleton talks here of a "hubris of the infinite," it seems that the human subject is indeed being expected to assume divine responsibilities. Indeed, we might say that this inflation of the self in Levinas's thought is such that it commends a degree of human responsibility that is, in reality, only appropriate to and realizable by God. The particularity, finitude, and limitations of human beings seem to drop from view, and humanity is being expected to love as God loves, namely, indiscriminately, and to exercise responsibility as God exercises it, namely, absolutely on behalf of all, and without reserve. In a sense, of course, this is not surprising, for we also saw that Levinas was writing in the wake of the death of God. After the death of God, it seems that the task of infinite responsibility is one that must now be assumed by human subjects themselves.

In the case of Žižek, we saw that he both converges with and radically diverges from Levinas in this respect. The divergence is found most radically, we noted, in that Žižek regards the face of the other not as issuing a call

---

3. Eagleton, *Trouble with Strangers*, 258.

Part IV: The Religious

to infinite responsibility but as a dangerous political lure to be resisted, one that threatens to blur the universal gesture of justice that would focus on the faceless Thirds. But if this unequivocal commitment to universal justice is a symptom of an undue elevating of the domain of the universal over the domains of the particular and the singular, we may further say that this elevation of the universal is in turn a symptom of the death of God. As we have seen, there is a sense in which, paradoxically, this "elevation" of the universal is necessary precisely because of the "death" of the universal. In other words, it is because God is dead that humans must assume God's role for themselves. The realization of the realm of universal justice should not be thought of as God's prerogative. Rather, it should be realized by humanity in the here and now, a realization that is inseparable from the violence by which it will be brought into effect. On Žižek's atheistic reading of Christianity, "we get a God who abandons [his] transcendent position and throws himself into his own creation, fully engaging himself in it up to dying, so that we, humans, are left with no higher Power watching over us, just with the terrible burden of freedom and responsibility for the fate of divine creation, and thus of God himself."[4] Humanity therefore takes up the divine burden, assuming responsibility for creation and its fate and, ultimately, for God himself.

So in the cases of both Levinas and Žižek, we found that both stilled the necessary interplay between the universal, the particular, and the singular through the elevation of one domain over the other two. Furthermore, this a priori elevation appears for both to be impelled by the death of God, even though the implications of that death are for each of them strikingly different. This difference may be explained by the fact that they each assume different aspects of the divine responsibility. Whereas in Levinas the subject is constituted by the call of responsibility for every singular other that appears before it, so that the subject takes on a divine responsibility for all, in Žižek the subject takes on divine responsibility for the universal task of instantiating justice. So Levinas takes on the task of responsibility for the salvation of each singular face, while Žižek takes on the task of ushering in the City of God here on earth. But both are impelled to assume or commend these tasks in the wake of the death of the God, who might otherwise be trusted to enact them. Can it be, then, that the interplay between the universal, the particular, and the singular—which we have seen to be ethically and politically necessary—is only possible through the invocation of a God who himself demands such an interplay in the "broken" or "fallen" domain of creaturely time?

4. Žižek in Žižek and Milbank, *Monstrosity of Christ*, 254.

Faith

Our discussions of the nature of the ethical and political as such would seem to suggest that this is so. With respect to the ethical, we have seen that ethical judgments are inseparable from the taking of risks. Decisions must repeatedly be made as to when the universal should be "suspended," how the universal should be instantiated in the realm of particularity, how this is to be done in singular instances. But the making of these decisions is always also the taking of a risk, for we never *know* that such decisions are justified. We are always deprived of the God's-eye perspective that would provide us with that guarantee. Transcendentally, it would seem that it is always necessary to invoke such a perspective, if only to remind us that it is a perspective that will always elude us. But the making of these judgments and the taking of these risks would become acts of arbitrary assertion were they not liable to be judged, in turn, from this higher perspective that is both transcendent and transcendental. Our decisions and risks are ethically meaningful to the extent that they are themselves open to a judgment from a perspective that transcends us. It is an awareness of that transcendental judgment that causes such risks to be taken in a spirit of fear and trembling (for we cannot from our perspective *know* what the content of the judgment might be) but also which allows them to be made at all (for equally, the perspective of transcendental judgment alerts us to the unavoidability of such risks). Such risks can only be taken in a spirit of faith and trust; they must be taken in good faith and with discernment, trusting that they are right, but with an awareness that the ultimate judgment is something that is beyond our ken. This perspective of transcendental judgment is something to which we are answerable but which we can never grasp as a substantive "present." The understanding of the ethical as the interplay between the universal, the particular, and the singular is inseparably connected with all of this, for it is the awareness of this transcendental divine perspective that prevents the a priori prioritizing of one domain over the others. When the God's-eye perspective dies, one is impelled to elevate either the universal (as does Žižek) or the singular (as does Levinas), and both in their different ways, as we have seen, betoken a "hubris of the infinite" with ultimately fatal ethical consequences.

In the domain of the political, we have seen something similar. We have seen the way in which we should conceive of the political task as being to represent a prior, shaping political order while simultaneously acknowledging that that order can never straightforwardly be *instantiated*. That is to say, we should never seek to represent or enact the universal in such a way that the particular is obliterated. The universal is always to be represented in the midst of the particular without thereby nullifying the latter. That gap or distance must always be transcendentally acknowledged. Once again, the attempt to unfold or represent the universal in the midst of the particular is the taking of a risk. To engage in the political task is interminably to exist in the domain of risk. Such risk may be avoided by a priori relegating the task of instantiating universal justice in favor of the demands of the neighbor immediately before me. It may also be avoided by a priori resisting the lure presented by the neighbor's face in favor of the revolutionary imperative. But in both cases, the avoidance of risk entails the death of politics. In one case, it gives rise to a passive quietism, while in the other, it gives rise to an inhuman totalitarianism; but in both cases, the political is betrayed. Once again, it seems that the political task must be undertaken at the behest of a transcendental judgment from elsewhere but also in such a way as to be open to judgment from that same perspective. It would seem that both the ethical and political can only be enacted under the gaze (enabling and judging) of the eye of God.

In these senses, it seems that the ethical and political themselves point to the unavoidability of religion. It would seem that the specter of religion or the Spirit of God has been haunting the preceding pages even without explicit theological invocation. In which case the primary purpose of this chapter is less to make new arguments than to make explicit what has been implicitly present in the earlier ones. That implicit argument has been that the great virtue of religion—specifically, in our context, Christianity, but doubtless other religions too—is that it can serve to *enable* the ethical and political through its universal content, its substantive conception of the Good. We have seen that a universal is indispensable for the ethical and political, and that this universal must be not merely procedural but constituted by a substantive content, a vision or *telos*. It is by this authoritative vision and its conception of the Good that the current social and political order—marked as it is by monadic atomism, wilful assertion, relentless acquisition, and shallow materialism—can be judged. As John Milbank has observed, "In the Christian socialist critique there is a distinct confrontation between Christian values and capitalist reality. The critique is seen as possible because of the difference from capitalism represented by Christianity, especially in its past history—the first Christian communities, the monasteries, the medieval towns, the guild associations. By contrast with this standard, capitalism appears as a kind of apostasy—according to John Ruskin, 'the most remarkable instance in history of a nation's establishing a systematic disobedience to the principles of its own religion.'"[5]

At the same time, religion also *prevents* the kind of immediately present instantiation of that Good in a way that obliterates particularity and

---

5. Milbank, *Future of Love*, 113.

thus ultimately destroys the ethical and political. This is because, at its best, it acknowledges that its own status as a universal can only be appropriated and enacted through a thoroughgoing interplay with the domains of the particular and the singular. Christianity's doctrines on the hiddenness of God, the "broken" and "fallen" nature of creation in time, the deferral of the eschaton, and the warnings against human hubris, all serve to guard against the unequivocal imposition of the universal on the particular in a way that would obliterate the latter. The dynamic at work here has been well articulated by Charles Taylor, who traces it back to the kind of political theology that finds its inspiration in Augustine. The universal Good (the City of God) must be represented in the earthly city; the earthly city both mirrors and participates in the heavenly city. It is imperative that this mirroring and participation be made a reality in the domain of the particular. But at the same time, there is a recognition that the earthly city cannot be *equated* with the heavenly city. The earthly city is fallen and corrupt, and it would be dangerous to pretend otherwise.

Taylor points out that Augustine had a strong sense of the gap between the city of God and the earthly city:

> the attempt by the magisterium, seconded by state power, to bring society more in line with the heavenly city would have certainly appeared extremely hazardous to him, at the least. Of course, reforming popes accepted that the fullness of justice, which for Augustine must include giving to God his due, cannot be expected in this world. Sinners will abound until the end. But a regime can be envisaged in which people are subordinated to rule which models itself on full justice. If kingly power really follows the injunctions of those speaking with the authority of God's will (the hierarchy of the Church), then an order can be established in which those truly good will rule, and the bad will be forced to conform.[6]

The universal is both necessary and impossible, an insight at the heart of the ethical and political as such and at the heart of religion at its best.

It must immediately be acknowledged, of course, that, historically, religion has appeared in forms that are far from its best. This is true of Christianity as it is of other religious traditions. There is an ever-present temptation for the religious universal to impose itself in precisely the way that I am suggesting that religion at its best guards against. This has been acknowledged by Rowan Williams when he speaks of the "almost infinite corruptibility of religious discourse. Those who claim to speak in the name

---

6. Taylor, *Secular Age*, 243.

Part IV: The Religious

of God will always be dangerously (exhilaratingly) close to the claim that in their speech, their active presence, the absent God who is never an existent among others is actually present: a claim of stupendous importance in legitimating any bid for power."[7] But, Williams continues, however frequently such religious discourse has developed in this way through history, it should not be forgotten that this is ultimately a distortion: "God is gracious, gratuitous: the creation of a world *unnecessary* to God reminds us that God is not 'needy'; the liberty of God challenges any notion that God can be reduced to a simple or tangible sameness with which we negotiate as we do with the other contingent presences in our mental and physical field. The passage of our speech about God into silence, the self-criticism of all doctrinal utterance in the context of contemplative worship, all this warns consistently against the ideological or hierarchical closures we have just mentioned."[8]

Thus, it should not be thought that an appeal to religion is any kind of easy panacea for our ethical and political difficulties. In this respect, there are two temptations in particular to which it is liable to succumb. On the one hand, as we have just been observing, there is the temptation immediately to substantiate the universal in the domain of the particular in such a way as to obliterate the latter. On the other hand, there is the temptation we observed in chapter 2, whereby religion or theology operates in the manner of a sedative that dissolves the tension and erases the difficulty at the heart of the ethical and political in favor of complacent resolutions. What both of these trajectories do—albeit in different ways—is to still the ethically and politically necessary interplay between the universal, the particular, and the singular. Sometimes—but not always—both of these paths may be pursued simultaneously. But insofar as either one of them is followed, it cannot but be to the detriment of the ethical and the political, and will end up repeating the problems from which the return to religion is supposed to deliver us.

It has to be said that to make a case for the return of religion is hardly novel in the context of contemporary theory. Even ostensibly secular thinkers and unequivocal atheists—some of whom we have been discussing in the preceding chapters—have been arguing similarly. It is not my purpose here, therefore, to unfold an apologia for the necessity of religion in contemporary ethical and political thought. For one thing, this has already been done implicitly in the foregoing chapters, and for another, it would be merely to recapitulate arguments made elsewhere by others. But in light of what has been said above, we begin to see how important is the question of the *manner* in which religion returns. There is a great deal at stake in

---

7. Williams, *Lost Icons*, 162.
8. Ibid., 163.

Faith

this question, for if religion returns in a way that succumbs to either of the temptations just mentioned, far from "saving" the ethical and political, it will end up by damaging them yet again. In what follows, therefore, I shall look in detail at the question of the *way* in which religion should return and, more particularly, the way in which religion should do justice to the necessary interplay between the universal, the particular, and the singular.

Religion and the "Triune Interplay"

We have seen that one of the advantages of religion is the way in which it acknowledges—as a universal—its own implication with the domains of the particular and the singular. We have also observed that throughout history, it has often forgotten the necessity of this interplay. The religious universal has often been turned into something one can *grasp*, and when this happens, we imagine we have a less mediated access to the universal than we do. This then gives license to that universal to impose itself upon and ultimately obliterate the domains of the particular and the singular. But just as there are better and worse ways in which religion may return, there are also better and worse ways for religion as a universal to pay due obeisance to the particular and the singular. I want to suggest that one way of attempting this, and one that has been particularly prominent in the twentieth century, is to enact a method that we might characterize as "folding" the particular and the singular into the universal itself. This method undercuts or dilutes the sovereignty of the universal by incorporating particularity and singularity into the universal. Indeed, it might be argued that, in very broad terms, this is precisely the method adopted by much modern liberal theology and by many variants of postmodern deconstructive theology in the twentieth century in particular. It is not difficult to see the attraction of such an approach in light of the violence brought by an unequivocal assertion of the sovereignty of the universal, an assertion that we have seen repeated in contemporary form in the thought of Badiou and Žižek. I further want to suggest, however, that while such a methodology might be laudable insofar as it is motivated by a concern to "balance out" the universal with the particular, it does so at the expense of eradicating the necessary tension and dialectical interplay between them that we have argued must be perpetuated.

In order to specify what I mean by these claims and to illustrate what is at stake here, I shall look at one specific example of what I take to be such an approach. If I am right in seeing this method as being enacted through much modern liberal and postmodern deconstructive theology, then one might invoke any number of possible examples, and the isolation of any one of them is bound to an extent to be arbitrary. But in what follows, I shall examine in particular the work of the feminist theologian Kathleen Sands. This is not because I think that her work is the most egregious example of what I take to be the problems intrinsic to this method. But her commendably clear discussion does much to bring into focus what I take to be at stake here, and the content of her analysis—not least her discussion of the nature of the Good—is particularly pertinent to some of the issues I wish to raise. Furthermore, her work has been analyzed in detail by Rowan Williams, and his own comments do much to illuminate the sort of concerns that I wish to express. In discussing Sands's work, therefore, I shall be making particular reference to her book *Escape from Paradise: Evil and Tragedy in Feminist Theology* (1994).

Sands's central contention in that book is that Christian orthodoxy in the West has tended to suffer from a stultifying closure that is manifested particularly in its conceptions of good and evil. These conceptions, she argues, are so ideal, abstract, and rigid that they fail to do justice to the complexities and contingencies of life. These problematic conceptions of good and evil are, of course, mutually implicated, and Sands spells out what she perceives to be particularly damaging about them. First, with respect to evil, Sands says that theology has dealt with it historically by means of one of two strategies which she dubs, respectively, rationalism and dualism. Of rationalism, she says that its "interpretations of evil are moved by the passion to render reality as a single intelligible whole" and "grew from the Platonic view of being as good and evil as nonbeing. . . . Ontic privation established the possibility of moral evil or error, in which contingent beings strangely attempted to rebel against the inviolable order of being. Though capable of wreaking havoc on each other, contingent beings remained fundamentally oriented toward the good. For Christian rationalism, moral evil was, at least in principle, never beyond comprehension or rehabilitation."[9] Dualism, on the other hand, understands reality as "a battlefield between good and evil. This *moral* division of reality has been the key to the ontological divisions that dualism also entails—for example, between spirit and matter, nature and civilization, or female and male. . . . By distinguishing the true from the good and the rational from the real, dualism provides ideological frameworks for strategies of withdrawal, resistance, and destruction. Dualistic patterns of thought are at work whenever evil is apprehended as generating its own counterreality and counterintelligibility."[10]

---

9. Sands, *Escape from Paradise*, 2–3.
10. Ibid., 3.

Sands maintains that while both strategies have their strengths, they suffer from a critical weakness: they both defend "an unequivocal good by erasing loss and negation, the one by denying the reality of the negated; the other by denying the entanglement of what is negated with what is affirmed." Instead, she seeks to "facilitate integral discourses about the risks and values of human existence amidst the elemental diversity of life."[11] She thereby attempts to rehabilitate the domain of contingency and, with it, the significance of the tragic. She invokes Martha Nussbaum's work in *The Fragility of Goodness: Luck and Ethics in Greek Tragedy and Philosophy* (1986), arguing against an "incorruptible, intelligible Good" that is untouched by the "chaotic force of circumstance"; she argues instead for a recognizably human understanding of goodness that is "more like a plant than like a jewel. Living, complex and delicate, humankind cannot partake of the more tenacious stability of the inorganic or the Ideal."[12]

While ultimately dissenting from her analysis, Rowan Williams nonetheless recognizes its force. He says that

> the case is an interesting and challenging one, which does not simply repeat standard feminist charges against Augustine, but allows his schema a degree of moral seriousness and weight. In effect, she is claiming that the tradition of which Augustine is the classical exponent—if not the creator—is preoccupied with what a contemporary critic would call "closure," a damaging impatience because, whatever the metaphysical good intentions, it is constantly slipping into polarisations of "the Good" and "the not-Good" in the present moment; polarisations that encourage the identification of actual agents here and now with the Good and the not-Good, and the projection of failure and lack on to certain classes and categories of existence (matter, woman).[13]

Williams goes on to say that what is interesting is that Sands's thoughts coincide with those of Augustine in several important respects: "there is no timeless and stable goodness in the world; there is no incarnation of evil. All creaturely good is realised in *time*, and the perfection of goodness exists not as something that issues from a *process*, but as the eternal standard and direction of creaturely good."[14] But the divergence comes on the notion of a "transcendent measure of good" over and above the contingencies of time. According to Sands, "Moral judgements . . . are strategic, contextual

---

11. Ibid., 36.
12. Ibid., 4–5.
13. Williams, "Insubstantial Evil," 118.
14. Ibid.

judgements about how the diverse goods of life might best be integrated and unnecessary suffering minimised in a particular place and moment."[15]

Sands thus seeks to *revise* orthodoxy's conception of the Good as well as its conception of evil. Rather than understanding the Good as being fixed, timeless and static, we have seen that she instead wants to understand the Good as being "various, mobile and vulnerable." In developing such an understanding, she hopes to overcome what she perceives to be orthodoxy's rigid understandings of good and evil that seem far removed from and inadequate to the contingencies of life. In other words (and to invoke the terminology of my own analysis), Sands believes that the *universal* (Christian) conception of the Good is fixed, timeless, and static and, as such, is far removed from the conditions of *particularity*, the domain of contingent existence, which is "various, mobile and vulnerable." She is clearly concerned that the attempt to impose the universal on the contingencies of life will result in the obliteration of particularity and will thus result in violent denial of contingent life itself. In this respect, she shares the concerns that we ourselves have already expressed. But in attempting to address this problem, she seeks to *erase* the difference between the universal and the particular, blending them into one unified account. The Good must itself become "various, mobile and vulnerable," which is to say that the universal must be *merged* with the particular. In other words, this seems to be an instance of the particular being incorporated or "folded" into the universal itself. But to what extent is this the most adequate way of addressing what I take to be the legitimate concerns that she has here identified?

First, with respect to her revised understanding of the Good, Rowan Williams has enumerated some penetrating criticisms. He notes that there is some difficulty in knowing quite what it would mean to understand the Good as being "various, mobile and vulnerable." He thus proposes three possible ways in which it may be understood and identifies the respective difficulties inherent in each of them. The first understanding would be "that the Good is different for different created subjects, to the extent that what is good for one subject is necessarily and permanently at odds with what is good for another."[16] But if this is so, then it "implies that there are genuine (truthfully conceived) creaturely goods that can be realised only at the expense of the genuine goods of others; a view hard to reconcile with any properly emancipatory ethic, since it is the argument, implicit or explicit, of the slave-master."[17] That is to say, where such genuine goods are con-

---

15. Sands, *Escape from Paradise*, 15. Quoted in Williams, "Insubstantial Evil," 118.
16. Williams, "Insubstantial Evil," 119.
17. Ibid.

ceived as being irreducibly conflictual, there is no overarching account of the Good for all, on which all genuine emancipation depends. Without this, it is difficult to avoid the conclusion that the tension between conflicting goods can only be solved by allowing to the strongest the consummation of their good. In other words, and again in the terms of my own analysis, what seems to be necessary for such an emancipatory ethic is the presence of an unequivocal universal. Once this becomes obscured by a merging or a blending with particularity, its emancipatory force seems inevitably to be weakened.

The second way of understanding the proposal would be to say that "the Good genuinely differs from circumstance to circumstance, without any 'grammar' of continuity." In which case, the difficulty arises from the consequent suggestion that "particular developments might render good what once was not, that torture or racial discrimination might be *made* good by historical changes."[18] It is, of course, the case that, historically and empirically speaking, *conceptions* of the good change. But the question that arises from this is whether this change is to be understood in relation to a notion of an "eternal" standard of Goodness, which would provide that grammar of continuity in the midst of this change, or, on the other hand, whether this change is ultimately arbitrary, so that there is nothing, in principle, that would prevent torture or racial discrimination, for instance, from being deemed "good" at some future stage. In other words, is there some *universal* conception of Goodness, however opaque and contested, that could serve to judge, however equivocally, between *particular* (and changing) conceptions of goodness? The third understanding would be to claim that "the Good of or for certain subjects might simply and finally fail and prove impossible of realisation," which "suggests that there are worldly subjects 'predestined' to final and irredeemable frustration."[19] Thus, just as there is a certain arbitrariness in relation to what is good for some creatures as opposed to others, so also there is a certain arbitrariness about which of those subjects will be able to realize their potential "goodness" and which of them will not.

Now although these three possible readings of Kathleen Sands's proposal are subtly different in their emphases, they all carry with them, according to Williams, an unavoidable Hobbesian outcome, namely, the assumption of "the war of all against all, the *inevitable* non-convergence of creaturely good." In order to avoid this, Sands appears to wish to appeal to "the notion of a viable balance in a community's life." But Williams argues

18. Ibid.
19. Ibid.

Part IV: The Religious

that this will not work, saying that "it assumes that the reconciliation of partial and competing goods is itself a good to be pursued, without qualification, it seems. There is no argument to establish why this good should be exempt from the general prohibition against general goods. An absolutist assumption is being smuggled in under the guise of pragmatism."[20] In this respect, Williams is surely right. A conception of the Good that is entirely particularist, if it is not to fall into a relativist free-for-all, seems inevitably and transcendentally to presuppose a "hidden" conception of the Good that is universal (as opposed to particular) after all.

What we are seeing here is a repetition of the structural phenomenon that we observed in the last chapter. There we saw that attempts to proclaim the sovereignty of particularity are always inverted, so that some kind of universal dimension gets unwittingly reinstated after all; attempts to proclaim the "end of metanarratives" are likewise inverted so that the very proclamation itself becomes yet another metanarrative. Here again, we are seeing that an attempt to understand the Good in particularist terms ends up by surreptitiously reinstating its necessary and universal aspect "behind the scenes" as it were. In so far as the latter is the case, there is inevitably an element of unconscious deception at work, in the sense that it invokes an unequivocal universal dimension without explicit acknowledgment.

If this is so, then it may lead us to question the methodological strategy Sands employs of seeking to *incorporate* the particular into the universal. This stands in contrast to the kind of disposition I have been defending throughout this study. In effect, both may be understood as alternative ways of restraining, limiting, or undercutting the comprehensive and totalizing pretensions of the universal, related in this case, especially, to its conception of the Good. But the respective ways in which this is done differ markedly. I have been arguing that the domain of the particular must be allowed to interrogate the universal, to put it into question, sometimes even to "suspend" it. And, of course, this process must happen in reverse: the universal must judge the particular, call it to an awareness of an "other" order by which it is enabled and to which it is accountable. But, critically, this dialectical process is enacted without thereby changing, revising, or destroying the universal. What we have here is a constructive tension, a dialectical dynamic between the universal, the particular, and the singular. The universal and particular must be kept distinct precisely in the interests of perpetuating the tension between them. This performs the limiting function sought by Sands (the "suspension" of the universal in the interests of the particular), but without weakening the internal integrity of the universal itself. The universal and

20. Ibid., 119–20.

necessary aspect of the Good is not thereby compromised, although it may momentarily be "suspended." In contrast, Sands's approach internalizes and incorporates particularity into the universal tradition itself, thereby revising and changing it.

This, I should argue, results in a fatal domesticating process that is enacted in two directions. First, the heterogeneous and transgressive character of the particular is destroyed as it is absorbed into the universal tradition itself. If the domain of particularity is effectively to perform its function of interrogating, restraining, and undercutting the universal, it must remain heterogeneous to it. The particular should not be "accounted for" or "included within" the universal, for then it would lose its power to "suspend" the universal. Second, the full force and impetus of the sovereign universal (in this case the conception of the Good) is dissolved and weakened, so that the strength of its ethical and political imperatives becomes increasingly constrained. When the universal is made to compromise with the particular by incorporating it within itself, its own heterogeneous judgments *upon* the particular become likewise compromised. For it can no longer judge with the force of an unequivocally external intervention. Indeed, this is reflected in the concerns expressed by Williams regarding the emancipatory efficacy of the sort of diluted conception of the universal Good advocated by Sands. The net result of these two associated processes is that the dynamic tension and interplay between the universal and the particular is replaced by an anodyne union between the two that is ultimately static and ethically and politically disabling. The paradox of this outcome is that we are left with a revised version of the universal that is, in its form if not in its content, static, homogenous, and totalizing, the very characteristics from which Sands sought to escape in her reconception of the universal Good. It seems that in purging the universal Good of these characteristics, she has unwittingly reinstated them at another level.

This, in turn, leads us to question the extent to which she has succeeded in her aim of doing justice to the contingency, particularity, and irredeemable tragedy intrinsic to the world we inhabit. She has attempted to incorporate such contingency and particularity into her revised version of the universal, the orthodox tradition, but, in doing so, has she not thereby emerged with a single, systematic, and coherent structure that itself betrays the very things she is seeking to respect? In attempting to *account for* and *incorporate* such contingency and jaggedness, has she not thereby smoothed it away? In other words, has she not developed yet another smooth, unitary account—albeit one that, in its content, attempts to "mirror" the contingent, jagged, and inconsistent nature of the reality to which she is seeking to do justice? To invoke Gillian Rose's terminology again, has she not "mended" that which should remain "broken"? Would not a more radical and effective approach be frankly to accept and embrace the phenomenon of incommensurability? It is only by resisting the temptation to incorporate contingency and particularity, I suggest, that these very things can genuinely be respected. In order to do justice to the brokenness of reality, one must cultivate a disposition of reconciliation to the brokenness of thought itself. Paradoxically, there is a sense in which this means conserving tradition rather than revising it, and my point here could thus be understood as a plea for doctrinal orthodoxy (although, of course, the question of what actually constitutes "orthodoxy" will always be contested). But critically, this orthodoxy is placed within the context of a wider dialectical backdrop in which it is implicated.

If the Christian universal is indeed to be placed within a wider dialectical backdrop in the manner I have been describing, this understandably raises a whole host of questions about the status of that universal, not least in its relationship to the wider dialectic that forms its backdrop. One might be tempted to ask whether it is the Christian universal or the dialectic itself that should be regarded as "ultimate" in philosophical terms. A related question would be whether the disposition I am here commending commits one to a substantive Christian (and therefore theistic) ontology, whether the Christian universal has ultimate ontological purchase as a true depiction of reality. Would it commit one to the ontological "truth" of this Christian universal? These are clearly important (and, doubtless for some, crucial) questions, and one can certainly understand why they might arise. For it would seem that the kind of methodology or disposition that I have been advocating throughout this study would leave them tantalizingly (or worryingly) unanswered. Such hypothetical interlocutors would be right to demand clarification, even if that clarification turns out to be that these questions (or at least some of them) should indeed, as a matter of principle, remain unanswered. It is to a consideration of this question that I turn in the final section of this chapter.

Ontological "Resolutions"

With a view to proffering a clarification of this kind, it will be helpful to see how the questions just raised may well take different forms and, in particular, we may anticipate two distinct versions of them arising from positions either side of the stance I am here advocating. From the theological side, it might be objected that my invocation of God, the theological tradition more generally, and doctrinal orthodoxy, is ultimately only a heuristic device,

Faith

somewhat akin, perhaps, to the status of Kant's transcendentals. Williams has asked a question of this kind, albeit arising from a kind of cultural analysis different from the one I have been discussing in this study. But arguing for the necessity of some kind of "noncontingent Other," or God, in the context of his own analysis, he asks, "Is the absent Other that makes possible my own saving absence and social presence simply a construct, a linguistic device to spring me from my trap and no more? It is, of course, *at least* a linguistic construct, it appears in and only in the ways in which we speak to each other, socially and 'privately'; but can it be read without remainder as a tactic to enable the soul to emerge?"[21]

John Milbank has articulated a more trenchant version of this question as part of his response to some of my own previous work. The terminology in this case is different—the point at issue is the question of the necessity/impossibility of the "metanarrative," but the underlying point is, I think, the same. On the one hand, one might argue (in the manner of Nietzschean postmodernism) that a metanarrative is impossible (and therefore that God or theology is merely a "fiction" or linguistic device), or on the other hand, one might argue that a metanarrative is unavoidable (and that the theological metanarrative is ontologically true). For Milbank, any attempt to transcend this either-or choice is ultimately unsustainable. He says that the Nietzschean postmodernists

> tended to protest that postmodernity makes any notion of a "metanarrative" impossible. Much more perceptively, the theologian Gavin Hyman accepted my assertion that [in that case] there is still a metanarrative (for example *The Genealogy of Morals*) but then argued to an *aporia*: there has to be/cannot be a single metanarrative. The upshot of this [according to Milbank] is to suggest an endless competition between metanarratives. Yet this is unthinkable: it would of course be agonistic, and no proponent of a single metanarrative would really accept the vailidity of the others. There would indeed have to be a "playful" (but the game is played with money and guns) wandering between these grand stories, implying once more that there is really one single nihilist metanarrative and ontology of violence.[22]

What both Williams and Milbank share here is the sense that we really are faced with an either-or choice: either the "noncontingent Other" is a "linguistic device" or it is "something more"; either there is one single metanarrative or there are no metanarratives (or, rather, only the nihilist

---

21. Williams, *Lost Icons*, 180.
22. Milbank, *Theology and Social Theory*, xx.

metanarrative of ontological violence). The possibility of a disposition that might transcend these either-or choices is not really considered. Milbank, indeed, does claim that any such attempt to transcend this dichotomy is ultimately illusory. It will finally collapse back into the anarchy of nihilism, and therefore the either-or choice will reinstall itself once again. But Milbank moves very quickly here, and does not give any sustained consideration to what such an attempt might look like. Perhaps there is more to living in the tension *between* these either-or choices than he is willing to credit.[23]

At the same time, however, this criticism might be made from the other side of the ontological spectrum, that is to say, from those committed to an ontological immanence or materialism. Indeed, while Žižek insists on the necessity of the return to religion, this return is necessary precisely because of the way it indirectly confirms the truth of atheism, however paradoxical this may appear to conventional thought. The return to Christianity is necessary *both* to deliver us from the illusion of "common sense empirical materialism" *and* to affirm a more thoroughgoing atheism. The "common sense empirical materialism" which Žižek rejects is constituted by the "assertion of material reality as fully ontologically constituted, 'really existing out there.'" In contrast, Žižek insists that the "basic axiom of today's materialism is for me the *ontological incompleteness of reality* . . . beneath the world of simply existing material objects we discover a different reality of virtual particles, of quantum oscillations, of time-space paradoxes, etc., etc.—a wonderful world which, while remaining thoroughly materialist, is anything but boring. It is, on the contrary, breathtakingly surprising and paradoxical."[24] In relation to this, "The necessity of religion is an inner one. . . . A truly logical materialism accepts the basic insight of religion, its premise that our commonsense reality is not the true one; what it rejects is the conclusion that, therefore, there must be another, 'higher,' suprasensible reality."[25] So the return to religion is necessary to rescue us from the materialism of modern atheism. (I shall return in more detail to the nature of this dialectical detour below.) At the same time, however, the return resolutely refuses any "higher" transcendent reality, and thus remains resolutely ontologically atheistic, even if this atheism is one that is ontologically incomplete.

On Žižek's reading, Christianity itself actually reinforces that atheism, as expressed in the logic of incarnation/death/resurrection. In an echo of Hegel's (and especially Thomas J. J. Altizer's) rendering of Christianity, this

---

23. For an attempt to sketch out such a disposition, see Hyman, *Predicament of Postmodern Theology*.

24. Žižek in Žižek and Milbank, *Monstrosity of Christ*, 240.

25. Ibid.

logic expresses an inexorable kenotic process, wherein God the Father dies in his becoming human in the incarnation; God the Son dies in the crucifixion; and God the Holy Spirit is brought to birth in the resurrection as a purely immanent manifestation of the divine in the human community. For Žižek, this is the true traumatic message of Christianity, which both orthodox theology and postmodern deconstructive theology have alike covered up. He asks, "what if the entire history of Christianity, inclusive of (and especially) its Orthodox versions, is structured as a series of defences against the traumatic apocalyptic core of incarnation/death/resurrection? What if Christianity comes near to this core only at its rare apocalyptic moments?"[26] It is therefore imperative, for Žižek, that the ontological status of Christianity be clarified in precisely this atheistic way, for this is in fact the core content of the Christian message:

> there is no transcendent God-Father who discloses himself to us, humans, only in a limited way. The reason God can appear incognito is that there is nothing to take cognizance of here: God is hidden not to hide some transcendent Truth, but to hide the fact that there is nothing to hide. This is, to my Hegelian view, the whole point of Christianity as the "religion of revelation": what is revealed in Christianity is not some new content, but the fact that Revelation belongs to the very nature of God, i.e., that God is *nothing but* his own Revelation to us.[27]

Although arising from opposite ends of the ontological spectrum, these questions actually converge on a common assumption, namely, that the question of the ontological status of the religion to which we are returning must be *resolved*—that the theological metanarrative must be thought to articulate an ontological reality that exceeds itself or else that the theological narrative must be evoked while denying that it has any ontological purchase, that is to say, that one must return to theology without in any way compromising one's ontological commitment to atheism. What both are demanding is a clear statement of the relationship of the universal religious narrative to "reality"; they both seek to specify the ontological status of the content of the universal. It is precisely this assumption on which these contrary standpoints converge that I wish to contest. I want to suggest that this question—which they both insist on answering—is one that should remain unanswered.

That it should remain unanswered was already suggested in chapter 2. There, I said that where there is an ontological "resolution" of the status

26. Ibid., 260.
27. Ibid., 235–36.

of the universal, we find that the inevitable effect of this is to mend the necessary equivocation that I have suggested is at the heart of the ethical and political as such. We saw there that where there is an unequivocal ontological resolution in favor of a theistic or nihilistic ontology, the result is to install an imbalance in the relationship between the universal, the particular, and the singular, an imbalance that produces problematic ethical and political results. In particular, we saw that where there is an unequivocal espousal of a theistic ontology, there is a tendency to allow the universal domain to "take care of itself" and for practical attention to be refocused on the domains of the particular and singular; contrariwise, where there is an unequivocal espousal of a nihilistic ontology, there is a tendency to allow the domain of contingency, of stubborn particularity, to "take care of itself" and to focus attention on the *production* of a universal. Indeed, we observed these contrary tendencies in the respective projects of Milbank and Žižek. But in both cases, we saw the problematic ethical and political implications of these resolutions.

In which case, our task would seem to be to accept the necessity of a universal, while at the same time leaving open—or refusing to answer—the question of its ontological status. Indeed, I should argue that we find such an approach being enacted within a dialectical disposition, a disposition that has been defended—albeit indirectly—throughout this study. In what follows, I want to develop this line of thought further by analyzing the respective ontological "resolutions" of Milbank and Žižek in precisely dialectical terms. I want to suggest that such an analysis will both help illuminate why they espouse the positions that they do, and also reinforce my suggestion that their respective "resolutions" must ultimately be resisted. In order to do this, we must first look a little more closely at the practice of dialectics as such, and the way in which the practice of dialectics is put to work within Žižek's texts in particular.

One would search with difficulty for an explicit discussion of this dialectical method in Žižek's works, although it is actually enacted in them time and again in many of his tantalizing and innovative analyses. Indeed, Fredric Jameson has identified this as being one of the few themes that have persisted throughout Žižek's now considerable oeuvre. Of the dialectic, then, Jameson says that

> The old stereotype is that Hegel works according to a cut-and-dried progression from thesis, through antithesis, to synthesis. This, Žižek explains, is completely erroneous: there are no real syntheses in Hegel and the dialectical operation is to be seen in an utterly different way; a variety of examples are adduced. Still, that stupid stereotype was not altogether wrong. There

is a tripartite movement in the Hegelian dialectic, and in fact, Žižek goes on, he has just illustrated it: stupid stereotype, or the "appearance"; ingenious correction, the underlying reality or "essence"; finally, after all, the return to the reality of the appearance, so that it was the appearance that was "true" after all.[28]

So it is the supposedly "stupid first impression" to which we ultimately return. But, of course, this is not a simple return or a straightforward restoration. The return to the first impression is one that is cognizant of the dialectical movement that has made this return possible. The "first impression" that is restored is not the same as the first impression that was left behind.

For Jameson, it is this very movement—this restoration that is at the same time a displacement—that constitutes the perversity of the dialectic. As he continues: "the dialectic is just that inveterate, infuriating perversity whereby a commonsense empiricist view of reality is repudiated and undermined. But it is undermined together with its own accompanying interpretations of that reality, which look so much more astute and ingenious than the commonsense empiricist reality itself, until we understand that the interpretations are themselves also part of precisely that 'first impression.'"[29] The radical implication of this, Jameson suggests, is the impossibility of philosophy as such, and the consequent displacement of philosophy by theory. This is because philosophy is predicated on the notion of a foundational subject that abstracts itself from the object under consideration in order to provide a complete and systematic account of the object ("reality") as a whole. Dialectics questions the very possibility of this abstract stance of subjective observation. The subject itself is always "caught up" in and is a part of that which is being observed. As Žižek puts it: "the subject's gaze is always-already inscribed into the perceived object itself . . . [which] means that the reality I see is never 'whole'—not because a large part of it eludes me, but because it contains a stain, a blind spot, which indicates my inclusion in it."[30] In light of this, therefore, one can see why a return to the initial impression—by means of this detour of dialectical negation—is not a simple return or a straightforward restoration. The paradox (or perversity) here is that the return to the origin is made possible precisely by this recognition (attained by means of the dialectical movement) that the origin in itself is impossible.

28. Jameson, "First Impressions," 7.
29. Ibid.
30. Žižek, *Parallax View*, 17.

Part IV: The Religious

But how does this analysis help to clarify the respective ontological "resolutions" espoused by Milbank and Žižek with respect to the Christian universal that they both invoke? I want to suggest that it provides us with one way of understanding the historical transition from theism to atheism and the way in which they each seek to move beyond both. Viewed dialectically, the "stupid first impression" is that God exists. In, admittedly, very broad terms, this would encapsulate the worldview of premodern Christianity. In this rendering of theism, there is a transcendent God who creates and sustains the world. We, as creatures, are "effects" of that God and, as such, are ultimately answerable to and utterly dependent on him. Truth is "given" or "revealed" as a divine gift, to be gratefully received by creaturely recipients. This worldview is for the most part an enclosed system, such that it can scarcely be contested. There were undoubtedly heresies and the persecution of heretics, but such acts of dissent took place *within* a system that itself remained uncontested. As numerous scholars have noted, "atheism" is virtually unknown in medieval Christendom and doesn't begin to rear its head until the early seventeenth century.[31] The possibility of dissent has not yet been created because the epistemological autonomy of the subject has yet to be asserted.

In time, however, this "stupid first impression," mired in ignorance and superstition, gives way to its "ingenious correction," the exposure of its underlying reality or essence. This is atheism—the realization that we are "really" on our own, that God was always a fiction, a projection of humanity, and that revelation was, after all, merely a myth. The story of the transition from theism to atheism is often portrayed as being a long and complicated one, constituted by a whole series of contingent shifts. In a way, of course, this was undoubtedly so, but there is another sense in which the transition was remarkably simple and abrupt. It can be traced, preeminently, to Descartes' self-reflexive establishment of foundational subjectivity. This revolutionary epistemological shift was effected by the *abstraction* of the human subject from the reality of which it was formerly an intrinsic part. This was a direct inversion of the previously prevailing epistemology. Hitherto, the subject had been an effect of, a creation of, that wider reality, whereas now the subject becomes the only certain reality which in turn has to found, justify, substantiate, and in a certain sense "create" a reality, the existence of which is otherwise radically uncertain. Initially, of course, Descartes must invoke God in order to secure the existence of the external world. But

---

31. The classic statement of this may be found in Febvre, *The Problem of Unbelief*, originally published in French in 1942, in which he claimed that atheism was "unthinkable" in medieval Christendom. Numerous subsequent scholars have made similar (if sometimes more understated) claims.

this God now has to be founded, in turn, on the rationality of the human subject. Over the ensuing centuries, this subjective "founding" of God is exposed as being what it is—a groundless projection. Ultimately, therefore, Descartes' atheistic methodology is shown necessarily to give rise to atheistic conclusions.[32] The subject is the only true reality and all conceptions of God are merely subjective projections. This is the "ingenious correction," the exposure of the real "essence" underlying the ignorant "appearance" of the premodern world.

But before long, this "ingenious correction" is itself put into question. In turn, the "real essence" it has exposed comes itself to be seen as yet another fictional appearance. In particular, the abstract subject, detached from its context, comes to be seen as a bizarre and peculiar projection, which ultimately shows itself to be unsustainable. This realization has been well expressed by Milbank when he says that "we should ask why the West gave birth to anything so fantastically peculiar and unlikely" as the notion of "a wholly artificial human being who has never really existed. . . . This is the pure individual, thought of in abstraction from his or her gender, birth, associations, beliefs and also, crucially, in equal abstraction from the religious or philosophical beliefs of the observer of this individual as to whether he is a creature made by God, or only material, or naturally evolved and so forth. Such an individual is not only asocial, he is also apsychological; his soul is in every way unspecified."[33] Not only is this abstract subject increasingly seen as being philosophically "peculiar and unlikely" in the way Milbank describes, but it is also seen as laying the foundations of a radical immanence, which has far-reaching and problematic implications, philosophically, socially, and culturally.

These implications are manifested in manifold ways. In general cultural terms, the philosopher Charles Taylor has illuminated what is at issue here when he says that "there is a generalized sense in our culture that with the eclipse of the transcendent, something may have been lost. I put it in the optative mood, because people react very differently to this. . . . But wherever people stand on this issue, everyone understands, or feels they understand what is being talked about here."[34] More specifically, Taylor identifies three forms that this "malaise of immanence" may take: "(1) the sense of the fragility of meaning, the search for an over-arching significance; (2) the felt flatness of our attempts to solemnize the crucial moments of passage in our

---

32. For further discussion of this, see Hyman, *Short History of Atheism*, especially chapter 2.

33. Milbank, "Gift of Ruling," 213.

34. Taylor, *Secular Age*, 307.

lives; and (3) the utter flatness, emptiness of the ordinary."[35] Furthermore, there is an increasing sense that, even on its own terms, the immanence, rationality, and objectivity of modern subjectivity are illusory. The development of Freudian and post-Freudian psychoanalysis has, of course, had a great deal to do with this. When Freud began his groundbreaking investigations, he did so from within rather than from without the framework of modern subjective rationality. But his work ultimately resulted in a subversion of that framework from within. The subject's immanence was shown to be saturated by an uncontrollable "excess," its rationality was seen to be underpinned by an irrationality that is in a sense more foundational, while its objectivity was shown to be, in many ways, a secondary construction.

These are all enormously complex processes and, in this context, we can do little more than gesture, vaguely, toward them. But in philosophical, cultural, and psychoanalytical terms, what we see is that the "ingenious correction" or "sophisticated interpretation" itself begins to crumble from within. As it does so, a suspicion emerges that the initial "stupid impression" was perhaps in a sense true after all. It is possibly in this context that the much-touted contemporary "return of religion" should be understood. At the very least, it is the context within which Milbank and Žižek's respective returns to religion should be understood. As we have seen, the return to the "stupid first impression" is not a simple or straightforward restoration of it. The return has been made possible precisely through the dialectical detour through the "ingenious correction," in this case, modern atheism. This antithesis is both canceled or annulled and also taken up or carried forward into the return to the initial thesis, the "stupid first impression." I should suggest that their respective returns to religion may both be understood in terms of this dialectical detour via the antithesis of modern atheism. Of course, Milbank has never explicitly endorsed dialectics in the way that Žižek has, and, indeed, he has often been directly critical of it. On the other hand, there are places where Milbank himself seems to understand his relationship to secular modernity in precisely dialectical terms.

Something of this ambivalence is well articulated when Milbank observes that "although I argue that the ultimate logic of history is not dialectical and that dialectical processes are never entirely necessitated, I acknowledge that certain historical developments can be understood in dialectical terms—such that aspects of my own metanarrative are, indeed, as Rowan Williams pointed out, transparently dialectical."[36] Furthermore, and more specifically, the dialectical character of Milbank's relationship to secu-

---

35. Ibid., 309.
36. Milbank, *Theology and Social Theory*, xvi.

lar reason or modern atheism is well expressed when he says of his book *Theology and Social Theory*, "The careful reader will realize that throughout the book, the attitude towards 'secular reason' is never as negative as it appears to be on the surface. For it is viewed not as what it primarily proclaims itself to be, namely the secular, but rather as disguised heterodoxy of various stripes, as a revived paganism and as a religious nihilism. In each case my attitude cannot be simply oppositional, since I regard Catholic Christianity as fulfilling the best pagan impulses. . . . It follows that there remains truth in all these distortions."[37] This is, of course, consistent with what Milbank has long argued, namely, that liberal values are parodies and distortions of Christian ones, and that the former ultimately lose their meaning and intelligibility unless "redeemed" by the original Christian insights from which they were derived.

But Milbank then goes on to take a step further when he says that it may even be the case that "just as Irenaeus learned much from Valentinus, the [secular liberal] distortions develop *better* certain aspects of orthodoxy which orthodoxy must then later recoup."[38] This is a significant move, for it is to admit that secular liberal atheism is not just, negatively, a distortion of Christian truth, but that, positively, it articulates certain aspects of that truth better than did Christianity itself.[39] What this implies is that Christianity has only become fully itself precisely by passing dialectically through its own negation. While Milbank himself may want to deny that this process is "entirely necessitated," he does seem to concede that, albeit contingently, the detour through secular liberalism brought to fruition Christianity's latent inner core. It was by means of this passage through secular atheism that Christian truth was fully explicated.

Thus, for both Milbank and Žižek, I suggest, their respective returns to religion can only be properly understood in light of this dialectical detour through secular atheistic liberalism. At the same time, however, it is also key to understanding the dispute between them over the manner in which they each return to religion. The dispute has been conducted at length in their book *The Monstrosity of Christ* (2009). But for all the complexities of their arguments, the difference between them may be straightforwardly expressed: Milbank returns to religion in a way that restores the ontological resolution of the *thesis*, premodern theism, while Žižek returns to religion in a way that perpetuates the ontological resolution of the *antithesis*,

---

37. Ibid., xiv–xv.
38. Ibid., xv. My emphasis.
39. For further discussion of this, see Hyman, "Postmodern Theology and Modern Liberalism."

Part IV: The Religious

modern atheism. Of course, such a statement must immediately be qualified because the very fact that their respective returns to religion are dialectically enacted means that Milbank's restoration of theism is not quite the same as the theism of the premodern thesis, just as Žižek's perpetuation of atheism is not quite the same as the atheism of the modern antithesis.

In Milbank's case, he has always explicitly acknowledged this, rejecting the claim that he is nostalgically and uncritically restoring premodern theism. Furthermore, he has not hesitated to point out some of the problems with premodern theism and to identify ways in which he seeks to move beyond them. In one of his earlier works, for instance, he makes clear that he is seeking to move beyond *both* the thesis of premodern theism *and* the antithesis of modern atheism: "If subjects and objects only are, through the complex relations of a narrative, then neither objects are privileged, as in pre-modernity, nor subjects, as in modernity. Instead, what matters are structural relations, which constantly shift; the word 'subject' now indicates a point of potent 'intensity' which can re-arrange given structural patterns." In light of this—and other such considerations—we can only make "a kind of *half* turn back to pre-modernity"; in this half-turn, the sovereignty of subjective inwardness has been renounced, we can speak again of things "external" to subjectivity, but now, "this externality is no longer, as for pre-modernity, an organised spatial realm of substances, genera and species, but rather a world of temporary relational networks, always being re-distributed with greater and greater 'freedom,' as one passes from mineral to vegetable to animal to cultural animal." Furthermore, he acknowledges that theology has "never fully escaped the grasp of a 'totalising' metaphysics."[40]

In all these (and other) ways, Milbank has made clear that his return to premodern theology does not entail a simple restoration of that which prevailed before. He has returned to this theme more recently, acknowledging that he seems to "face in two directions at once: towards a call for a return to the pre-modern prior to 1300 on the one hand, but towards an invocation of modern romantic expressivism and 'postmodern' ultra-constructivism on the other."[41] He goes on to suggest that this is why some critics have accused him of nostalgia and fideism, while others have accused him of being unduly rationalistic, liberal, and modern. Still others have suggested that he "incoherently or else inevitably tend[s] in both these directions at once."[42] He then goes on to sketch out a rationale for how these two apparently contradictory elements in his thought hang together. But regardless

---

40. Milbank, "Postmodern Critical Augustinianism," 225, 226, 227. My emphasis.
41. Milbank, *Theology and Social Theory*, xxii.
42. Ibid., xxiii.

Faith

of the specific way in which this synthesis is effected, the fact that these two elements coexist in Milbank's thought is perfectly explicable in terms of the kind of dialectical analysis outlined by Žižek and Jameson. As we saw, the return to the "stupid first impression" (in this case, premodern theism) is made possible—indeed is impelled—by the dialectical detour. At the same time, however, that which returns or is restored is simultaneously *transformed* precisely by this same dialectical detour. The "stupid first impression" to which we return is not the same as the "stupid first impression" that was left behind.

We see the same logical mechanism at work in Žižek's simultaneous return to religion and perpetuation of atheism. In the move from the antithesis of modern atheism to the return of the "stupid first impression," the return to Christianity, the antithesis of modern atheism is *both* perpetuated (the return to religion remains, for Žižek, resolutely atheistic) *and* annulled (the atheism that is sustained is not the same as the atheism that has been left behind). Indeed, the perpetuation of atheism is sustained precisely on the basis of its annulment. The logic here is rather like the one that pertains to Žižek's parallel perpetuation of materialism. As we observed in chapter 2, the materialism to which Žižek is committed is not the inert, static, immanent materialism of secular modernity. Rather, materialism itself contains an excess—a transcendence—that exceeds itself. This excess or transcendence is not dualistically other than or set over and against the material, but rather is an intrinsic facet of the material as such.

The application of this logic to the question of atheism is enacted directly by Žižek himself when he says that "I don't think one can translate theology into secular humanism. Not because of any secret, obscure reason but because there must be a moment of thinking that it is not we who are acting, but a higher force that is acting through us. This element has to be maintained."[43] In other words, there is an excess to human subjectivity that is beyond its control, a transcendent excess that immanent humanistic atheism cannot countenance. The latter wants to maintain a conception of subjectivity understood unequivocally in nominative terms, whereas Žižek wants to return to the theological understanding of subjectivity as existing fundamentally in an accusative tense—to retain the sense of a "force" or "power" by which we are addressed and which acts through us. At the same time, this "force" or "power" does not constitute some kind of occult, hidden, transcendent realm. Rather, it is a necessary aspect of subjectivity as such. He goes on to say that at the crucifixion, the Roman soldiers "thought they had destroyed everything in Christ, but that little bit of alien residue

---

43. Žižek, "Meditation on Michaelangelo," 179–80.

remained and started to organize itself into the community of believers. That is a crucial point. Again, what I'm saying here cannot be reduced to simplistic humanism. I think this is the legacy of Christianity—this legacy of God not as a big Other or guarantee but God as the ultimate ethical agency who puts the burden on us to organize ourselves."[44] In other words, the repudiation of God as a big Other is, in effect, a perpetuation of atheism. But this is not an atheism of absolute immanence—the atheism of secular modernity. Rather, it is an atheism that acknowledges the necessity of God as a "force" or "power" that is an effect of immanence itself. But although it is an effect of immanence, it is not simply "produced" or "projected" by humanity. As an "excess," it is something that exceeds our grasp or control.

In light of all this and in terms of the "old stereotype" of Hegelian dialectics, we may say that modern atheism is an embodiment of the *antithesis* in relation to religion, whereas Žižek's atheism is an embodiment of the *synthesis* (while acknowledging that Žižek has questioned the reality of any such syntheses in Hegel's work). If this is so, we can see that Žižek's atheism is as different from modern secular atheism as the latter is from theism itself. For Žižek, as for Hegel, a simple movement from thesis to antithesis will always be inadequate and incomplete. What is needed is a return to the "stupid first impression," albeit in such a way that both annuls and perpetuates the antithesis. The latter is annulled in so far as there is a repudiation of absolute immanence, of the final truth of humanistic atheism, and a return to Christianity itself. At the same time, the atheistic antithesis is perpetuated in so far as this movement is one that remains resolutely atheistic and materialist.[45]

We thus begin to get a sense of what it is that divides Milbank and Žižek, and also of what it is that brings them together. While both move from thesis and antithesis to a third, they disagree as to the ontological status of this third. For Milbank, it is theistic (whereby he ontologically privileges the thesis), whereas for Žižek it is atheistic (whereby he ontologically privileges the antithesis). In other words, this fundamental disagreement between them rests upon an underlying convergence, namely, their conviction that the question of the ontological status of the third to which they both return must be "resolved." Milbank resolves the question by prioritizing the theism of the thesis, while Žižek resolves it by prioritizing the atheism of the antithesis. But what if we were to contest both Milbank and Žižek on the point at which they converge? What if we were to join with them in the dialectical return to the "stupid first impression," to the Christian universal,

44. Ibid., 180.
45. For further discussion of this, see Hyman, "Dialectics or Politics?"

while refusing to prioritize either the theism of the thesis or the atheism of the antithesis? This would be to refuse, in principle, to answer the question of whether the Christian universal has a corresponding ontological underpinning. As such, it would neither affirm nor deny such an underpinning, and, indeed, it would insist on the necessity of refusing such an affirmation or negation.

Could it not be said that this is the more genuinely dialectical move? Is not the dialectical imperative to move decisively beyond both thesis and antithesis? This would still be so, I suggest, even if we were to accept Žižek's criticism of the "old stereotype" of the Hegelian dialectic, even if the dialectical move beyond thesis and antithesis leads not to synthesis, but to a return to the thesis. For we have seen that if the dialectical outcome is not a synthesis, not a "resolution," but rather a return to the initial thesis, there are two important things to note about this process. First, the "outcome" of the movement, the return to the initial thesis, is less important than the activity of the process itself. It is not that the dialectical process is "merely" a methodology, something provisional to be discarded once one has reached one's destination. Rather, as Žižek has insisted, the dialectical process is itself revelatory of the truth of incommensurability, of the "brokenness" of reality, of creation as "fallen." In which case, perhaps the return to the thesis should be effected in such a way that does not annul the dialectic but, rather, perpetuates it. In other words, the return to the thesis should not "overcome" the dialectic by means of a decisive ontological resolution. Rather, the dialectic between the theism of the thesis and the atheism of the antithesis should be carried over into the return to the thesis itself. This would be to enact a return to the thesis, the Christian universal, in such a way that perpetuates the very dialectic between theism and atheism that has made this return not only possible but unavoidable.

Such an approach would seem to be demanded not only by the dialectical analysis being sketched out in this chapter, but also by the ethical and political analyses undertaken in this book as a whole. The burden of the previous chapters was to argue that the ethical and political are alike constituted by a dynamic interplay between the domains of the universal, the particular, and the singular. We also observed that an unequivocal ontological resolution seemed inevitably to give rise to a corresponding ethical-political resolution, a resolution that is ultimately disabling. Paradoxically, however, we saw that in whichever direction the ontological resolution was effected, the ethical-political resolution was effected in the opposite direction. As we saw in chapter 2 in particular, and as has been reiterated earlier in this chapter, where there is an ontological resolution in favor of universality (theism), in the practical domain of the ethical-political, attention is shifted

Part IV: The Religious

onto the domain of particularity. Contrariwise, where there is an ontological resolution in favor of particularity (atheism), ethical and political efforts become focused on the instantiation of universality. In both cases, the tension between universal and particular demands is severely weakened, with detrimental effects on the ethical and political themselves. The dynamic interplay at the heart of both threatens to be stilled or displaced by a complacent particularism on the one hand and a violent universalism on the other. If our analysis of the ethical and political in the preceding chapters is accepted, it would seem that while it is necessary to invoke a universal, it is also necessary to keep open and unresolved the ontological status of that universal. Otherwise, the open-ended interplay between the domains of the universal, the particular, and singular is in danger of being skewed or stilled. So while it is necessary to return to the Christian universal, it is also necessary for the question of its ontological status to be kept in suspension.

But while we might make a case for such a suspension on dialectical or on ethical and political grounds, we might also make such a case on specifically religious grounds. In other words, in terms of the discourse of the Christian universal itself, there are good reasons for keeping open the question of its ontological underpinning. In this respect, it is worth remembering that one of the characteristic features of Christian discourse (and indeed of other religious discourses) is that faith itself is or should be characterized by an indifference to outcomes, guarantees, or underpinnings, even if this has been distorted or forgotten in much of the historical tradition. That is to say, faith is not a "bargain," a commitment now that will be retrospectively justified by rewards to come. Neither is faith some kind of philosophical "wager" on the ontological structure of reality that will turn out to have been futile if, from an Absolute perspective (by definition inaccessible to finite human creatures in time), that reality turns out not as faith has imagined it to be. On the contrary, true faith is indifferent to rewards or justifications and, at its most radical, should be indifferent to the question of its ontological underpinnings, of its philosophical or empirical "correctness." The faith that deems the content of the Christian universal to be "true" is doing something other and higher than making a mundane philosophical judgment about ontological "correspondence." Again, even if, from the perspective of the Absolute, there is no such correspondence, the commitment of faith would in no way be invalidated. There is a sense in which faith is indifferent to its own ontological guarantee, indeed, would be destroyed by any such guarantee.

Admittedly, I am here pushing this theme further than the historical tradition has generally thought it proper to do. Nonetheless, I am drawing on a stream of thought that has undoubtedly been part of this tradition, and it is one to which Rowan Williams has drawn attention. He has written of the ways in which people of faith "make gestures and take stands, not for the sake of dramatizing their beliefs or for the sake of any result that may be guaranteed, but because there is simply nothing else that can be done with honesty."[46] With respect to this, he turns to the biblical narrative in the book of Daniel in which three young men have been condemned to death by King Nebuchadnezzar for refusing to worship the king's false gods: "Shadrach, Meshach and Abednego answered the king, 'O Nebuchadnezzar, we have no need to present a defense to you in this matter. If our God whom we serve is able to deliver us from the furnace of blazing fire and out of your hand, O king, let him deliver us. But if not, be it known to you, O king, that we will not serve your gods and we will not worship the golden statue that you have set up'" (Dan 3:16–18). As Williams comments, "'Even if he does not'—the act does not depend on the outcome, it is simply what has to be done. The author of Daniel would have had in mind all those in his own day who had resisted the persecution of King Antiochus and who had not been rescued, as the three young men in the story were. He is recording the bare fact that those who resisted did so knowing that miraculous rescues were not in the contract."[47]

Religion testifies to such "useless" witness that is not underpinned by any guarantee. Williams himself, of course, places this way of thinking within the context of an unequivocally theistic ontology, as would Milbank. Nevertheless, it is a way of thinking that can and should be radicalized, and in being so radicalized, it should be noted that the lack of a guarantee, the embracing of ontological suspension, may be seen as an extension of a principle that is at the heart of religious discourse itself. When extended in this way, we may say that even if, from the perspective of the Absolute, reality is structured in a way other than that conceived by faith, this would in no way invalidate the judgment of faith that the Christian universal is "true." As has now often been said, but still needs repeating, truth is by no means limited to that which modern philosophy has deemed it to be. As Raymond Geuss has pointed out in the context of a discussion Badiou's work, "The basic sense of 'true' is that in which Jesus says of himself that he is the truth. To say that Jesus is the truth is to say that his life is the true life, i.e., the good life, the exemplary lie, the life that is a model for humans, the life to which we should all aspire to be faithful."[48] It is, in other words, the life by which all other lives are to be judged. That such a conception of truth

46. Williams, *Christ on Trial*, 10.
47. Ibid.
48. Geuss, review of *Ethics*, 410. Quoted in Critchley, *Infinitely Demanding*, 43.

Part IV: The Religious

echoes an older, Platonic conception is obvious; that it is not irrelevant to modern conceptions of truth relating to ontological "correspondence" is also clear. But the former conception of truth is by no means synonymous with or constrained by the latter. The former could conceivably survive (and possibly be strengthened) even if, in principle (and, of course, this is something that could only happen in principle), it failed the test of ontological "correspondence."

In many ways, of course, this is to do little more than to make a point that was made long ago by Kierkegaard when he said that

> an objective uncertainty held fast in an appropriation-process of the most passionate inwardness is truth, the highest truth attainable for an *existing* individual . . . there objective knowledge is placed in abeyance. Thus the subject merely has, objectively, the uncertainty; but it is this which precisely increases the tension of that infinite passion which constitutes his inwardness. The truth is precisely the venture which chooses the objective uncertainty which is the passion of the infinite. . . . But [this] definition of truth is an equivalent expression for faith. . . . If I wish to preserve myself in faith I must constantly be intent upon holding fast the objective uncertainty, so as to remain out upon the deep, over seventy thousand fathoms of water, still preserving my faith.[49]

These comments of Kierkegaard lead me to make one final point. As we have emphasized previously, all the talk of labor, abeyance, and suspension that has pervaded this entire study should not in the slightest be taken to imply a practical disposition of indecisive paralysis. On the contrary, decisive action and equivocation belong together; they are not alternatives between which we must choose. The decision must be made in the context of equivocation, and equivocation is the necessary purgative preface to the decision. Both equivocation and decision are necessary; each is incomplete without the other.

In a parallel way, we have argued that while the ethical and political impel a return of the Christian universal, it must nevertheless return in such a way that the question of its ontological status is suspended rather than resolved. Thus, the return of the Christian universal is neither unequivocally theistic, as for John Milbank, nor unequivocally atheistic, as for Slavoj Žižek. It is precisely such an ontological suspension, I have suggested, that is best able to preserve the open-ended interplay between the universal, the particular, and the singular, which we have seen to be a defining feature of

---

49. Kierkegaard, *Concluding Unscientific Postscript*, 182.

the ethical and political as such. But again, such ontological suspension, such traversing of the middle, should not be seen as an accomplice of indifference or agnosticism. Agnosticism takes such an ontological suspension as a license for the abdication of faith, whereas what is being commended here entails precisely the opposite outcome. As was the case for Kierkegaard, such ultimate ontological suspension should intensify rather than weaken faith and its concomitant ethical and political commitments. To these commitments we must hold fast, and do so all the more strongly given their suspension over an ontological abyss, over seventy thousand fathoms of water.

BIBLIOGRAPHY

Badiou, Alain. *Being and Event*. Translated by Oliver Feltham. London: Continuum, 2006.
———. *Ethics: An Essay on the Understanding of Evil*. Translated by Peter Hallward. London: Verso, 2001.
———. *Saint Paul: The Foundation of Universalism*. Translated by Ray Brassier. Stanford: Stanford University Press, 2003.
Badiou, Alain, and Slavoj Žižek. *Philosophy in the Present*. Edited by Peter Engelmann. Translated by Peter Thomas and Alberto Toscano. Cambridge: Polity, 2009.
Balthasar, Hans Urs von. *The Glory of the Lord: A Theological Aesthetics*. Vol. 5, *The Realm of Metaphysics in the Modern Age*. Translated by Oliver Davies et al. Edinburgh: T. & T. Clark, 1991.
Bowlin, John. *Contingency and Fortune in Aquinas's Ethics*. Cambridge: Cambridge University Press, 1999.
Caputo, John D. *Against Ethics: Toward a Poetics of Obligation*. Bloomington: Indiana University Press, 1993.
———. "Atheism, A/Theology and the Postmodern Condition." In *The Cambridge Companion to Atheism*, edited by Michael Martin, 267–82. Cambridge: Cambridge University Press, 2006.
———. Review of *The Monstrosity of Christ: Paradox or Dialectic?*, by Slavoj Žižek and John Milbank. *Notre Dame Philosophical Reviews* (2009). Online: http://ndpr.nd.edu/news/24179-the-monstrosity-of-christ-paradox-or-dialectic/.
Caygill, Howard. *Levinas and the Political*. London: Routledge, 2002.
Certeau, Michel de. *The Possession at Loudun*. Translated by Michael B. Smith. Chicago: University of Chicago Press, 2000.
Ciaramelli, Fabio. "Levinas's Ethical Discourse between Individuation and Universality." In *Re-Reading Levinas*, edited by Robert Bernasconi and Simon Critchley, 83–105. London: Athlone, 1991.
Critchley, Simon. *The Ethics of Deconstruction: Derrida and Levinas*. 2nd ed. Edinburgh: Edinburgh University Press, 1999.
———. *Ethics-Politics-Subjectivity: Essays on Derrida, Levinas and Contemporary French Thought*. London: Verso, 1999.
———. *Infinitely Demanding: Ethics of Commitment, Politics of Resistance*. London: Verso, 2007.
Cupitt, Don. *Taking Leave of God*. London: SCM, 1980.
———. *The Time Being*. London: SCM, 1992.

Bibliography

Derrida, Jacques. *The Gift of Death*. Translated by David Wills. Chicago: University of Chicago Press, 1995.

———. *Given Time: I. Counterfeit Money*. Translated by Peggy Kamuf. Chicago: University of Chicago Press, 1992.

Eagleton, Terry. *Reason, Faith, and Revolution: Reflections on the God Debate*. New Haven: Yale University Press, 2009.

———. *Trouble with Strangers: A Study of Ethics*. Oxford: Wiley-Blackwell, 2009.

Febvre, Lucien. *The Problem of Unbelief in the Sixteenth Century: The Religion of Rabelais*. Translated by Beatrice Gottlieb. Cambridge: Harvard University Press, 1982.

Frank, Thomas. *One Market Under God: Extreme Capitalism, Market Populism and the End of Economic Democracy*. London: Vintage, 2002.

Geuss, Raymond. Review of *Ethics*, by Alain Badiou. *The European Journal of Philosophy* 9 (2001) 408–12.

Hardt, Michael, and Antonio Negri. *Empire*. Cambridge: Harvard University Press, 2000.

———. *Multitude: War and Democracy in the Age of Empire*. London: Penguin, 2004.

Hegel, G. W. F. *Science of Logic*. Translated by A. V. Miller. London: Allen & Unwin, 1969.

Heidegger, Martin. *The Question Concerning Technology and Other Essays*. Translated by W. Lovitt. New York: Harper & Row, 1977.

Hyman, Gavin. "Augustine and the Nihil: An Interrogation." *Journal for Cultural and Religious Theory* 9:1 (2008) 35–49.

———. "Dialectics or Politics? Atheism and the Return to Religion." *Approaching Religion* 2 (2012) 66–74.

———. "Must a Post-metaphysical Political Theology Repudiate Transcendence? The Case of Gianni Vattimo." *Journal for Cultural and Religious Theory* 8:3 (2007) 124–34.

———. "Postmodern Theology and Modern Liberalism: Reconsidering the Relationship." *Theology Today* 65 (2009) 462–74.

———. *The Predicament of Postmodern Theology: Radical Orthodoxy or Nihilist Textualism?* Louisville: Westminster John Knox, 2001.

———. *A Short History of Atheism*. London: I. B. Tauris, 2010.

Isherwood, Christopher. *Diaries, Volume One: 1939–1960*. Edited by Katherine Bucknell. London: Methuen, 1996.

Jameson, Fredric. "First Impressions." *London Review of Books* 28:17 (2006) 7–8.

———. *Postmodernism, or, the Cultural Logic of Late Capitalism*. Durham: Duke University Press, 1991.

Kant, Immanuel. *Critique of Practical Reason*. Translated by Lewis White Beck. Indianapolis: Bobbs-Merrill, 1956.

———. *Religion within the Limits of Reason Alone*. Translated by Theodore M. Greene and Hoyt H. Hudson. New York: Harper & Row, 1960.

Kierkegaard, Søren. *Concluding Unscientific Postscript*. Translated by David F. Swenson and Walter Lowrie. Princeton: Princeton University Press, 1941.

Kirk, Kenneth E. *The Vision of God: The Christian Doctrine of the Summum Bonum*. London: Longmans, 1931.

Kristeva, Julia. *Tales of Love*. Translated by Leon S. Roudiez. New York: Columbia University Press, 1987.

Lacan, Jacques. *Le séminaire, livre 21: Les non-dupes errent* (unpublished transcript, 11 December, 1973).

Levinas, Emmanuel. *Difficult Freedom: Essays on Judaism.* Translated by Sean Hand. Baltimore: Johns Hopkins University Press, 1990.

———. *Otherwise than Being or Beyond Essence.* Translated by Alphonso Lingis. The Hague: Martinus Nijhoff, 1981.

Lloyd, Vincent. *The Problem with Grace: Reconfiguring Political Theology.* Stanford: Stanford University Press, 2011.

Lyotard, Jean-François. *Économie Libidinale.* Paris: Minuit, 1974.

Marion, Jean-Luc. *God without Being.* Translated by Thomas A. Carlson. Chicago: University of Chicago Press, 1991.

McInerney, Ralph. *Ethica Thomistica: The Moral Philosophy of Thomas Aquinas.* Washington, DC: Catholic University of America Press, 1997.

Milbank, John. *Being Reconciled: Ontology and Pardon.* London: Routledge, 2003.

———. "Can a Gift Be Given? Prolegomena to a Future Trinitarian Metaphysic." *Modern Theology* 11 (1995) 119–61.

———. *The Future of Love: Essays in Political Theology.* Eugene, OR: Cascade Books, 2009.

———. "The Gift of Ruling: Secularization and Political Authority." *New Blackfriars* 85 (2004) 212–38.

———. "'Postmodern Critical Augustinianism': A Short *Summa* in Forty-Two Responses to Unasked Questions." *Modern Theology* 7 (1991) 225–37.

———. "The Return of Mediation." In *Paul's New Moment: Continental Philosophy and the Future of Christian Theology*, by John Milbank, Slavoj Žižek, and Creston Davis, 211–38. Grand Rapids: Brazos, 2010.

———. "Sublimity: The Modern Trasnscendent." In *Religion, Modernity and Postmodernity*, edited by Paul Heelas, 258–84. Oxford: Blackwell, 1998.

———. *Theology and Social Theory: Beyond Secular Reason.* 2nd ed. Oxford: Blackwell, 2006.

Miller, J. Hillis. *Poets of Reality: Six Twentieth-Century Writers.* New York: Atheneum, 1969.

Negri, Antonio. "The Political Subject and Absolute Immanence." In *Theology and the Political: The New Debate*, edited by Creston Davis, John Milbank, and Slavoj Žižek, 231–39. Durham: Duke University Press, 2005.

Peperzak, Adriaan. "Autrui, Société, Peuple de Dieu." *Intersoggettività Socialità Religione, Archivio de Filosofia* 54 (1986) 309–18.

———. "Giving." In *The Enigma of Gift and Sacrifice*, edited by Edith Wyschogrod, Jean-Joseph Goux, and Eric Boynton, 161–75. New York: Fordham University Press, 2002.

Pickstock, Catherine. "Theology and Post-modernity: An Exploration of the Origins of a New Allegiance." In *New Directions in Philosophical Theology: Essays in Honour of Don Cupitt*, edited by Gavin Hyman, 67–84. Aldershot: Ashgate, 2004.

Ram-Prasad, Chakravarthi. *Eastern Philosophy.* London: Weidenfeld & Nicolson, 2006.

———. "The Great Divide." *Prospect* 119 (2006) 20–25.

Reinhard, Kenneth. "Toward a Political Theology of the Neighbor." In *The Neighbor: Three Inquiries in Political Theology*, by Slavoj Žižek, Eric L. Santner, and Kenneth Reinhard, 11–75. Chicago: University of Chicago Press, 2005.

Rose, Gillian. *The Broken Middle: Out of Our Ancient Society.* Oxford: Blackwell, 1992.

Bibliography

———. *Hegel contra Sociology*. London: Athlone, 1981.
———. *Judaism and Modernity: Philosophical Essays*. Oxford: Blackwell, 1993.
Sands, Kathleen M. *Escape from Paradise: Evil and Tragedy in Feminist Theology*. Minneapolis: Fortress, 1994.
Schwarz, Regina. "Revelation and Revolution.'" In *Theology and the Political: The New Debate*, edited by Creston Davis, John Milbank, and Slavoj Žižek, 102–24. Durham: Duke University Press, 2005.
Stratton, David. Review of *Sleepers. Variety*, September 2, 1996. Online: http://www.variety.com/review/VE1117911068.html?categoryid=31&cs=1.
Streng, Frederick. *Emptiness: A Study in Religious Meaning*. Nashville: Abingdon, 1967.
Surin, Kenneth. "Rewriting the Ontological Script of Liberation: On the Question of Finding a New Kind of Political Subject." In *Theology and the Political: The New Debate*, edited by Creston Davis, John Milbank, and Slavoj Žižek, 240–66. Durham: Duke University Press, 2005.
Szabari, Antónia. "The Scandal of Religion: Luther and Public Speech in the Reformation." In *Political Theologies: Public Religions in a Post-Secular World*, edited by Hent de Vries and Lawrence E. Sullivan, 122–36. New York: Fordham University Press, 2006.
Taylor, Charles. *A Secular Age*. Cambridge: Belknap Press of Harvard University Press, 2007.
Taylor, Mark C. *Altarity*. Chicago: University of Chicago Press, 1987.
———. *Confidence Games: Money and Markets in a World without Redemption*. Chicago: University of Chicago Press, 2004.
———. *Erring: A Postmodern A/Theology*. Chicago: University of Chicago Press, 1984.
———. *The Moment of Complexity: Emerging Network Culture*. Chicago: University of Chicago Press, 2001.
Williams, Rowan. "Between Politics and Metaphysics: Reflections in the Wake of Gillian Rose." *Modern Theology* 11 (1995) 3–22.
———. *Christ on Trial: How the Gospel Unsettles our Judgement*. London: HarperCollins, 2000.
———. "Insubstantial Evil." In *Augustine and His Critics: Essays in Honour of Gerald Bonner*, edited by Robert Dodaro and George Lawless, 105–23. London: Routledge, 2000.
———. *Lost Icons: Reflections on Cultural Bereavement*. Edinburgh: T. & T. Clark, 2000.
———. "'Religious Realism': On Not Quite Agreeing with Don Cupitt." *Modern Theology* 1 (1984) 3–24.
Wood, David. *The Step Back: Ethics and Politics after Deconstruction*. Albany: State University of New York Press, 2005.
Wyschogrod, Michael. "Response to the Respondents." *Modern Theology* 11 (1995) 229–41.
Žižek, Slavoj. "A Meditation on Michaelangelo's *Christ on the Cross*." In *Paul's New Moment: Continental Philosophy and the Future of Christian Theology*, by John Milbank, Slavoj Žižek, and Creston Davis, 169–81. Grand Rapids: Brazos, 2010.
———. "Neighbors and Other Monsters." In *The Neighbor: Three Inquiries in Political Theology*, by Slavoj Žižek, Eric L. Santner, and Kenneth Reinhard, 134–90. Chicago: University of Chicago Press, 2005.
———. *The Parallax View*. Cambridge: MIT Press, 2006.

———. "Selfhood as Such Is Spirit: F. W. J. Schelling on the Origins of Evil." In *Radical Evil*, edited by Joan Copjec, 1–29. London: Verso, 1996.

———. *Violence*. London: Profile, 2008.

Žižek, Slavoj, and John Milbank. *The Monstrosity of Christ: Paradox or Dialectic?* Cambridge: MIT Press, 2009.

Žižek, Slavoj, Eric L. Santner, and Kenneth Reinhard. *The Neighbor: Three Inquiries in Political Theology*. Chicago: University of Chicago Press, 2005.

INDEX

agnosticism, 197
akedah, 11
Altizer, Thomas J. J., 182
antithesis. *See* thesis–antithesis–synthesis
anxiety (ethical), 28, 29ff.
aporia (ethical), xiv, 45–46, 65–66
Aquinas, Thomas, xiii, xv, 50–56, 58
atheism, xix–xx, 168, 182, 183, 186, 187, 189, 190, 191, 192, 193, 196
autonomy (ethics), 7ff.
Augustine, 54, 143, 171, 175
    Augustinian theology, ix

Badiou, Alain, ix, x, xii, xviii, 4, 86, 104–13, 136, 138, 139, 141, 142, 146–52, 154, 158, 160, 165, 166
Balthasar, Hans Urs von, 17
"Bartleby politics" (Žižek), xviii, 152ff.
Benjamin, Walter, 61
"broken middle" (Rose), 140, 158, 179–80
Buddhism, 98

capitalism, ix, 109, 111, 113, 128–33, 137, 138, 150, 170, 171, 180
"capitalo-parliamentarianism" (Badiou), 138, 149
Caputo, John D., 36–38, 40, 94, 152
Carcaterra, Lorenzo, 72
Caygill, Howard, 83–85

Certeau, Michel de, 18–19
Chinese revolution, 107
Chinese thought, 4
Christianity, xix, 63–64, 127, 150–51, 168, 170, 174, 182–83, 189, 191–96
Ciaramelli, Fabio, 87–88
City of God (Augustine), 171
complacency (ethical), 49ff.
Critchley, Simon, xvii, 84–85, 113–22, 136
coercion, 143, 146, 148
communism, 107
complexity theory, ix
consent (to truth), 145
content/form (of universal), 164ff.
conversion, 142–43, 145–47, 149, 159
Cupitt, Don, 76, 134–36

Daniel, Book of, 195
"death of God," 94, 95, 167, 168
decision (ethical/political), 196
deconstruction (Derrida), 114, 116, 117, 122, 134, 141
democracy, xvii, 109
"dependent co-origination," xvi, 98
Derrida, Jacques, 11, 20–21, 37, 65–66, 114, 116–17, 122, 133–34, 141
Descartes, René, 124, 186, 187
dialectics, 184–94
distinterestedness, xiv, 16ff., 36–37
dualism, 27
    (Christian), 174

Index

Duns Scotus, John, 123–24, 127–28, 135

Eagleton, Terry, ix, 5, 42, 60–61, 100, 129, 149–50, 158–59, 167
Eckhart, Meister, 64
ego, 118
"Empire" (Hardt and Negri), 94–95, 109, 123, 129, 134
equivocation (of ethical and/or political), xi–xii, xiv, xv, 5ff., 27, 33, 58, 61–62, 65, 68–69, 70, 71ff., 77, 92–93, 145, 146, 147–48, 149–51, 160, 184, 196
ethical/political, xi, xii, xiii, 81ff., 88ff., 91ff.; see also equivocation (ethical/political as), "triune" (ethical/political as)
ethical/political origin, 97ff., 155
ethics/ethical, ch. 1 *passim*, ch. 2 *passim*, ch. 3 *passim*; see also system (ethical)
"Event" (Badiou). See "Truth–Event" (Badiou)
"exteriority" (in political theory), 126–32, 134

face (Levinas), 30ff., 89, 90, 97, 99, 100, 118, 141, 145, 155, 170
faith, ch. 6 *passim*, 169, 194, 195, 197
fascism, 118
Fénelon, François, 23
"Five Ways" (Aquinas), xiii
form/content (of universal), 164ff.
Freud, Sigmund, 118, 188

Geuss, Raymond, 195
God, xv, 3, 22–25, 42, 50ff., 62, 63, 67, 69, 167, 168, 170, 171, 172, 181, 183, 186, 187, 192; see also "death of God"
Good, the, 8, 9, 50ff., 164–65, 166, 170, 171, 174–79
gift, 20–21, 37

Hardt, Michael, ix, xvii–xviii, 94, 95, 110, 113, 122–36, 153
Harvey, David, 137
Hegel, G. W. F., 133–34, 151–52, 182
Heidegger, Martin, 126
heteronomy (in ethics), 8ff.
Hobbes, Thomas, 124
humor, 118

immanence, 93–94, 95, 123, 126, 127, 128–29, 130, 131, 132, 134, 182, 183
Indian philosophy, 4
instrumentalism, 126–27
Isherwood, Christopher, 3

Jameson, Fredric, ix, 137, 184–85, 191
Judaism, 12, 13
justice, xix, 82ff., 90, 97, 100, 154–56, 160, 168, 170

Kant, Immanuel, xi, xiv, xv, 8, 9, 15, 16ff., 33, 34, 36, 38, 40, 47–48, 92, 124, 164–65, 166
Kristeva, Julia, xv, 50ff.
Kierkegaard, Søren, 11, 12, 76, 196

labor (ethical), 71ff.
language (implicated with violence), 139–40
Lacan, Jacques, 53, 61, 133
Lacoue-Labarthe, Philippe, 115
Lefort, Claude, 115
legality (Kant), 17
Levinas, Emmanuel, xiv, xv, xvi, 8, 9, 15, 22, 29ff., 54–55, 88ff., 91ff., 114, 115, 116, 117, 118, 119, 121, 122, 134, 141, 146, 154, 155, 158, 160, 167, 168, 169;
and the political, 82ff.
Levinson, Barry, 71
liberalism, 83–84, 109, 113, 115, 145, 147, 148, 150, 154, 189
liberation (politics of), 128
Lloyd, Vincent, xvii, 104, 109

love, 12, 13, 27, 42, 50ff., 89ff., 92, 157
  of neighbor, 12ff., 16, 25, 26, 30, 39, 40, 50ff., 58ff., 64, 104, 157
Luther, Martin, 18
Lyotard, Jean-François, 132–33, 136

Marion, Jean-Luc, 31
Marx, Karl/Marxism, ix, xvii, 105, 106, 107, 111, 129, 130, 132, 133
materialism, 68, 182, 191
mercy, xix, 160
metanarrative, ix, x, 150–51, 181
metaphysics, 31–32, 126–27
Milbank, John, ix, xii, xix, 26, 43, 62–67, 69–70, 129, 130, 132–33, 136, 138, 139, 140–41, 146–47, 149, 150, 154, 157, 170, 181, 182, 184, 187, 188, 190, 191, 192
Miller, J. Hillis, 31–32
Missionary imperative (and universalism), 144, 145
modern philosophy/thought, xi, xv; see also western philosophy
morality (Kant), 18
Muller, Jean-Marie, 139
multiculturalism, 113
multitude, 155
"multitude" (Hardt and Negri), 95, 97, 99, 125–26, 130, 132

Nagarjuna, 98
Nancy, Jean-Luc, 115
Negri, Antonio, ix, xvii–xviii, 94, 95, 110, 113
neighbor, xiv, 5, 12, 13, 14, 25, 149, 155, 157, 158, 170; see also love of neighbor
network culture, ix
Nietzsche, Friedrich, 32, 94
nihil/nihilism, xv, 50, 54–57, 57ff., 67, 68, 93–94, 95, 150, 184
norms/practices, xvii, xviii, 104, 105, 107, 108, 109, 111, 143, 150, 158, 159

Nussbaum, Martha, 175

ontology/ontological, xix–xx, 31, 68, 70, 94–95, 115, 128, 183, 184, 192, 193, 194, 195
  ontological "correspondence," 194, 196
  ontological "resolution," 70–71, 99, 180ff., 192, 193
other, xv, 14, 27, 30ff., 58ff., 98, 145, 181

particular/particularism, x–xi, xii, xvi, xvii, 4, 5–6, 9–10, 28, 34, 45–46, 63, 69, 81–82, chapter 3 *passim*, 111–112, 116, 117, 114–22, 125, 137, 143, 144, 145, 146, 148, 149, 150, 155, 156, 158–60, 168–69, 175, 178, 194, 196; see also "triune" (structure of ethical/political; universal/particular/singular)
Paul, Saint, 147
Peperzak, Adriaan, 39, 86–87
persuasion, 143, 145, 146, 149, 151, 159
politics/political, xvi, 82ff., 103ff., ch. 3 *passim*, ch. 4 *passim*, ch. 5 *passim*
  end of politics, xvii, xviii, 105, 107, 111, 159, 160, 170
postmodern philosophy/thought, ix, x, xi, xii, xv, 94–95, 122–23, 137, 138, 141, 155, 181
postmodernism, x–xi, xii, 94–95, 139
"poverty" (Hardt and Negri), 131
practices/norms. See norms/practices
pre-modernity, 190
psychoanalysis, 118

rationalism (Christian), 174
radical orthodoxy, ix
Ram-Prasad, Chakravarthi, 4
Reinhardt, Kenneth, 13–14, 16, 25, 53–54, 59, 121

Index

reciprocity (in ethics), 63ff.
relativism, 143, 144
religion/religious, xii, xiii, xix,
    76–77, 163ff., 170, 172–73,
    173ff., 182, 191, 194, 195
    return of, 188–89
responsibility (ethical), 35–36, 39,
    40–41, 97, 167, 168
revolution
    "revolutionary politics," 110,
    124–25, 130, 158, 159
    revolutionary terror, 154
    see also Chinese Revolution,
    Russian Revolution
risk (ethical/political), 10, 75–76,
    77, 111, 169, 170, 175
Rose, Gillian, xvii, 5, 10, 11, 12, 34,
    44–47, 50, 109, 135, 140,
    179–80
Rousseau, Jean-Jacques, 148–49
rumspringa (Žižek), 153–54, 157
Russian revolution, 107

Sands, Kathleen, 60, 174–79
Santner, Eric, 13–14, 16, 25, 59
saying/said (Levinas), 44–45
Schwarz, Regina, 85, 141, 146
self/selfhood, xv, 5, 14, 27
    self, love of, 50ff., 58ff., 104
    self-denial/self-annihilation,
    21–222, 27, 33, 36, 38,
    39–40, 42, 43, 158
    self-promotion, 23–24, 25, 27,
    33, 36, 38, 39–40, 41, 42, 43;
    see also subject (human)
singular/singularity, xii, xiv, xvi,
    5–6, 10, 32ff., 45–46,
    63, 69, 81–82, 86ff., ch.
    3 *passim*, 112–113, 118,
    122ff., 156, 158–60; *see
    also* "triune" (structure of
    ethical/political; universal/
    particular/singular)
Sleepers (1996), 71–75
Spinoza, Benedict de, xv, 54–56, 94,
    127–28, 135
state (nation), 105–9

"state of the situation" (Badiou),
    105–9
Stratton, David, 72
subject (human), 3, 4, 23, 28, 98,
    99, 104, 167, 185, 186, 187,
    188, 191
superego, 118
sublimation, 118
Surin, Kenneth, 127
suspension
    ethical, 10, 11, 74–75, 169
    of universal, 165, 166, 167, 178,
    179
    ontological, 195, 196, 197
subjects–objects, 190
synthesis. *See* thesis–antithesis–
    synthesis
system (ethical), xi, 3, 4, 71, 117
Szabari, Antónia, 18

Taylor, Charles, 171, 187–88
Taylor, Mark C., ix
teleology, 129, 130, 132, 133, 134
telos (ethical/political), 9, 170
theism, 184, 186, 190, 193, 196
theology/theological, xiii, xvi, xix
    50ff., 57ff., 77, 150, 163, 170,
    172, 174, 181, 183, 184
    theology, modern liberal, 173
    theology, postmodern
    deconstructive, 173
thesis–antithesis–synthesis, 189ff.,
    192
totalitarianism, 115, 118, 119, 141,
    149, 159
transcendence, 123–24, 125, 127,
    128, 129, 132, 134, 182,
    187–88, 191
"trauma" (Critchley), 118–19
"triune" (structure of ethical/
    political; universal/
    particular/singular), xi, xv,
    xvi, 5, 34, 45–46, 62ff., 168,
    172, 173ff., 193, 194, 196
truth, 145, 149, 154, 194, 195, 196
"Truth-Event" (Badiou), 104, 112,
    142, 146–52, 165–66

unilateralism (in ethics), 63ff.

universal/universalism, ix, x, xii, xiv, xvi, xviii, xix, 5–6, 9–10, 11, 28, 34, 45–46, 63, 69, 76–77, 81–82, 86ff., ch. 3 *passim*, 112–13, 117, 118, 119, 125, 128, 134, 135, 136, 137, ch. 5 *passim*, 163ff., 168, 169, 171, 175, 177, 178, 179, 193, 194, 196; *see also* "triune" (structure of ethical/political; universal/particular/singular)

"universal of all universals" (Milbank), 150, 151

violence, xviii–xix, 11, 69, 70, 85–86, 92, 93, 115, 118, 119, 137ff.

subjective/systemic, 140–41

western philosophy, 3, 4, 32, 185; *see also modern philosophy/thought*
Williams, Bernard, 26
Williams, Rowan, 6ff., 23, 108, 171–72, 174–78, 181, 195
Wood, David, 36, 42–43, 58, 159

Žižek, Slavoj, ix, xii, xiv, xv, xvi, xviii, xix, 13, 16, 25, 40, 41, 42, 54–56, 57, 67–69, 70, 86, 88ff., 91ff., 121, 133, 138, 139, 140, 141, 143–44, 152ff., 160, 165, 166, 167, 168, 169, 182, 184, 188, 190, 191, 192, 196

www.ingramcontent.com/pod-product-compliance
Lightning Source LLC
Chambersburg PA
CBHW031356230426
43670CB00006B/560